THE WORST SONGS IN THE WORLD

THE WORST SONGS IN THE WORLD

The Terrible Truth About National Anthems

DAVID PATE

DUNDURN PRESS

Publisher: Meghan Macdonald | Acquiring editor: Kathryn Lane | Editor: Dominic Farrell
Cover designer: Karen Alexiou
Cover image: trumpet: Katsiaryna Pleshakova/istock.com; flag: StockSmartStart/shutterstock.com; light rays: Freepik.com
Interior decoration: macrovector/Freepik.com

Library and Archives Canada Cataloguing in Publication

Title: The worst songs in the world : the terrible truth about national anthems / David Pate.
Names: Pate, David (Journalist), author.
Description: Includes bibliographical references and index.
Identifiers: Canadiana (print) 20240372247 | Canadiana (ebook) 20240372255 | ISBN 9781459754560 (softcover) | ISBN 9781459754584 (EPUB) | ISBN 9781459754577 (PDF)
Subjects: LCSH: National songs—History and criticism.
Classification: LCC ML3545 .P38 2024 | DDC 782.421/599—dc23

Canada | Canada Council for the Arts | Conseil des arts du Canada | Ontario
ONTARIO ARTS COUNCIL
CONSEIL DES ARTS DE L'ONTARIO
an Ontario government agency
un organisme du gouvernement de l'Ontario
ONTARIO CREATES

We acknowledge the support of the Canada Council for the Arts and the Ontario Arts Council for our publishing program. We also acknowledge the financial support of the Government of Ontario, through the Ontario Book Publishing Tax Credit and Ontario Creates, and the Government of Canada.

Printed and bound in Canada.

Dundurn Press
1382 Queen Street East
Toronto, Ontario, Canada M4L 1C9
dundurn.com, @dundurnpress

To Gemma, for never doubting.

CONTENTS

OVERTURE

Patriotism is your conviction that this country is superior to all other countries because you were born in it.

— George Bernard Shaw

The Saturday evening audience at London's Drury Lane Theatre was anxious and restless. The news from the north was not good. They needed distraction — and reassurance. They did not realize they were about to witness an event that would change the world.

News had reached the city of a terrible calamity. A Scottish army under Bonnie Prince Charlie had defeated a much stronger English force at the Battle of Prestonpans outside Edinburgh a week earlier. The battle lasted just thirty minutes and was the first significant military engagement of the 1745 Jacobite Rising. What had seemed like a minor Scottish rebellion that would be quickly put down was now causing panic in London. The British Army's best forces were deployed in Europe, fighting in one of the almost continuous wars that occupied the continent during the eighteenth century.* It appeared nothing could stop the Jacobite rebels from marching on London. They wanted to place Charles Stuart on the throne his grandfather had been ousted from almost sixty years earlier.

There was talk of King George II, the German-born monarch viewed by the Jacobites as a usurper, fleeing the country. Newspapers warned that the country was facing great danger. There was a run on London banks. It was no wonder the theatre audience was restless and concerned. The play that evening — September 28, 1745† — was a revival of a classic comedy by Ben Jonson. Written in 1610, *The Alchemist* was an audience favourite. It's still performed and enjoyed today. With a cast of bumbling con artists and a plot filled with swindles, double-crosses, and extravagant humour, it was just the kind of light relief needed to distract the worried theatregoers.[1]

Once the play was done and the actors had received their applause, there was an unexpected development. Three of London's most famous singers walked onto the stage, led by Susannah Cibber, a performer so accomplished that Handel wrote the contralto arias in the *Messiah* specifically for her. She was in the original cast of Handel's masterpiece when it was first performed in Dublin in 1742.

Susannah Cibber was a remarkable woman. She entranced not just Handel but the entire English public. She was the highest-paid actress in the country at a time when women in public life were a rarity — and when a career as an actress was viewed with suspicion by a society that did not in general like the idea of independent women taking charge of their own lives.

---

* This one was the War of the Austrian Succession from 1740–48.

† In 1745 Britain was still using the Julian calendar, which, due to a mistake in calculating leap years, was now eleven days out of sync with the actual date. In 1752 Britain adopted the more accurate Gregorian calendar, which meant that September 2 was followed by September 14. All this means is that while the Drury Lane Theatre crowd thought they were out for a Saturday night, a Google search will show that September 28, 1745, fell on a Tuesday.

On that Saturday night in 1745, Cibber was joined on the Drury Lane stage by two more of Handel's favourite singers — tenor John Beard and bass Henry Reinhold. All three had recently performed together in a London revival of the *Messiah*. The audience would certainly have known who they were but would have had no idea why these superstars were unexpectedly standing before them.

Their appearance on the Drury Lane stage wouldn't have been hard to organize. Susannah Cibber's father-in-law was the theatre manager; her brother, Thomas Arne, led the orchestra. He was an accomplished composer, best known for his song "Rule, Britannia!" He had just arranged another patriotic work, which he wanted to introduce that night to counter the gloom and pessimism sweeping the capital in the wake of the Prestonpans defeat, and he wanted his sister to sing the song because of her unique voice. That voice was praised by Charles Burney, a pupil of her brother's, who became a composer and prominent music historian. He wrote that "by a natural pathos, and perfect conception of the words, she often penetrated the heart, when others, with infinitely greater voice and skill, could only reach the ear."[2]

Thomas Arne arranged the music that Saturday night to bring out the best in Cibber, setting it in the key of E flat. He followed the example of Handel, who so loved Cibber's voice that he chose the same key for her solo, "He Was Despised," in the *Messiah*. When she performed it at the oratorio's premiere in Dublin in 1742, a cleric, the Reverend Patrick Delaney, leapt to his feet and cried out, "Woman, for this be all thy sins forgiven thee!"*[3]

* Susannah Cibber's "sins" went on full public display in 1738, when her husband sued her lover for "ravishing and carnally knowing" his wife. The trial's salacious details were widely published and eagerly read, showing that the public's appetite for sordid celebrity gossip was as strong in the eighteenth century as it is today. Cibber's husband sought £5,000 in damages. The jury's sympathies clearly lay with his wife. They awarded him just £10.

Cibber was used to rapturous receptions. She was about to get another one. She, Beard, and Reinhold sang this song:

> God bless our noble King,
> God Save great George our King,
> God Save the King.
> Send him victorious,
> Happy and glorious,
> Long to reign over us,
> God save the King.

We don't know who composed the tune. Its origins have been traced back to medieval times, and over the centuries, it was used as the music for other songs. The author of the words is also unknown, although the phrase "God Save the King" was a common one. Handel wrote music for George II's coronation in 1727, featuring the lyrics "God save the king / Long live the king." A version of the song similar to the one performed at Drury Lane Theatre — and using the same music — is believed to have been sung in the late seventeenth century. And the words and music that Thomas Arne used as the basis for his arrangement were first published together in 1744. But it was not until that Saturday night in 1745 that the song became a national phenomenon.

The *Daily Advertiser* described the audience reaction, reporting that "the universal applause it met with, being encored with repeated Huzzas, sufficiently denoted in how just an abhorrence they hold the arbitrary schemes of our invidious enemies."

It was an immediate hit. Other theatres took up the practice of performing the song. An advertisement in the *General Advertiser* on October 2, 1745, promised, "At the Theatre in Goodman's Fields, by desire, God save the King, as it was performed at the Theatre Royal, Drury Lane, with great applause."[4]

Morale improved. The Scottish rebellion was crushed the following year at Culloden, and soon, everyone who wanted to show their loyalty to the king was singing the song. What started out as a one-off attempt to show support for the king in a time of national crisis became a song played every time George II showed up at an event. And then it was realized the anthem could apply to any monarch with just a slight tweaking of the words.

A little over forty years later, the noted novelist and diarist Fanny Burney* — the daughter of Charles Burney, mentioned above — wrote in her journal about a royal visit to Cheltenham by the next king, George III. "All the way upon the road we rarely proceeded five miles without encountering a band of the most horrid fiddlers, scraping 'God Save the King' with all their might, out of tune, out of time, and all in the rain."

By the time of Burney's diary entry, the song was firmly entrenched as a national anthem. No occasion was too small for the song to be played, as Burney noted about the king's visit to the seaside town of Weymouth in July 1789: "The King bathes, and with great success; a machine follows the royal one into the sea, filled with fiddlers, who play 'God Save the King,' as his Majesty takes his plunge!"[5]

It wasn't long before other European monarchs took note and wanted their own song. Some just took the same tune and a version of the same "God save me" theme in their own language. These were not yet songs aimed at promoting a ruler — or a country — to the rest of the world. This was about self-promotion at home, a musical loyalty test to reassure nervous monarchs that, yes, the people truly did love them. But once it started, there was no stopping the trend. A new era was born that Saturday night in 1745. An era of national anthems.

---

* Several of her novels as well as editions of her diaries and letters are still in print, including *Evelina*, *Cecilia*, and *Camilla*.

♫

We are about to take a journey around the world. A journey into the music and lyrics of the national songs that every nation now possesses. And it all began in that Drury Lane theatre. And like "God Save the King," most national anthems are shouted statements of intent: don't mess with us, God is on our side, we are prepared to slaughter our enemies, and if we can't kill you all, we'll die in the attempt. This is the dirty reality of national anthems: they are not nice songs.

In writing this book, I compiled a database of 218 countries, from Afghanistan to Zimbabwe. That's really an arbitrary number: I started with the 193 countries of the United Nations and then expanded it to include the nations that compete in the Olympics (206) and the countries that vie for football's World Cup (211).* If that seems like a heavy emphasis on sporting organizations, that's because, as we'll find out, sports — and the Olympics and FIFA in particular — have pretty much created the modern national anthem. Most people will only hear another country's national song if they are watching a televised international sporting event.

Here's the reality: if it wasn't for sports, lots of countries wouldn't even bother with anthems. Most of the anthems we hear today are designed to be played at sporting events like the Olympics, which

* I use "football" rather than "soccer" for the sake of consistency, not because I think one word is better than the other. Nothing provokes a contemptuous sneer more in an English football fan than the use of the term "soccer" by a North American. This is strange, because the word "soccer" was regularly used in the United Kingdom up until the early 1980s, when people decided, for no clear reason, that it was an Americanism and pretty much banned it from polite conversation. The word itself started in England, derived from "association football" (so called to distinguish it from rugby football). The name was abbreviated to "assoccer" and then just "soccer." I grew up using soccer interchangeably with football. When a plane carrying Manchester United's team crashed in Munich in 1958, killing many of its stars, the headline in London's *Daily Mirror* read "Soccer Air Tragedy." A popular English weekly publication from 1952 to 1970 was *Soccer Star*.

limits them to no more than eighty seconds in length. FIFA, which runs international football, has a ninety-second rule. And they've been pushing to make them even shorter — preferably less than a minute — to suit these fast-paced times. Those limitations have forced countries to come up with an official abridged version of their anthems. For example, the music for Uruguay's anthem lasts about five minutes in its full form. And be thankful that Greece decided to adopt a shorter version of its national anthem; the original runs to 158 verses and takes about an hour to sing.

The countries that devote the most time, attention, and laws to national anthems tend to be the most dictatorial (like China) or the most militaristic (like the United States). In both cases, an obsession with being seen as Top Dog means a massive amount of national pride is tied up in an often unsatisfactory song. Nations with less to prove — or less insecurity about their place in the world — don't really care about anthems (like San Marino, which doesn't even have any lyrics for its anthem and doesn't seem to miss them).

And yet, there is power in music. As the poet Alfred Lord Tennyson wrote, "The song that nerves a nation's heart / Is in itself a deed."[6] We'll look into why music is so important to people as part of their regional and national identity — and has been for as long as humanity and music have existed. But because music holds so much power, it needs to be managed carefully. As we'll see, that hasn't been done. Most anthems share one of three fatal flaws: violence, sexism, or sectarianism. Many have all three. Of the 193 UN members, just thirteen have anthems that meet criteria that any civilized society would apply to an elementary-school play. And three of those anthems don't have lyrics.[7]

We'll find out how hard it is to change anthems to make them more inclusive and less nasty — but it has been done. And campaigns to either rewrite or create new anthems exist in many nations. Sometimes, that happens by just dropping or forgetting the more contentious parts of the anthem; many countries have much longer songs than even their own citizens realize, and the bits that are no longer sung are usually even worse than the bits that remain. There's a reason why no one sings the third verse of "The Star-Spangled Banner."

We tend to think of national anthems as ancient and unchanging symbols of proud nations. And yes, for some countries, their anthem has been around for a long time — since at least 1745. Most of the older ones are creations of the nineteenth century. The U.S. national anthem has been the nation's official song since only 1931. Before that, it was just one of several popular nationalist songs. But most of the world's anthems are actually very recent because most of the countries we recognize as nations today didn't exist until recently. In 1960 the UN had ninety-nine member states — a little more than half the number it has today.

The decolonization of Europe's empires led to the creation of dozens of new countries, all needing anthems. And the collapse of the Soviet Union led to the emergence — or re-emergence — of more. And those massive changes also led to orphaned anthems, songs that belonged to countries that no longer exist — or that venerated individuals or political systems that were no longer wanted. We're going to take a trip around a virtual warehouse of abandoned anthems that no longer have a home.

Along the way, I'll be making the case for getting rid of anthems altogether and asking why people think we need them. But if people insist on a national song, why stick with just one? Why not have a selection of songs appropriate to the occasion? And if you must pick an anthem, make sure the words reflect what you want your country to be — and include everyone who lives there. Don't base it around an ancient grievance that only you care about.

It's one of those problematic anthems that got me started on all this. From the time I was young, I haven't been a fan of anthems.

That's probably because I come from a country where I've had to stand through three different bad anthems at sporting events and other occasions over the years. I am originally from Scotland, which is part of the United Kingdom. That makes its official anthem "God Save the King." I'll confess my bias: I have never been a fan of the monarchy and have never sung the song. Many Scottish people feel the same way, which has led to the anthem being booed at public events and a move to replace it with something less antagonizing.

"Scotland the Brave" served for a time as a sporting anthem, but it never inspired the fans, and so it was pushed aside in favour of "Flower of Scotland," which is now the de facto anthem of the nation. And that makes me sad because it is a really terrible song. I'll explain why, even though it won't make me popular in my homeland.

We'll hear about the strange corporate obsession with having a company song — or, in the case of IBM, a whole songbook — and the extreme measures companies will take to eradicate those songs when they are rightly ridiculed for being truly awful. You see, that's the difference between a company anthem and a national anthem: national songs get the state's official endorsement. They are deemed good and right and proper, and we are expected to stand and sing along when they are played.

On the other hand, corporate anthems are judged by the cold light of day. We don't have to sing them. We assess them purely on their merits, and that judgment is inevitably harsh. We owe no loyalty to KPMG. We will not rise to our feet and place our hands over our hearts when the song it commissioned, presumably at vast expense, is played. We listen in astonishment to lyrics like "KPMG, we're strong as can be, a dream of power and energy" and mock it mercilessly. We wonder at the vanity and hubris of the executives who approved the song and then when it proved to be an international embarrassment hired lawyers to prevent people from sharing it online.

But there is a lesson to be learned from the reception given to corporate anthems, one that we should apply to our national songs. Let the people judge if your song is really worthy of national recognition — or derision. We seem to discard our critical thinking when it comes to national anthems, possibly out of a very sensible concern for avoiding the inevitable abuse that will come our way if we criticize the song. We need to get over that. We need to take a long, hard look at our national anthems and ask ourselves: "Can we do better?"

The answer, my friends, is "Yes, we can." Read on and find out why.

1

LIVING FOR MUSIC

The tiny figure who walked onto the huge stage wasted no time. Amelia Anisovych wore a traditional Ukrainian costume, a simple white dress embroidered with red, white, and blue flowers. Her long blonde hair was braided into pigtails. She stood in the spotlight in front of a sold-out crowd of ten thousand people in the Atlas Arena, the largest venue in the Polish city of Lodz. Millions more were watching on television around the world.

Amelia was the opening act in a charity concert organized to raise funds to help refugees from the war in her homeland. The microphone obscured much of her small face as she lifted it to her lips and sang the Ukrainian national anthem. Her self-assurance would have been remarkable for a seasoned professional, but Amelia Anisovych was just seven years old and had never done anything like this in her short life.

Amelia had shot to fame a few weeks earlier after the Russian army invaded Ukraine. When her family took refuge in a bomb shelter in Kyiv, she decided to lift people's spirits by singing one of her favourite songs: "Let It Go" from the Disney movie *Frozen*. Other people in the bomb shelter recorded her singing and posted the video online. It instantly went viral. The sight of the little girl singing her heart out while above her air raid sirens warned of Russian attacks captured the hearts of people around the world. Shortly afterwards, Amelia's parents sent her to stay with her grandmother in Poland, making her one of the many millions who fled from the invaders.

Organizers of the charity event "Together With Ukraine" invited Amelia to open the fund-raising concert in Lodz. In her high, clear voice — familiar to so many from that viral video — Amelia sang the Ukrainian national anthem with its eerily appropriate opening lines:

> The glory and freedom of Ukraine has not yet perished,
> Luck will still smile on us, brother Ukrainians.
> Our enemies will die, as the dew does in the sunshine,
> And we, too, brothers, we'll live happily in our land.

Amelia Anisovych captured the nation's mood and the power of an anthem in the sweet voice of a child. We are here. We have hope. We will triumph.

Within days of Russia's attack on its western neighbour, the Ukrainian national anthem achieved global recognition. Choirs gathered to share the country's national song, from New York's Metropolitan Opera to London's Royal Albert Hall, while sports fans rose to their feet for it in National Hockey League arenas across North America. Ukrainians gathered in the ruined streets of their hometowns to sing it, their voices sometimes distorted by tears and anguish.

♫

There is no denying the power of music. And it is because music is so powerful that we need to be very careful about the songs we select for our national anthems and the stories they tell. Political leaders have always known they can rouse the populace with the right message and the right song. Andrew Fletcher of Saltoun, a Scottish politician who laboured unsuccessfully to prevent the 1707 Act of Union with England, recognized this more than three centuries ago. "I knew a very wise man [who] believed if a man were permitted to make all the ballads he need not care who should make the laws of a nation," he wrote to a friend, "and we find that most of the ancient legislators thought that they could not well reform the manners of any city without the help of a lyric, and sometimes of a dramatic poet."[1]

Control what the people sing, and you control the people. Things get complicated when you realize that people *want* to be controlled by music. Singing together is so wonderful that we seek to participate in communal sing-a-longs. The political scientist and historian Benedict Anderson of Cornell University wrote in his book *Imagined Communities: Reflections on the Origin and Spread of Nationalism*: "Take national anthems, for example, sung on national holidays. No matter how banal the words and mediocre the tunes, there is in this singing an experience of simultaneity. At precisely such moments, people wholly unknown to each other utter the same verses to the same melody."[2]

Music binds people together. A study published in the American journal *Evolution and Human Behavior* in March 2016 looked at the impact of singing in choirs on social bonding and the participants' ability to tolerate pain. It found that people singing together in large groups produced more endorphins, a stress-relieving hormone, which gave them a potentially higher pain threshold and brought them closer together. The authors noted, "The finding that singing together fosters social closeness — even in large contexts where individuals are not known to each other — is consistent with evolutionary accounts that emphasize the role of music in social bonding, particularly in the context of creating larger cohesive groups than other primates are able to manage."[3]

Other studies show that listening to music encourages the brain to release dopamine, which makes us feel pleasure. We get an even bigger buzz when we actively perform music by singing or playing. We can't help ourselves; we're hard-wired to love a good tune. Of course, that doesn't mean we have no choice in the matter. We don't all love the same music; your favourite band as a teenager may not have had the same impact on your parents, who — far from feeling a dopamine-induced moment of pleasure — may have ended up screaming at you to "turn down that damned noise!" The trick is to find the tune that inspires most people most of the time.

As mentioned, music can also make us more tolerant of pain. That's been well known for generations, even if the scientific reasons behind it weren't understood. Early on, people figured out that marching into battle with a song on your lips or a band at your back was a great way to get troops all psyched up for the fight. The ancient Egyptians knew it. So did the Chinese. The famous military strategist Sun Tzu wrote in *The Art of War* about using drums and music to get soldiers to focus on the task at hand: "Gongs and drums, banners and flags are means whereby the ears and eyes of the host may be focused on one particular point. The host thus forming a single united body, it is impossible either for the brave to advance alone or for the cowardly to retreat alone. This is the art of handling large masses of men."[4]

Not all music is suitably martial. In the eighteenth century, an outbreak of what was known as "Swiss Illness" plagued European armies. Many of Europe's monarchs hired Swiss mercenaries to pursue their complicated and seemingly perpetual conflicts. The tough

Swiss soldiers were much in demand.* But there was a problem. These battle-hardened troops could be reduced to quivering masses of emotion by music — a particular type of music called *Ranz des Vaches* played by Swiss cattle herders. Every valley had its unique melody, played on the Swiss alphorn, but they shared a melancholic tone described by the eighteenth-century Swiss philosopher Jean-Jacques Rousseau in his book *A Complete Dictionary of Music.* He wrote that it "was so generally beloved among the Swiss, that it was forbidden to be played in their troops under pain of death, because it made them burst into tears, desert, or die, whoever heard it; so great a desire did it excite in them of returning to their country."[5]

A Swiss doctor who studied this phenomenon invented the word "nostalgia" to describe what was seen as a genuine and potentially deadly illness. The word was formed from two Greek words meaning "homecoming" and "pain." Literally "homesickness."[6] Nostalgia was listed in textbooks as a medical condition until the twentieth century, although no one could figure out why it seemed to affect Swiss soldiers more than anyone else. It spread to other armies and nationalities and was dealt with brutally. The last thing an army commander needed was soldiers losing the will to fight over a bout of homesickness.

During the American Civil War, Dr. J. Theodore Calhoun, who served with the Union Army, presented a paper titled "Nostalgia as a Disease of Field Service." He held that battle was "the great curative agent of nostalgia in the field." Dr. Calhoun had a low opinion of those who suffered from nostalgia, accusing them of being unmanly. "Any influence that will tend to render the patient

---

* The Swiss later settled down and became a more peaceful nation, but their tradition of military prowess lives on in the famous Swiss Guard that protects Vatican City. And Switzerland has one of the highest rates of gun ownership in the world. Swiss soldiers are encouraged to hang onto their weapons after completing compulsory military service, creating a well-armed populace ready to deter any invader.

more manly, will exercise a curative power," he wrote. "In boarding schools, as perhaps many of us will remember, ridicule is wholly relied upon, and will often be found effective in camp. The patient can often be laughed out of it by his comrades, or reasoned out of it by appeals to his manhood."[7]

And if bullying and ridicule didn't eliminate an outbreak of nostalgia, then generals could always rely on the rallying power of the right kind of music. Writing about the use of bagpipes in 1584, Irish historian Richard Stanihurst explained, "This sort of instrument is held among the Irish to be a whetstone for martial courage: for just as other soldiers are stirred by the sound of trumpets, so they are hotly stimulated to battle by the noise of this affair."[8]

The bagpipes weren't created as a martial instrument, but their power to rally troops (and to mourn their passing in graveside laments) was adopted by Scottish clans when they fought each other, then when the Scottish fought the English, and later by Scottish regiments in the British Army. Such was the perceived power of the pipes that a Scottish bagpiper captured after the defeat of Bonnie Prince Charlie at the Battle of Culloden was sentenced to death, despite not being an active participant in the fight. James Reid's lawyer asked for mercy on the grounds that his client was just a piper, but the judge ruled that as a Highland regiment never marched without a piper, he was a member of the army, and his bagpipes were, therefore, an instrument of war.

The noise of the pipes may have struck terror into the hearts of the enemy, but these instruments of war didn't do much to protect the men who wielded them. Their lives were a price the British Army was willing to pay in the First World War in return for encouraging young men to charge toward German machine-gun fire. The pipers were easy targets for the enemy because they generally led the charge and very loudly advertised their positions. Of the

2,500 bagpipers who served in the war, an estimated 1,100 were killed or wounded.

One such piper was James Richardson from British Columbia. He was twenty years old when he enlisted in the 16th Infantry Battalion of the Canadian Expeditionary Force. In October 1916 Richardson performed an extraordinary act of bravery during the later stages of the Battle of the Somme that won him the Victoria Cross, the British military's highest award for valour.

The award announcement was made in an official British government notice.

> For most conspicuous bravery and devotion to duty when, prior to attack, he obtained permission from his Commanding Officer to play his company "over the top."
>
> As the Company approached the objective, it was held up by very strong wire and came under intense fire, which caused heavy casualties and demoralised the formation for the moment. Realising the situation, Piper Richardson strode up and down outside the wire, playing his pipes with the greatest coolness. The effect was instantaneous. Inspired by his splendid example, the company rushed the wire with such fury and determination that the obstacle was overcome and the position captured.[9]

Richardson didn't survive the battle; shortly after leading his comrades to victory, he left his pipes behind while helping a wounded soldier to safety. He went back to get them and was never seen again.

Richardson's body was unearthed in a farmer's field in 1920 and buried in a war cemetery in France. Amazingly, his pipes were also found, buried in mud, although it took more than eight decades to identify them as Richardson's. They are now on display at the British Columbia legislature in Victoria.

The practice of leading troops into battle with bagpipes continued into the Second World War, despite an order restricting pipers to the rear of the battlefield to cut down on their losses. The most famous example was during the D-Day invasion in 1944 when Canadian-born Scottish piper Bill Millin waded ashore on Sword Beach from a landing craft wearing a kilt and playing his pipes. He marched up and down the beach playing his pipes while soldiers died around him. British commando Tom Duncan was there that day: "I shall never forget hearing the skirl of Bill Millin's pipes. It is hard to describe the impact it had. It gave us a great lift and increased our determination. As well as the pride we felt, it reminded us of home, and why we were fighting there for our lives and those of our loved ones."*[10]

The strong links between music, the military, and nation-building survive in many of the world's more violent national anthems. It's hard to imagine a national day in almost any country that doesn't involve a military band playing the country's anthem along with soldiers marching and warplanes screaming overhead. It all speaks to the power of music in human affairs. Songs were a vital part of creating a uniform culture long before national anthems were created. In our world of instant access to almost all global knowledge, we tend to forget that there was no way of sharing and preserving information for much of human existence. Mass literacy has been

* Millin continued leading men into battle as the Allied forces fought across Europe. Captured German soldiers said they didn't try to shoot him because they thought he had gone mad. Millin lived until 2010.

achieved only relatively recently. It's estimated that in 1820 only 12 percent of the world's population could read and write. When survival was based on agriculture, there was little need for most people to be literate. But people still wanted stories, and the easiest way to record the past and preserve it for the future was through song — something understood by those who wanted to get their version of events into the public record.

In the Overture of this book, we saw how London theatre audiences responded to a Scottish military victory by adopting "God Save the King" as a national rallying cry. But the 1745 Battle of Prestonpans also inspired other music, including the song "Hey, Johnnie Cope," written in the immediate aftermath of the battle by a local farmer. Sir John Cope was the English general who lost the battle, and he is brutally mocked in the song for fleeing the field at the sound of the Highland bagpipes. This was pure propaganda, and the Jacobites ensured the song was spread far and wide to make their famous victory known. Of course, Scots have depressingly long memories when it comes to fighting the English, so the song is still popular today, along with later, sadder songs about the crushing of the rising. And the fact that so many of those Jacobite* songs are still sung in Scotland shows how powerful and successful they were. If you have a version of history set to a catchy tune stuck in your brain, it will be very hard to shift it. In largely oral societies, that's how national histories, tragedies, and heroic deeds were passed down through the generations.

In the introduction to his 1856 book, *The Ballads of Ireland*, Irish scholar Edward Hayes wrote, "No nation can afford to despise its ballads. They are an important portion of its history — the first efforts of its civilization. And in the record of a nation's

* The word "Jacobite" means a supporter of Jacobus, which is Latin for James. The last Stuart king was James II, and those who tried to get him — and then his son and then his grandson — back on the British throne were called Jacobites.

ballads, we find the history of its progress and its triumphs — or its decay and death."

We have always turned to poets and singers to explain our world and tell our tales. But the inspirational power of music worries governments. While it can be used to create conformity and support for the state, it can also help to motivate revolution. France's "La Marseillaise" was a revolutionary song composed to inspire people to fight back against foreign invaders intent on destroying the new republic. But the song was banned when the French monarchy was restored in 1815. It wasn't reinstated as the anthem until 1879.

Vladimir Lenin recognized the power of all art to sway the people's mood. The founder of the Soviet Union wrote, "Every artist and everyone who considers himself such has the right to create freely, to follow his ideal regardless of everything."[11]

Sounds great — total freedom for artists in the new workers' paradise. However, if you think there's a giant "but" hovering over that sentence, you're right. Here it comes: "But then, we are Communists and ought not to stand idly by and give chaos free rein to develop. We should steer this process according to a worked-out plan and must shape its results."

All totalitarian states attempt to control music. They ban anything seen as deviating from the party line. Performers of unapproved music can find themselves imprisoned or exiled because if there is one thing a dictator fears, it is the sound of people singing about freedom. And with good reason, because music makes humans hopeful, and hope can topple regimes.

In 1988 the "Singing Revolution" broke out in the Baltic states. The Soviet Union had annexed Estonia, Latvia, and Lithuania during the Second World War. But the dream of regaining independence never faded in those countries, and when Moscow started to loosen its iron grip in the mid-1980s, new pro-independence movements began to emerge. This was the era of *glasnost* and *perestroika* — the opening of the Soviet Union to economic and political reforms. People began to speak — and sing — about a better future.

No one really knew what the Soviet promise of reform actually meant. The secret police, the KGB, kept monitoring crowds and suspected political activists. But people sensed real change in the air and began to test this new freedom's limits. The goal, of course, was independence, but that seemed like an almost impossible dream. Could non-violent protests really bring an end to Soviet rule?

The demonstrations began in Estonia when people gathered to sing banned patriotic and protest songs. The singers expected to be arrested. The police did nothing. More songs were sung. After a 1988 music festival in the capital city of Tallinn, thousands of people started singing Estonia's unofficial national anthem, "Mu Isamaa On Minu Arm" (My Fatherland Is My Love). The crowd kept singing long into the night. The next day, they were back. They did that for five nights, with the crowd growing to one hundred thousand people. They sang about their country, drank beer, laughed, cried, and waved the Estonian flag in public for the first time in almost half a century.

After the spontaneous concerts, Estonian artist and political activist Heinz Valk wrote an editorial in the weekly newspaper *Sirp Ja Vasar* (Sickle and Hammer). The title was "Singing Revolution." "A nation who makes its revolution by singing and smiling should be a sublime example to all. It is impossible to even imagine in Estonia's city streets the riots, barricades, burning automobiles, and similar features of mass revolt by large nations. This is not our way!"[12]

The movement now had a name. The authorities still didn't know how to react. The crowds continued to gather and sing. Entire families — mothers, fathers, children, grandparents — joined hands and raised voices. Lacking orders from the top to break up these musical gatherings by force, the police were reluctant to intervene. The Singing Revolution spread to the other Baltic states,

Latvia and Lithuania, and became more organized. Now the goal was not just to sing for freedom but to win it. In September 1988 an estimated three hundred thousand people attended the Song for Estonia Festival in Tallinn. That was about 20 percent of the country's population at the time. It was an openly pro-independence event, with speeches from political activists, including Heinz Valk, who, in addition to naming the revolution, now gave it its most famous slogan: "One day, no matter what, we will win!"

And there was music. Video from the concert shows people holding hands, waving Estonian flags, and singing along. There was a sense the movement was now unstoppable. The following summer, people took to the streets throughout Estonia, Latvia, and Lithuania. What became known as the Baltic Way was a demonstration to join all three capitals — Tallinn, Riga, and Vilnius — with a human chain. About two million people held hands to create an unbroken connection 690 kilometres long. And they sang. It was the ultimate demonstration of people power. Two years later, the Baltic states were again independent nations. They had sung their way to freedom.

♫

We turn to music in times of our greatest happiness and deepest despair. It's what lifts and soothes us. When the *Titanic* sank, the ship's band played to help calm the passengers. The musicians kept playing even as the water washed across the deck. All the band members died, but the survivors always remembered their sacrifice.

Music is like oxygen; it acts as an accelerant to our emotions. Researchers at the University of London found that listening to music can change how we feel about things. The study "Crossmodal Transfer of Emotion by Music" examined what happened when people listened to a short burst of music before looking at an emotionally neutral face. When the music was happy, the face appeared happy. And when the music was downbeat, the face seemed sad.[13]

We take our emotional cues from music; this is why movies have soundtracks. Our eyes can see what is happening on screen, but it is the music that augments our emotions. That is why music was vital to the movies even before soundtracks were invented. The silent movies from the early days of Hollywood were accompanied by live orchestras or piano players. Their music helped audiences laugh and cry at the right moments. Think of how the music from *Jaws* defines the entire movie. Or how so many of us are moved to tears when Elliott has to say goodbye to E.T. It's the music that taps into our emotions.

One of the most powerful scenes in the movie *Casablanca* is when patrons at Rick's Café burst into "La Marseillaise" to drown out a group of German officers singing an anti-French song. The camera focuses on one young woman who ends the song with shouts of "*Vive la France!*" and "*Vive la démocratie!*" while tears stream down her face. It's probably the most powerful scene in the movie — and deliberately so, because *Casablanca* is a proudly anti-Nazi film.

There was more than just acting going on in that scene. Madeleine Lebeau had just turned nineteen when the movie was shot in 1942. She had arrived in Hollywood two years earlier, having fled Paris ahead of the invading Germans. Like the plot of the movie, her escape also involved travelling to Portugal using purchased transit passes of dubious origins. The tears she cried on film were real.

To learn more about why music affects us so strongly, I contacted Michael Dean at the University of California in Los Angeles. Dean is a professor of voice performance and a renowned classical singer who performs in operas and concerts worldwide. He knows about the power of music. And he has a rather surprising view of why Olympic anthems have such a great impact: "In my opinion, the most emotion-evoking performance of our national anthem that ever happens is the instrumental version at the Olympics when no one's singing at all."

That seems like a strange opinion for a voice performance professor to hold, but he goes on to explain why. He describes that shared moment — the athlete on the podium, us watching at home, the camera in close-up on the winner's face — as one when "we all wordlessly share a sense of unity." The words don't matter. What we are experiencing together is the familiarity of the music. We, the audience, may never know what it is like to win Olympic gold, but for those few seconds while the anthem plays, we feel a connection to the athlete and each other. We share the emotion and the joy. We cry as one.

That moment was perfectly illustrated in the medal ceremony for the men's 10-metre synchronized diving platform event at the 2021 Tokyo Olympics. British diver Tom Daley was one of the gold medal winners. "To hear the national anthem play — I was gone," he said in a BBC interview. "I couldn't even sing. I was halfway singing, and I was blubbering. I just can't believe it."

Daley's emotions were shared by others. One fan wrote on Twitter (now X), "I'm crying watching Tom Daley crying at the National Anthem." For that minute when the anthem was played, there was a powerful musical connection shared by participants and observers.

"The reason music is such an integral part of human existence is because notes, melodies, harmonies, and rhythms that we associate with certain events in our experiences go into our brains," Dean says. "Music works on the brain in a way that almost no other thing does, which is why people who have dementia can still play instruments or can still recognize songs."

Dean describes the feeling we have when we hear music that transports us back to life's important moments, good and bad. Like the song on the radio when you first kissed your high-school crush, or the hymn played at your mother's funeral. For Dean, emotions come flooding back whenever he hears songs featured on the mixtape his parents played during drives to the beach. "When I hear those songs, I can smell the salt air, and I can feel the heat on my skin, and I am inexplicably happy when I hear those chords and those melodies, no matter what the words mean."

National anthems tap into those deep associations between familiar music and important events to create a common sense of purpose and unity. We cry for the athlete from our country but not for the winner from another nation. Even if we recognize their anthem, it doesn't generate the same emotional connection. We have been programmed from birth to react to our own national songs. But we can still be moved by new music and raw emotion. That's why seven-year-old Amelia Anisovych touched so many people when she sang the Ukrainian national anthem at that Polish fundraiser. Few of us watching or listening understood the lyrics, but we understood the context of her performance as one of millions of refugees fleeing a terrible conflict.

A translation of Ukraine's anthem doesn't carry the same poetic power. The formal and stylized structure of anthems with phrases like "twilight's last gleaming" or "true north strong and free" are hard to recreate in another language. So, when we listen to the Ukrainian anthem, we react not to the words but to the music and the emotion. We do this all the time; think of Shakespeare and how the language of his plays can seem incomprehensible when we read it in a book, and yet, when we hear it spoken on stage, the same words suddenly resonate.

Most of the audience for Amelia's anthem performance would not have understood what she was singing that night in Lodz. But they recognized the music's power, holding up their phones to brighten the darkened arena in the same way previous generations would have held candles to bring hope through light. The message they heard from Amelia was clear: one of defiance and survival. You don't need to understand the lyrics to know that. What we respond to is the music. And that is why national anthems — even if the lyrics are violent, sexist, and sectarian — resonate with us. The tunes are planted in our consciousness. We can't help ourselves.

2
TO ARMS!

The man who climbed onto our wooden patio table at the beer garden was wearing a large French flag around his shoulders and a hat shaped like a chicken. He started marching up and down, forcing us to grab our pint glasses before they were kicked to the ground. He sang as he marched, a familiar tune.

Allons enfants de la Patrie,
Le jour de gloire est arrivé!

Other chicken-wearing and flag-draped Frenchmen quickly joined in singing their national anthem, "La Marseillaise." The sound swept along the crowded street.

Aux armes, citoyens,
Formez vos bataillons,
Marchons, marchons!
Qu'un sang impur
Abreuve nos sillons!

The anthem over, the man who started it all jumped off the table and gave a quick bow. We raised our glasses as the crowd poured past us, heading for Auckland's Eden Park where France was getting ready to meet New Zealand's All Blacks in rugby's 2011 World Cup. We trailed in their wake, ticketholders but not so invested in the outcome that we'd wear rubber chickens on our heads.

The chicken — technically, a *coq gaulois* or Gallic rooster — is a French national symbol. It's woven into the jerseys of football and rugby players. It's not uncommon for supporters to smuggle live roosters into stadiums and release them onto the playing field. I've seen it happen. The sight of groundskeepers chasing a rooster is hugely entertaining for the crowd.

But what struck me on that sunny September afternoon wasn't the chickens (real or rubber) but the words of "La Marseillaise." I knew it was a revolutionary song calling on the people of France to rise up, but now I wanted to know exactly what they were being called on to do. My French wasn't good enough, so I turned to Google for a translation. I was shocked at what I found.

> Do you hear, in the countryside
> The roar of those ferocious soldiers?
> They're coming right into your arms
> To cut the throats of your sons, your women!

It gets worse. After marching on, the citizen army is encouraged to kill their enemies and let their impure blood water the fields of France. Stirring stuff. But really? Is this the kind of message any country wants to send about itself? Go after us and we'll slaughter you?

Lots of countries do the same. The songs we sing to honour our nations aren't always kind and gentle. In fact, many of them are downright bloodthirsty. Or religious. Or sexist. Or all of the above. Of course, most of us are unaware of what other people's national anthems actually say because we rarely hear them, and when we do, they're often in a language we don't understand.

Even the songs that don't call for death or claim a special relationship with a deity could often do with improvement. But as we'll see, suggesting minor changes to a country's national anthem can generate massive outrage or even, in the case of some countries, a lengthy prison sentence and some major state-mandated re-education.

There is a certain pattern to national anthems. Countries born out of revolution tend to have bloodthirsty anthems that involve a lot of marching. It's hard to beat the French anthem on both counts, but plenty of others are in the running. China's "March of the Volunteers" encourages its people to brave the enemy's gunfire by marching toward it, building a new Great Wall with their own flesh and blood. Vietnam urges its people to march along the path of glory over the bodies of their foes. And when it comes to glorifying warfare, Algeria sets the standard with lyrics that take "the noise of gunpowder as our rhythm and the sound of machine guns as our melody." The author of Algeria's anthem allegedly wrote the words on the wall of his jail cell in his own blood while being held for interrogation by French colonial authorities. Which probably explains the verse that warns France about a day of reckoning.

Most of the revolutionary anthems are also big on praising liberty and throwing off the shackles of tyrants. That pretty much describes every anthem in the Americas. Except for Canada's, which we'll get to in later chapters.

♫

Let's work our way down the Americas. It's the part of the world where we find the greatest global concentration of violent anthems. That's because the countries of North and South America were mostly born from revolution. They often won their freedom in wars of independence, which became the foundations of their national identities. Their anthems were written to celebrate glorious victories and those who died fighting the oppressor. To make those deaths meaningful, the fight for freedom had to be portrayed as a mystical cause worth dying for.

It all began in the United States, the home of the original people's revolution. The United States, of course, is the land of the free and the home of the brave and celebrates bombs bursting in air. But we know that those bombs don't burst for everyone; the promise of freedom remains an aspiration for some, as we've seen in protests from the 1968 Olympics with the Black Power salute to the anti-racist gesture of knee-taking at sporting events, both of which we'll revisit in later chapters.

Most of the countries of Central and South America were carved out of the Spanish and Portuguese empires. By the early nineteenth century, those empires were in decline. The American and French revolutions inspired leaders like Simón Bolivar to take up arms against Spanish colonial rule. But the Spanish weren't the only enemy to inspire national anthems.

Mexico's anthem promises no mercy to anyone who threatens the nation, tosses in a "Marseillaise"-like reference to watering fields with blood, has a lot of stuff about roaring cannons, and comes with a big shout-out to liberty. That's a lot of fighting for a country that hasn't seen a foreign invader since the end of the Mexican-American War in 1848. The anthem was written shortly after that conflict, when the country lost more than half its territory — including Texas and chunks of what are now the states of Arizona, California, Colorado, Nevada, New Mexico, and Utah. It was a traumatic national defeat, so it does seem odd to opt for an anthem that relishes the prospect of war when your only real opponent has just humiliated you on the battlefield. It seems unlikely that, after the deaths of twenty-five thousand Mexicans, many families would have felt comfortable with lyrics thanking heaven for giving them a soldier in every son.

The message of most Latin American anthems is clearly aimed at their former Spanish rulers. The words "tyrant" and "slaves" appear a lot. Guatemalans sing lustily about how they'll die before being enslaved and how they hope that tyrants will never spit upon their faces again. Such lyrics might lead one to believe that Guatemalans fought bravely to liberate their country from Spain; in fact, though, it left peacefully in 1821. Independence was achieved through administrative edict rather than revolution. There was no war of independence. Mexico and the Central American provinces of the Spanish Empire negotiated their way out of Spain's control, although it took several more decades of joining and leaving alliances before the current independent nations were created. That turmoil meant that Guatemala saw no pressing need for an anthem until seventy years later.

The one it got was written by a Cuban poet who basically described his own experiences in Cuba's wars of independence against Spain, which were still going on at the time he wrote the lyrics in 1896. He just assumed that what happened in Cuba must have happened in Guatemala too. José Joaquín Palma submitted his poem anonymously when Guatemala's president announced a competition for the country's anthem. He didn't admit to being the author until 1910, probably because he was also a member of the jury that selected his own work as the winning entry.

The lyrics were reworked in the 1930s to more accurately reflect the reality of Guatemala's peaceful path to independence. The stuff about tyrants and wishing death over slavery remained, but the bits about torrents of blood and clashing of steel were dropped in favour of lines about how the road to nationhood was "managed without bloody clash."

Nicaragua has had several goes at picking the right anthem, starting in 1876. There was another attempt in 1889, one in 1893, and yet another in 1910. In 1939 it finally settled on the anthem still used today. And it's something of an exception in Latin American anthems — and probably shouldn't be featured here at all. Because it's a deliberately anti-violent song. It was written in 1918, while the country was under American military occupation following a civil war. The writer was anxious to avoid inflaming nationalist passions. The lyrics do feature cannons — but only to note they no longer roar across the land. Instead of calling on sons to lay down their lives, it instead asks for peace to shine beautifully in the sky.

A nice message, but one that doesn't reflect Nicaragua's bloody experience of civil war. Most nations have the problem of a bloody anthem sung in peacetime; during the brutal battles of the Contra wars of the 1980s, Nicaraguans sang about peace while thirty thousand people died in the fighting.

♫

Once we get into South America, the anthem violence really heats up. This is where most of the fighting against Spanish rule took place. An estimated six hundred thousand people died in the various wars of independence. The vast majority of the deaths were revolutionary fighters or civilians, so it's no surprise the anthems of these new South American nations were filled with fury and venom aimed at their former rulers.

It's fair to sum up the entire range of anthems in South America as promoting freedom, with various degrees of sacrifice — from hard work to death — on offer in the pursuit of liberty. Better to die than to live as a slave is a common theme. You should remember that most of the people doing the singing didn't seem too concerned that the Indigenous Peoples of the conquered lands didn't feel very liberated or free.

Argentina's anthem is one of the oldest on the continent, adopted in 1813. Memories of brutal Spanish rule were still fresh and were reflected bloodily and at length in the song. Here we find the lines, "Don't you see them devouring as wild animals all people who surrender to them?" It may have captured popular sentiment at the time, but times change.

By the start of the twentieth century, Argentina was one of the richest economies in the world. Immigrants and capital were pouring into the country. There was talk of Argentina rivalling the United States as an economic power in the Americas. Playing the victim when you were now as rich as your former subjugator seemed inappropriate. And then something unusual happened in the history of nations. Argentina took a reflective look at its anthem and decided to behave — and there's no better way of putting this — like an adult.

It all reached a head in 1900 during a visit to Spain by the Argentine naval training vessel *Presidente Sarmiento.* The tall ship's voyage to ports around Spain was both a diplomatic and public triumph, with huge crowds turning out to see the frigate.* The visit was seen as a symbol of a new relationship between not just Argentina and its former colonial master, but also with the world. Argentina had arrived, and it was time to grow up.

Among the many visitors to the ship were members of the Spanish royal family and the country's political leaders. There were several occasions when the Argentine national anthem was sung. That meant a bunch of Argentinian sailors singing lyrics that described their hosts as tyrants, oppressors, and bloodthirsty tigers. The Spanish listened politely. There were no official complaints, but

* The *Sarmiento* continued to serve as a training ship with the Argentine navy until 1961 and is now a museum ship in Buenos Aires.

politicians back in Buenos Aires thought it was maybe time to dial back the rhetoric.

A presidential decree was issued saying the anthem "contains phrases written as a product of another era and have since lost their relevance. Such phrases denigrate the patriotism of the Spanish people and are incompatible with international relations of friendship, union, and harmony that today unite the Argentine Nation with Spain."[1]

The decree approved a much shorter anthem that dropped all the anti-Spanish stuff, but Argentinians still get to swear they will die with glory if required. Unfortunately, there wasn't much glory ahead. A corrupt political system, an economy that relied heavily on agriculture, and the sale of key national assets to foreign companies all contributed to economic decline, threats of revolution, and military dictatorships. The early promise of an Argentine superpower was never fulfilled.

Other South American nations have also reworked their anthems to shed some of the more incendiary verses. Chile no longer warns Spain that if it invades, the people will draw arms and know victory or death. Colombia, on the other hand, actually added a verse to its anthem during a border war with Peru in the 1930s, where the singers promised — in the depressingly familiar way of violent anthems — to give their lives for their country, "Since to die for the fatherland is not to die, it is to live." Fortunately, not too many had to die on that occasion — and hardly any were killed in battle. Most of the four hundred or so deaths in the war were due to jungle diseases. The wartime verse is no longer part of the official Colombian anthem. But they still sing how "the horrible night has ceased," and there's plenty of blood in there, enough when mingled with tears to make a river.

Perhaps the strangest route to independence in South America happened in Brazil, where the fight was more of a civil war. The

Portuguese royal family moved from Lisbon to Rio de Janeiro in 1807 to escape Napoleon's invading army. They obviously liked it there, because after Napoleon's defeat, they decided to stay and even declared a new, transatlantic state: the United Kingdom of Portugal, Brazil, and the Algarve. This move did not go down well in Portugal, where people didn't like their former colony now being treated as an equal. Protests turned into a revolution with a demand that the king return to Lisbon to "restore the metropolitan dignity."

King John VI set sail for Portugal in 1821, but his son remained behind to act as his regent in Brazil. When the Portuguese parliament voted the following year to dissolve the Kingdom of Brazil, Brazilians were furious. They weren't prepared to accept the reduced status of a colony. They were backed by Prince Pedro, who declared that "by my blood, by my honour, and by God: I will make Brazil free." When troops arrived from Portugal to take control, he ordered them to return home. But not all of them left, and fighting broke out in what was now a war for independence. Prince Pedro was declared emperor of Brazil in 1822.

All that history is necessary to understand why the anthem that Brazil initially adopted was later replaced. The new emperor took time out from the struggle for independence to compose the music, while the lyrics were provided by a local poet who followed the well-established South American trend, penning words that spoke of breaking chains, sneering at tyrants, and a readiness to die for freedom. It was also, like many anthems at the time, very long, with ten verses and a chorus, including some that pay tribute to Pedro — always a wise move when writing lyrics for an emperor.

However, songs written by and for a particular monarch generally don't have a long shelf-life, and this particular anthem was promptly replaced when he was forced to abdicate in 1831. The new anthem was mostly played without words. It wasn't until 1922 that the lyrics that are sung today were finally approved. Despite being written decades after the fight for independence, they still draw from that same well of predictable revolutionary clichés. They promise that no son of Brazil will "run away from the fight / Nor fear, who adore you, death itself."

Interestingly, Emperor Pedro still gets a shout-out in the anthem, although the reference would likely be lost on anyone outside Brazil. The opening lines recount how "the resounding shout of an heroic folk" were heard along the shores of the Ipiranga. That's the river in São Paulo where Pedro made his promise to fight for Brazilian freedom. It's now the site of a monument to the independence of Brazil. It's also where Pedro's body is buried. And remember that anthem Pedro composed the music for? It's now known as the "Independence Anthem" and is still sung today every September 7 as part of Brazil's Independence Day celebrations. The verses praising Emperor Pedro are omitted.

♫

It's frustrating that so many countries see their national identity deriving from the amount of fighting and dying that had to be done through the ages. China's civilization stretches back thousands of years, but apparently the only stuff that's a source of anthemic pride is the fight of volunteer armies against Japanese invaders in the 1930s.

"March of the Volunteers" was originally part of the soundtrack for a 1935 movie. *Children of Troubled Times* was a pro-Communist film made at a time when China was ruled by a right-wing military dictatorship. The country was embroiled in a civil war between the government and Communist rebels. This situation was further complicated by the Japanese invasion of Manchuria. These were definitely troubled times. The movie tells the story of two friends in Shanghai. One joins the Communist resistance against the Japanese; the other is more interested in pursuing a glamorous widow. But when his friend dies, he abandons love and joins the fight against the invaders.[2]

Children of Troubled Times ends with the protagonist and the rest of the volunteers grabbing guns, swords, pickaxes, and clubs and marching off to battle while singing the theme song.

The movie's theme song was written by the playwright Tian Han. The music was composed by Nie Er, but he never got to see the movie or to know how famous his tune would become; he died in a swimming accident shortly after completing his composition. Tian Han survived the fighting and continued writing plays but fell afoul of the authorities during China's Cultural Revolution in the 1960s. He died in prison but was rehabilitated posthumously as a national hero.

"March of the Volunteers" became a song of resistance throughout the war against the Japanese. When the Communists took power in 1949, the party adopted the song as the national anthem of the People's Republic of China. It calls for a literal sacrifice from the people of China. "Arise, we who refuse to be slaves," it begins. "With our very flesh and blood / Let us build our new Great Wall!"

That's an image baked into modern Chinese culture. When President Xi Jinping spoke in 2021 to mark the centenary of the founding of the Chinese Communist Party, he referenced those opening lines when he said, "The Chinese people will never allow any foreign forces to bully, oppress, or enslave us. Anyone who dares to try to do that will have their heads bashed bloody against the Great Wall of Steel forged from the flesh and blood of over 1.4 billion Chinese people."[3]

When your supreme leader uses violent imagery like that, the idea that anyone in China would criticize the anthem is laughable. It's an untouchable piece of the Chinese state. The government describes the anthem as expressing "China's admirable tradition of courage, resolution, and unity in fighting foreign aggression."[4]

You can see why this piece of musical propaganda was valuable during the long wars against internal and external opponents. But surely China's four thousand years of civilization contain something more inspiring for an anthem.

♫

It's hard for newly liberated nations to let go of the idea that the most glorious thing in their past is warfare. In the euphoria of independence, the song that helped get you there may seem like the inevitable choice for the future. But as the years pass and revolution turns into the more mundane struggle of daily living, an anthem glorifying death in battle seems out of touch with what people want. When the first word in your anthem is "soldiers," you have a pretty good idea of what's coming. Vietnam has the dubious honour of owning one of the world's bloodiest national songs — it's right up there with those of France and Algeria. Like China's anthem, it was written during a period when Vietnam's citizens were suffering from Japanese occupation and engaged in an ongoing war of independence against the French colonial power, which still administered the country even during Japanese rule.

"Tiến Quân Ca" (March to the Front) has the soldiers of Vietnam hurrying along the road to the battlefield. The flag they carry is red with blood. The path they march along passes over the bodies of their foes. And of course, it's not just a regular everyday path; it's a path to glory, on which is heard the distant rumble of guns. The Vietnamese are told it's time to fight, because for too long "we have swallowed our hatred."

Vietnam is a country that should be sick and tired of war. The Vietnamese government estimates that 3.1 million people — soldiers and civilians — died in fighting between 1955 and 1975. Bear in mind how traumatic the Vietnam War was to the United States, which saw no fighting on its soil and lost just over fifty-eight thousand soldiers — less than 2 percent of the Vietnamese total. Seeking a path that leads to peace, hope, and reconciliation would seem a better choice than marching on one whose end is war.

Right next door to Vietnam, Cambodia was also destroyed by war. There, Khmer Rouge Communist soldiers battled government forces in the 1960s and '70s. The United States intervened in support of the government, launching massive bombing campaigns. An estimated three hundred thousand people died in the fighting, but what came next was far worse.

The victorious Khmer Rouge tried to turn the country into a self-sufficient agrarian society. All of the country's culture and traditions were to be destroyed in a great reset of the nation, which began with a declaration that the revolution marked the start of "Year Zero": a new beginning for Cambodia. The cities were emptied at gunpoint, and the population was forced into rural labour camps. Those suspected of disloyalty or being intellectuals (and just wearing glasses was sufficient proof of guilt) were massacred in what came to be known as the Killing Fields. The weapon of choice was the pickaxe, used to save the expense of using bullets. In less than four years, an estimated two million people died — a quarter of the country's population.

The national anthem adopted by the Khmer Rouge opens with blood, like so many other revolutionary songs. There's so much blood that it floods the towns and plains of the country, but that apparently was the necessary cost for a glorious victory. The anthem and other patriotic songs were played constantly while starving people were forced to work in the fields.

One of the people who played for the Khmer Rouge was Arn Chorn-Pond. He was from a musical family, which probably saved his life. Chorn-Pond was eleven years-old when he was taken to a work camp. He described what that was like: "We were starving. Three or four times a day, they would kill people and force us all to watch. I was forced to push people into graves. If you didn't do what the Khmer Rouge told you to do, they'd kill you too."

Chorn-Pond, who now devotes his life to reintroducing music to a country that lost an entire generation of musicians, described how he survived when so many others died: "In the middle of all the killing, the Khmer Rouge forced us to play music. They told us they were going to start a music class and asked who would like to play. So, I raised my hand because I knew if I became a musician, they might give me more food."[5]

The audiences for these musical performances had no choice but to sing along and cheer enthusiastically. One of the most popular singers of the Khmer Rouge era was San Yoeun, who both recorded patriotic anthems and performed them live. She spoke about her singing career in an interview with the *Phnom Penh Post* in 2022:

> My feelings at that time up on stage were very happy. There was applause and cheering by the people who came to see my performances who seemed excited and emotional about the songs I was singing. But now I think of their applause bitterly because they had no other choice and their lives were very difficult because they did not get enough food to eat, unlike us artists up on stage. We were always fed well.[6]

An invading Vietnamese army overthrew the murderous Khmer Rouge regime in 1978. It took another fifteen years before the country regained its full independence. The monarchy, which had been ousted in 1970 by a military coup, was restored, under the same king. And the old anthem was also reintroduced. It's a traditional "God Save the King" type of song, opening with a call for heaven to protect the king. But then it moves on, with an invitation to remember the past and "temples asleep in the forest." The anthem is a gentle piece, slow and reflective, about a country where "songs rise up from the pagodas to the glory of the holy Buddhist faith." There's no death, no marching, no blood, no talk of revenge.

♫

The idea that it would be nicer to replace gruesome anthems with ones that celebrate a little peace, love, and understanding seems obvious. But nations can't or won't let go of their pasts. And it doesn't seem to matter how long ago the blood flowed or what's changed in the meantime, armchair warriors love their battle hymns. Unfortunately, we're usually so caught up in the moment that we often miss that message.

Among the Rugby World Cup games I attended in 2011 was the only one that mattered for many Scottish fans: England and Scotland. England's team, of course, was serenaded with "God Save the Queen." Scotland's song was its de facto anthem, "Flower of Scotland." I had sung it often. But this time, because of my experience with the French anthem, I listened to what the lyrics said. And here's what you need to know about "Flower of Scotland."

It was composed in the 1960s by Roy Williamson of the Scottish folk group The Corries. By 1990 it was being played before rugby games. The football team was slower to adopt it, but it's now hard to imagine a Scottish sporting event — or indeed any Scottish occasion that requires the playing of a national song — without hearing "Flower of Scotland." This all just happened. It wasn't planned, and there's nothing official about it. Scotland isn't technically a nation in the UN sense of the word, so it doesn't require an official anthem. But it's difficult to envision any other song taking its place if Scotland should ever regain its independence.

And that's a pity. Because the people of Scotland should really think about what kind of song they want to sing to celebrate their nation. Most countries are stuck with their bad anthems (Really France? You'd go with throat-cutting lyrics if you had to write your national anthem today?), but a new country has a choice. And you'd like to think it would look forward rather than backward. "Flower of Scotland" is all about defining Scottish identity as the need to beat the English.

Fair enough, you may say, because let's face it, that's a situation that's shared by a considerable number of nations around the world. More than a quarter of today's countries were part of the British Empire at some point in their history — from Afghanistan to Zimbabwe. And a fair number of them have pretty good reasons to cheer on Anyone But England. It's quite surprising that so few of those nations have anthems that target the English in the way that South American nations trash-talk the Spanish. Ireland's "Amhrán na bhFiann" (The Soldier's Song)* does (it has cannons, rifles, despots, and slaves). The United States' "The Star-Spangled Banner" celebrates a two-hundred-year-old military victory over British forces. But countries like India, Kenya, and Jamaica have preferred to take the high road of hope over settling scores with their brutal imperial overlord. Instead of refighting old battles, these anthems talk of blessings, peace, wisdom, love, and liberty. It's a lesson that Scotland should learn from.

There's a marvellous video that was produced for the BBC to promote the 2012 Six Nations rugby tournament. It starts in

* The Irish national anthem was originally written in English. It was only after its approval as the anthem of the Irish Free State that an Irish-language translation was adopted and eventually became the standard. While both versions are deemed official, the anthem is now rarely if ever performed in English.

bewildering fashion, with fans from Ireland, Scotland, and Wales all shouting out "England!" with apparent joy. Why, viewers might momentarily wonder, are all these people supporting their traditional enemy with such passion? And then words appear on the screen…. "The Six Nations. It's not about who you want to win … it's about who you want to lose." And then it cuts to a bunch of slightly hapless English supporters in a pub saying, "Scotland, France, Wales, definitely Wales" before the final caption appears, "The Six Nations on the BBC. United in Rivalry." It's hilarious, though the BBC refused to air it, calling it "inappropriate."[7]

But the promo makers knew exactly what they were doing. Because for the Irish, Scots, and Welsh, beating the English is what it's all about. That used to be done — or at least attempted — on the battlefield. And it usually didn't go well for the smaller nations. That fight has now transferred to the less-violent world of sports, which, as George Orwell observed, "is bound up with hatred, jealousy, boastfulness, disregard of all rules and sadistic pleasure in witnessing violence: in other words, it is war minus the shooting."[8]

The trouble is, Scotland has to go a long way back to find a significant military victory over the English. All the way back to 1314. That's more than seven hundred years. The Battle of Bannockburn* saw a vastly outnumbered Scottish army under Robert the Bruce defeat the invading army of England's King Edward II. The victory was vital in securing Scottish independence. And that's what "Flower of Scotland" celebrates, an ancient battle against "proud Edward's army" that "sent him homeward tae think again."

You have to wonder. Scotland is a small country but one with an extraordinary history of influencing the world through contributions from writers, scientists, economists, political thinkers,

* This is not the battle at the heart of *Braveheart*. That fight, at Stirling Bridge in 1297, was indeed a major victory, but it didn't end the war, and William Wallace's army was defeated when the English regrouped and returned the following year.

inventors, and industrialists. There's much for a proud nation to honour. And yet it chooses to sing about the last time it gave the English a really good thrashing.*

Suggesting alternatives for an anthem is a game no one can win. "Flower of Scotland" has acquired extraordinary momentum for a song that's only been in the mass consciousness for a little over a generation. It will be hard to shift it. But how about a little reconciliation as the basis for a national song? Or there's always Robert Burns to turn to. There have been campaigns to have his song "A Man's a Man for A' That" selected as Scotland's anthem. Or even "Auld Lang Syne." There's merit to the latter suggestion. It would instantly become the only anthem in the world that everyone would sing along to, making it possibly the only anthem worth having.

Public petitions to push the Scottish government into adopting an official national anthem have been rejected or ignored. You don't get to be a ruling politician without recognizing a minefield when you're asked to walk across one. In 2015 the governing Scottish National Party responded to one of the periodic official anthem calls by saying, "Scottish ministers believe that consideration of whether Scotland should officially adopt a national anthem, and if so, what that might be, should not be led by the Scottish government or by any single political party. We, therefore, have no current plans in this regard."[9]

This hot potato will not be handled until it can no longer be ignored. If the experience of other countries is anything to go by, the decision will involve parliamentary committees, public consultation, competitions, and a referendum — all so the blame for the

---

* That's not technically correct. There has been a more recent landmark victory. It happened in 1967 when Scotland's football team stunned England at London's Wembley Stadium, where England had won the World Cup just a year earlier. The 3–2 Scottish victory is seen by many as their greatest sporting victory over the "Auld Enemy." But it's hard to imagine it as the basis of a great national anthem.

inevitably disappointing choice can be dumped on as many people as possible.

The better option, of course, would be to have a debate on whether an official anthem is necessary at all. Or to just decide that with so many great songs to pick from, all of them will be equally acceptable and used randomly. You'd never know what song to expect at a Scotland national event. Maybe today it'll be "Loch Lomond." Or maybe it will be "Scotland Will Flourish." Or "Yes Sir, I Can Boogie."*

At least Scotland will have a choice if it ever gets around to deciding on an official anthem. People will have the opportunity to object, raise questions, and propose alternatives. If, after all that, they still don't like what happens, they can just refuse to sing along. But as we're about to find out, not singing can be as big a statement as belting your heart out.

---

* Seriously. The 1970s disco hit became a Scottish football fan favourite after a video of player Andy Considine performing the song for his stag party became so popular his Scottish teammates sang it to celebrate their qualification for the 2020 European Championships. Video of the post-match song and dance was tweeted out by the team. Then fans started singing it at matches. It would be a great national anthem.

3

HUMMING ALONG

Most of us only get to hear other countries' national anthems while watching international sporting events. The tradition of doing that is likely the fault of New Zealand's famous All Blacks rugby team. The New Zealanders have been intimidating international opponents with their haka since the late nineteenth century. Teams around the world have tried to come up with ways of countering the impact of the intimidating pre-game dance. Countries like Samoa, Tonga, and Fiji perform their own war dances before games. Other nations have adopted a stare-down approach. The French rugby team chose to march toward the haka-performing New Zealanders in a V formation during the final of the 2011 World Cup, played in Auckland's Eden Park. The confrontational approach didn't help the French team (they lost), and it earned them a £2,500 fine from the International Rugby Board, which actually has a rule about how opponents should behave during the haka — they must remain, standing still, at least ten metres on their side of the halfway line.

That rule wasn't in place on December 16, 1905, when the All Blacks took to the field in Cardiff to play Wales. Conditions at

Cardiff Arms Park were perfect. It was a beautiful day, more like spring than winter. The sunshine and warm weather encouraged people to show up hours before the game to guarantee a good spot for what was expected to be a classic encounter. The New Zealand team, who were already a powerhouse in international rugby, were on a tour of the Northern Hemisphere. They tore apart every opponent on that tour, winning all but one of their thirty-five matches. Then, as now, they started out with the haka. And then, as now, their opponents didn't really know how to respond. But the capacity crowd of more than forty-five thousand Welsh supporters knew what to do. The correspondent for Cardiff's *Evening Express* wrote that there is a "time when a Welshman must either sing or crack and he sings. He did it on Saturday." The crowd launched into the Welsh national song "Hen Wlad Fy Nhadau" (Land of Our Fathers).

Here's how the *Evening Express* described the scene:

> The Blacks had brought over the Maori war song with them, and it reeked of blood. With arms extended, and with stamping feet, they faced the Welsh team, and said the most cruel things. It was good Maori, phonetically rendered, but it was in the waving of arms, stamping of feet, and screwing of chins that the strength lay. In answer came the rolling heart tones of the Welsh singing, strident with calm confidence, greatly comforting. This had a great effect on the Colonists. They have since acknowledged that it took immediate hold of them, and that Wales had already scored.[1]

Inspired by the crowd, the Welsh rugby team handed the All Blacks their only defeat of their tour. And their supporters started the tradition of singing anthems at international sporting events.

However, there really weren't very many international sporting events taking place at the time of that famous Cardiff rugby game. Basically, the only international teams that competed against each other in team sports were parts of the British Empire, playing rugby, football, and cricket. The arrival of the modern Olympics started to change that, but the founder of the revived Games wanted to bring people and nations together rather than to celebrate nationalism. That was the idea behind granting the Olympics to cities rather than countries. For Baron Pierre de Coubertin, the founder of the modern Olympic movement, the goal of the Games was not to celebrate national achievements but individual victories. He wrote, "The important thing in life is not the triumph but the struggle, the essential thing is not to have conquered but to have fought well."[2]

As we know, that dream did not last long. Sports quickly became identified with national success. They became political. From the very beginning, national success was defined by the number of medals won, flags raised, and anthems played. The slow blend of nationalism and sporting prowess was completed at the 1936 Berlin Olympics, hosted by Nazi Germany. By then, the games were no longer about the struggle; international sports were purely about victory.

Emotional though they can be, Olympic anthem ceremonies are pretty passive affairs. The occasional athlete will sing along to the recorded instrumental anthem, but there is no sense of a massive national occasion. For that, you need two teams, a stadium, and as many fans as you can pack into the grounds. There's only one competition that brings all that to a truly global stage: the FIFA World Cup. Casual followers of football probably don't realize that the World Cup competition every four years is just the final part of a process that begins pretty much as soon as the world champions are crowned. FIFA recognizes more countries than either the United Nations or the Olympics. Most will never appear at a World Cup, but they do play in qualification tournaments in their regions. Tiny San Marino may not have won a single official international game, but they still get to play top-ranked teams like England and have their national anthem played in front of thousands of fans.

That is where you need to experience the full impact of anthem singing: a major stadium in a nation where the sport means everything. Preferably with a live band to accompany the crowd. The flags and banners waving; the voices of the fans combining in a way that makes it sound as if they are actually all singing in key. It's a staggeringly emotional and powerful moment that can't really be captured on video. You have to be there.

I was there in 2011 when Canada's men's rugby team took on New Zealand's All Blacks in Wellington. I got to sing "O Canada" along with the rest of the small but passionate group of Canadian supporters. We did our best to motivate a team that even the most delusional fan knew was about to get steamrolled by the best team in the world playing in their home stadium. And hey, it seemed to work. Two minutes in, Canada was in front. I took a picture of the scoreboard and prayed for a hurricane, lightning storm, or tornado. The immediate cancellation of the game due to catastrophic weather conditions seemed like the only way Canada could end up ahead.

The weather stayed fine, and five minutes later, New Zealand scored the first of a depressingly long list of tries, eventually winning 79-15. Sometimes, pouring passion into a song really makes no difference to the outcome.

♫

Television helped make the singing of a national anthem a political event in and of itself. It used to be that the focus of the cameras when an anthem was played was on the stadium itself. For example, at the 1966 World Cup final between England and West Germany, the only close-up shots during the pre-game anthems were of Queen Elizabeth — who wasn't singing along. No one was paying much attention to what the players were doing.

Eight years later, at the 1974 World Cup, hand-held cameras were down on the field, capturing the players' faces during the pre-game anthems. England didn't qualify for the finals that year, but Scotland did. And the close-up shots of the team's reaction when they heard "God Save the Queen" before the match against Brazil are priceless. They certainly weren't singing. Check it out on YouTube. Perhaps the players were recalling the extra verse of the British anthem that was occasionally added on appropriate occasions after Bonnie Prince Charlie's failed Scottish rising in 1745.

> Lord, grant that Marshal Wade*,
> May by thy mighty aid,
> Victory bring.
> May he sedition hush,
> and like a torrent rush,
> Rebellious Scots to crush,
> God save the King.

The opinion of the Scottish players — and many of their supporters — in 1974 was clear: "God Save the Queen" was not their national anthem. It took a little while to figure out what should replace it. As mentioned in the previous chapter, "Flower of Scotland" is now the song of choice for Scottish sporting events.

"God Save the Queen" (now "God Save the King") remains the anthem for England's football team and, somewhat perversely and very politically, for Northern Ireland's team — this at least cuts

* Field Marshal George Wade was commander-in-chief of the British forces during the 1745 Jacobite rebellion.

down on anthem-playing time when the two sides play each other.

The tune for "God Save the King" has also been used by other countries for their anthems — although with different words. Russia had "The Prayer of the Russians." Prussia had its own version, "Heil dir im Siegerkranz" (Hail to Thee in Victor's Crown), which was adopted as the imperial anthem after Germany was unified under Prussian leadership in 1871. This meant that when the First World War broke out in 1914, Britain and Germany shared the same tune for their national songs. The German anthem was changed to the tune we recognize today after the war.

Switzerland also adopted the tune and stuck with it until 1961. And of course, random bits of the British Empire — like the Falkland Islands — still have "God Save the King" as their official anthem. But one country, with no colonial connection to Britain, saw no reason to change. Liechtenstein, a tiny nation of forty thousand people squeezed between Switzerland and Austria, uses the tune for its national anthem, "Oben am jungen Rhein" (High on the Young Rhine). So, when Liechtenstein's football team played Scotland in Glasgow in 2010, the fans were understandably surprised to hear what they thought was "God Save the Queen" being played at a Scottish game. The Liechtenstein players — and presumably the small group of their fans present in a stadium that could easily accommodate the entire population of the country — thought it very unsporting of the crowd to boo their national anthem. The Scottish Football Association issued a public apology and condemned the booing fans for unsporting conduct.[3]

There was also some confusion when England played Liechtenstein in 2003 and both anthems were played, with English fans uncertain about whether they should be singing along to both.

This kind of confusion doesn't just happen at football games. The same tune popped up at the inauguration of Donald Trump as president of the United States in January 2017. In that country, the tune has been adopted for the patriotic hymn "America" ("My Country, 'Tis of Thee"). And Norwegians also recognize the tune, because it's used as that country's royal anthem — it is played at events involving the monarch, but it is not the country's national song.

♫

There are certain protocols that most people follow when a national anthem is played. You stand, and you're usually expected to sing. You usually want to, particularly at a major sporting event. As Wales found out back in 1905, the power of a national song belted out by thousands of people can inspire you to victory. It's all about intimidating your opponents. But until recently, it was usually just the crowd that sang along. The camera that tracked the unimpressed faces of Scotland's football team in 1974 didn't catch any of them singing. And it wasn't just because they didn't like the anthem. Players of all countries were usually seen staring ahead, silently, thinking of the game to come. The occasional player would mouth the words. Most did not.

By the 1990s, players were expected to sing along. Failure to sing at all — or with insufficient gusto — led to criticism in the media. German football players with Turkish roots were carefully scrutinized to make sure they were sufficiently enthusiastic about the anthem. Mesut Özil made more than ninety appearances for the German national team between 2009 and 2018. But he never sang the anthem. In his autobiography, *Gunning for Greatness*, Özil — a devout Muslim — wrote that he prayed in Turkish while the anthem was being played. There was no shortage of critics for his decision, but it seems odd to accuse a player who helped his country win a World Cup of a lack of patriotism.

The arrival of the internet and social media allowed fans to join in with complaints about players not singing. National coaches ordered their players to sing, and some even handed out lyrics of the anthem to deal with the sometimes-awkward fact that not all players actually knew the words.

Sport is both big business and a symbol of nationalism.* Governments have long used sports to push their political or ideological agendas. Hitler famously turned the 1936 Berlin Olympics into a propaganda tool for his Nazi state. The Cold War saw both East and West fighting proxy battles on sports fields. The drive to "win" the Olympics by topping the medal table motivates major countries like the United States and China. Even Canada gets into the game as a winter sports powerhouse, although for most Canadians the only sport that matters — and to be honest the only major team sport in which Canada is a real contender — is hockey.

The pressure on national teams can be massive. England's football team has failed to win a major tournament since the 1966 World Cup and has never topped the FIFA world rankings, but its supporters and the country's tabloid press treat every game and every tournament as one they are destined to win. English fans chant "football's coming home" at major tournaments — a reference to the fact that the modern game originated in England. Defeats are seen as calamities. Managers will do whatever they can — and recruit whatever athletes are available — in order to win. Results are everything, and all things can be forgiven as long as the team — and the country — ends up on top.

In the 1980s, the Football Association of Ireland recruited a legendary English footballer to manage its national team. Jack Charlton was part of the 1966 World Cup–winning side and had no Irish roots. What he did have was a desire to win. Charlton used what was called the "granny rule" to recruit foreign-born players who qualified for Irish citizenship through a grandparent.

* The management consulting firm Kearney estimates that the global sports industry is worth up to $620 billion. That's more than the gross domestic product of most countries.

The result was a team mostly made up of people who had never lived in the country and in some cases hadn't even visited until they showed up to play for Ireland. One player, Tony Cascarino, qualified through his Irish grandfather — although it turned out his mother was adopted. In 2000 Cascarino wrote in his autobiography, "I didn't qualify for Ireland. I was a fraud. A fake Irishman."[4]

At first, there was deep suspicion of Jack Charlton's methods. He fielded teams with as few as three Irish-born players. Charlton didn't care. He knew the critics would collapse under the weight of success. And he was right. His team of "plastic Paddies"* qualified for Ireland's first-ever major tournament, Euro 1988, and their first game was (and this may actually be evidence of karma or a deity) against England. The fans sang their hearts out during the pre-game anthem, but many of the players stayed silent. This was not a national anthem many of them knew, and it was sung in Irish — a language few of them understood.

The game is still remembered as one of Ireland's greatest sporting triumphs. The men in green defeated the heavily favoured English team, and Jack Charlton instantly became an Irish national hero.

Anthems are designed to bind a tribe. They are a test of loyalty. At their most provocative, they are designed to exclude as well as bond. Across the border from the Republic of Ireland lies a remnant of England's empire: Northern Ireland. And for reasons that are not entirely clear, it has its own football team, recognized along with the other constituent parts of the United Kingdom — England, Scotland, and Wales — as a country by the global body that regulates football, the Fédération Internationale de Football Association, or FIFA. It's strange, because most sports on the island

* A term coined in the 1980s to describe people who call themselves Irish but actually know very little about the culture and have never been to the country.

are organized on an all-Ireland basis that survived the partition of the 1920s. The Irish rugby team, for example, draws on players from both Northern Ireland and the Republic. But when the island was divided into an independent Irish state and British-ruled Northern Ireland, football was also divided.

The political and religious differences that separate so much of Northern Ireland's life also percolate into sport. Football was traditionally seen as a Protestant working-class game (the middle class often preferred rugby and never seemed too bothered about describing themselves as Irish on the rugby pitch and British in the bar afterwards). And in a deeply suspicious country where loyalties were defined by allegiance to the right (or wrong) religion, the governing body for football in Northern Ireland (confusingly called the Irish Football Association, as opposed to the Football Association of Ireland, which runs the game elsewhere on the island) insisted that it would show its loyalty to the British monarchy by selecting "God Save the King" as its national anthem.

As you might expect, a large part of Northern Ireland's population will not sing that song, either on the field or in the stands. This is partly the point: it guarantees that the team will only be supported by the pro-British section of the country. Some people want to change that, including former players like Gerry Taggart, who played fifty-one games for Northern Ireland.

"There's one slight issue left to go and that is the anthem. Why can't we get our own anthem?" Taggart asked in an interview with Irish public broadcaster RTÉ in 2019.[5] It's a good question, but in a part of the world where almost every facet of daily life has political undertones, just selecting a song would likely be impossible. The obvious candidate might appear to be "Danny Boy," which has been used by Northern Ireland at the Commonwealth Games. But it's not free from sectarian baggage; the tune is known by some as the "Londonderry Air," but only pro-British Unionists in Northern Ireland refer to that city as Londonderry: the mostly Catholic nationalist community calls it Derry.

Intractable though the Northern Irish anthem issue may seem, it has been resolved by another sport: rugby. Unlike football, there is only one Irish rugby team, drawn from the whole island — north and south. When Ireland plays games at its home stadium in Dublin, two anthems are played: the Republic's national song "Amhrán na bhFiann" (The Soldier's Song) and an anthem that was specifically commissioned for the team, called "Ireland's Call." When the team competes in other countries, only "Ireland's Call" is played. The Northern Irish players don't tend to sing the Irish anthem and aren't obliged to, but everyone joins in for "Ireland's Call." It's a little messy, but it seems to work.

Just who sings along to an anthem has become a contentious issue in many countries, where failure to sing can leave a player's loyalties open to question. Or even have them kicked off the team. In 2012 Adem Ljajić was a rising star on Serbia's national football team. But when he refused the coach's instruction to sing the national anthem, he was suspended. Ljajić never spoke about exactly why he wouldn't sing, just saying that it was for personal reasons. At a news conference, he said, "I'm sorry. I love Serbia, but I have to respect my beliefs. I've always wanted to play for this country. The coach asked me to sing the national anthem, but if you do not respect yourself, no one can respect you."[6]

What is known is that Ljajić's hometown was at the centre of violent ethnic cleansing during the many civil wars that raged during the break-up of Yugoslavia. The town's Muslim population, including Ljajić's family, was forced to flee their homes. Serbia's national anthem, "Bože pravde" (God of Justice), is seen by many Serbian Muslims as only speaking to the country's Orthodox Christians. Adem Ljajić didn't play for Serbia again until two years later, when a new coach was appointed, one who didn't insist on all the players singing the anthem.

Policing athletes for not singing a national anthem is truly a global practice. American football (soccer) star Megan Rapinoe refused to sing "The Star-Spangled Banner" and has often knelt during the anthem, which she said she has done to show her opposition to white supremacy and police brutality against Black people. The reaction has been predictable, ranging from the almost-inevitable Twitter threats of violence and death to hyperbolic claims from conservative commentators, including a former Trump White House aide turned right-wing pundit who said Rapinoe was out "to destroy everything that is wholesome in our country and in our Judeo-Christian civilization."[7] That's a big agenda for a football player, even one as good as Megan Rapinoe.

There are probably many athletes who choose to sing their country's national anthem even if their heart really isn't in it just to avoid being attacked online and in the media. But it's unusual to single out an entire team for failing to sing. That's what happened during a semi-final game at the Euro 2020 football tournament (confusingly played, like the 2020 Olympics, in 2021 because of the Covid-19 pandemic). Italy was playing Spain. A Northern Ireland politician didn't like what he heard. Or rather, didn't hear. John Taylor, who served as a British MP and member of the European Parliament before becoming a peer in the British House of Lords, turned to Twitter to express his disappointment: "Amazing that every member of the Italian team sang its National Anthem whereas every single member of the Spanish team remained totally silent. Not one sang the Spanish Anthem!"

The reaction on Twitter was instant and predictably savage. While Taylor — whose title is Lord Kilclooney — wasn't the only person to criticize the Spanish silence, you'd think that as a former European politician he would have known better. Spain's anthem,

"La Marcha Real," has no lyrics. The most the Spanish players could have done was hum along to the music.[8]

Spain isn't alone in having a wordless anthem. Three other countries have also opted for music only: Bosnia and Herzegovina, Kosovo, and San Marino. It's unclear why San Marino never bothered. The tiny state — with a population of fewer than thirty-five thousand — is entirely surrounded by Italy. It adopted its music-only anthem at the end of the nineteenth century. Lyrics were written for it by well-known poet Giosuè Carducci, who later became the first Italian to win the Nobel Prize for Literature. That's a pretty good pedigree for an anthem writer, but San Marino's government clearly wasn't impressed — nor were the people. The words never caught on and were never officially adopted. The Sammarinese seem to prefer their anthem the way it is: wordless.

Spain, Bosnia and Herzegovina, and Kosovo are countries that have experienced bitter civil wars, and there remain deep divisions that have not yet healed. Bosnia and Herzegovina and Kosovo were born from the violent collapse of Yugoslavia in the 1990s. The international agreement that ended the Bosnian war required that national symbols in the new nation should be inclusive of the country's main ethnic groups.

A competition was held for a new anthem, one without words. But even that has proved controversial; the winning composer was a Bosnian Serb who was condemned as a traitor by those members of his ethnic group who wanted Bosnia to become part of Serbia. Croats and Bosnians didn't like that a Serb composed the anthem. It's one of the rare national anthems (like "God Save the King") that gets booed by some of its own citizens, although it remains unique in that there are no actual words to condemn.

There have been several attempts over the last twenty years to adopt lyrics for the anthem, but even verses with such hopeful phrases as "we go into the future together" have proved unacceptable to some, presumably those who don't actually want to go into the future together.*

Kosovo faced a similar anthem problem to Bosnia and Herzegovina. It also held a national competition for a new anthem; it, too, has failed to find a set of lyrics that would satisfy all ethnic groups. And it has to walk a fine line politically because more than half the members of the United Nations do not recognize Kosovo as an independent state; Serbia claims it as part of its territory, a claim that is backed by UN Security Council members Russia and China. Finding words for its anthem is probably pretty low on the Kosovo government's list of priorities. But it does get to compete as a country at the Olympics and the FIFA World Cup.

Most people haven't had the opportunity to hear the anthems of San Marino, Bosnia and Herzegovina, and Kosovo. But Spain is a different matter. The Spanish anthem is one of the world's oldest. "La Marcha Real" dates back to the 1700s. It has had lyrics associated with it over the years, although none were ever officially adopted. The right-wing Spanish dictator General Francisco Franco approved lyrics that were used during his rule, which ended with his death in 1975. Franco came to power after a bitter civil war in the 1930s. The ghosts of that war still haunt the country today. The constitutional monarchy that replaced Franco sought to eliminate divisive symbols, and the national anthem went back to its original wordless state. There have been half-hearted attempts since to find new lyrics, but most people seem quite happy to just hum along.

There's a lot to be said for a wordless national anthem. You can't complain about who's included — and who's left out. Of course, you also can't have sixty thousand fans inspiring your football team to victory with a powerful rendition of the nation's song. But

* Opponents of the anthem have also accused the composer of plagiarism because of the tune's similarity to — of all things — the theme music from *National Lampoon's Animal House*. The composer denies stealing the tune.

despite the Welsh experience that launched all of this back in 1905, the power of anthem singing may be overrated. The lack of words didn't stop the Spanish team from winning back-to-back European Championships in 2008 and 2012 and the World Cup in 2010. That may be one reason why a popular chant at Spanish games is simply called "Campeones" (Champions). Spanish fans also have some quite specific chants to motivate their team, depending on the opposition, like "Es Ingles El Que No Bote" (It's the English That Don't Jump) and "Gibraltar Español" (Gibraltar Is Spanish). When it comes to football, everyone likes to trash-talk England.

The point is, there are plenty of songs and chants that fans can use to boost team spirit on the field. "Vamos Vamos Argentina" raises the passion of Argentina's football fans. The Irish ballad "The Fields of Athenry" can be heard soaring around Irish football and rugby stadiums. You don't actually need an official tribal chant to give your country a sense of worth. You don't need God. You don't need glorious victory over a historic enemy. And that's what was really happening back in 1905 when those Welsh rugby fans rallied their team to a famous victory over New Zealand's All Blacks. It was just a song that every Welsh person could share. The national implications — the identification of a song with the nation — came later.

So, here's what you need to ask yourself about a national anthem: if the words and music don't include everyone, is it really a national song? If some choose not to sing because it doesn't speak to them, is that the fault of the silent minority or the words? It is probably impossible to find a national anthem that every person in the country can accept as perfection. So maybe Spain, Bosnia and Herzegovina, Kosovo, and San Marino have it right: better to grumble about the lyrics you don't have than to deal with words you can't sing. The result is the same: you stand mute when the anthem is played, but at least if you're Spanish, the only people who will criticize you for staying silent are fools.

4

BADLY PLAYED AND MONOTONOUS

The head of the International Olympic Committee didn't pull any punches: "The national anthems are badly played," he said. "They are also monotonous. I think it would be better to play some sort of Olympic song."[1]

It was an extraordinary statement coming from the man running the Olympic movement. Avery Brundage was the president of the IOC from 1952 to 1972. He mostly got what he wanted. And in the 1960s, he wanted to get rid of national anthems and flag-raising ceremonies. He went public with his thoughts at a news conference just before the closing ceremonies of the 1964 Tokyo Summer Olympics.

Brundage was involved in the Olympic movement first as a competitor at the 1912 Stockholm Games and then as a sports administrator in the U.S. Olympic movement before his election as IOC president. He was a passionate supporter of amateurism and fought losing battles against both payments to athletes and the growing commercialization of the Olympic movement. He believed that athletes should compete purely for the love of the game. Of course, he was speaking from a position of privilege. While he came from humble beginnings, by the time he became a major power in the Olympic movement, Brundage was a wealthy man, thanks to his construction and real estate businesses.

Brundage was continually on the wrong side of history, not just on the issues of commercial involvement in sport and the rise of professionalism, but also on politics and the Olympics. He initially opposed calls to expel white-ruled South Africa and Rhodesia from the Olympic movement. He refused to take on the Soviet Union for its use of athletes who were professionals in all but name. And at the 1968 Mexico City Games, he was furious at the Black Power salute by U.S. athletes Tommie Smith and John Carlos, who raised black-gloved fists during the playing of the American national anthem after winning gold and bronze in the 200-metre sprint. Brundage demanded they be expelled from the Games and threatened to ban the entire U.S. track team if it didn't comply. The two sprinters were suspended from the team and sent home (although they did keep their Olympic medals).

Despite all that, his efforts to take nationalism out of the Olympics have a certain charming and naive idealism it's hard not to admire. He believed flags and anthems helped generate extreme nationalism. His 1964 news conference wasn't the first time Brundage had raised the issue. He'd already tried to convince the IOC to eliminate victory ceremonies but had been voted down. The Soviet Union representative commented that athletes should not be deprived of their pride in representing their country.

There's no doubt that athletes — and fans — can be deeply moved by medal ceremonies. After all, winning a world championship or an Olympic medal is the pinnacle of any athlete's career. But sometimes, strange things can happen on the medal podium. At the 2020 Tokyo Olympics (the one that was actually held in 2021 because of the Covid-19 pandemic), Flora Duffy of Bermuda won gold in the women's triathlon. Her country, with just sixty-four thousand people, was the smallest ever to win an Olympic event.

However, Bermuda isn't actually a full country — it's officially a British Overseas Territory: not quite a colony but not an independent nation either. It doesn't get a seat at the United Nations, but it does get to compete under its own flag at the Olympics. Its own flag but not its own anthem. When Bermuda's standard was raised at the medal ceremony, the music that was played was "God Save the Queen." There was a delightful moment when Flora Duffy, on recognizing the tune, turned on the podium to smile at the silver medallist, British athlete Georgia Taylor-Brown, who — happy to hear her own national anthem — shrugged her shoulders in confusion.

At least that anthem wasn't the wrong one (Bermuda does have its own territorial anthem, "Hail to Bermuda," which is played at events on the island). Possibly the worst anthem fail of all time took place in Kuwait at a shooting competition in 2012. Gold medallist Maria Dmitriyenko expected to hear the Kazakhstan national anthem, but what was played instead was the parody anthem created for the movie *Borat: Cultural Learnings of America for Make Benefit Glorious Nation of Kazakhstan*. Along with praising Kazakhstan industry for inventing toffee and trouser belts, the song also celebrates the cleanliness of the country's prostitutes.

Dmitriyenko stood stoically, hand on heart, only reacting at the very end with a laugh and a smile. Kazakhstan's team managers, however, didn't think it was funny. They asked for an apology, which of course they got, and for a new medal ceremony, which this time was accompanied by the correct anthem. Organizers said they downloaded the wrong anthem from the internet. They apparently didn't think it odd that the Kazakhstan anthem was sung in English. And they obviously didn't bother listening to the words.

Playing the wrong song can ruin what is supposed to be one of the greatest moments in an athlete's life. So, it's understandable if they get upset. Violetta Skvortsova of Belarus won gold in the triple jump at the 2017 U20 European Athletics Championships in Italy. She stood to attention as the flags were raised, but as soon as the first notes of the anthem played over the loudspeakers, it was clear from Skvortsova's face that something was very wrong. She grimaced, looked around, and then climbed down from the podium and wandered around the field until the anthem was done, before telling an official what had happened. The person responsible for playing the anthem had clicked on Bosnia and Herzegovina by mistake.

♫

It's clear to most of us that sports and national pride are inextricably linked. One of Canada's most successful athletes ever is Rosie MacLennan, a double Olympic gold medallist in trampolining in 2012 and 2016, a three-time World champion, and winner of many Pan American and Canadian titles. She was the only Canadian gold medal winner at the 2012 London Games* and was the Canadian flagbearer at the 2016 Olympics. After winning her first Olympic gold, MacLennan wrote in her blog about the highlight of the whole experience: "Completing my final routine was a highlight because that's the moment I was doing what I loved and was really in the zone but I have never felt so proud to stand on top of the podium, watching the flag raise and hearing the anthem play. I will never forget that moment or all the people that helped me get there."[2]

---

* A second gold-medal winner was later confirmed. Canadian weightlifter Christine Girard finished third in the women's 63 kg category in 2012, but both the gold and silver medallists subsequently tested positive for banned substances. Girard was named champion and received her gold medal at a ceremony in 2018. She also received a bronze medal at the same ceremony for the 2008 Beijing Olympics, where she finished fourth but moved up a spot after a reanalysis of blood samples led to the disqualification of the silver medallist.

The Olympic movement has always tried to present itself as an apolitical sporting organization with the motto *Citius, Altius, Fortius — Communiter* (Faster, Higher, Stronger — Together).* The founder of the modern Olympics, Pierre de Coubertin, wanted to create a competition between athletes where the goal was to foster unity and peace. And it wasn't supposed to be about winning. De Coubertin said, "Winning medals wasn't the point of the Olympics. It's the participating that counts."† The participants were supposed to be competing against each other, not on behalf of their respective nations. The Olympic Charter states that the "Olympic Games are competitions between athletes in individual or team events and not between countries."

Of course, no one is fooled by that disingenuous Olympic statement. The IOC tried for years to maintain the pretence that the Games weren't about countries, refusing to even entertain the idea of an official Olympic medal table. But from the very beginning, athletes were there to represent nations. As early as 1924, the IOC authorized the playing of anthems when the winner of each event was announced — but medals weren't awarded at the same time, because the tradition then was to hand out all the medals as part of the closing ceremony.

The American actor and newspaper columnist Julia Hoyt described an anthem ceremony she witnessed at the 1924 Paris

* The words "*Communiter*/Together" were added to the motto in 2021 to recognize "the unifying power of sport and the importance of solidarity."

† Pierre de Coubertin didn't just found the Olympics: he competed in them. It's not widely known that the Olympics also used to award medals for artistic endeavour — for literature, music, architecture, painting, and sculpture. De Coubertin won the gold medal for literature at the 1912 Summer Olympics for his poem "Ode to Sport," which he submitted under a pseudonym. The arts events weren't successful, largely because professional artists couldn't compete. The music category was particularly limited, as the judges had to base their decision on sheet music rather than listening to performances. The art competitions were eliminated after 1948, which is rather a shame. It would have been nice to see them evolve into a genuine competition. Who wouldn't want to see a sing-off between Adele and Beyoncé? Or a timed sculpture competition?

Summer Games that showed that even back then anthems weren't always treated with respect by supporters of other nations:

> It is a custom of the Olympic games that at the end of each competition the flag of the countries placed first, second, and third are raised, and the national anthem of the winning country is played. A large number of the people after the diving contests refused to stand up during the playing of *The Star Spangled Banner* and kept up their hooting and yelling during it. It was really shocking. A woman and two men next to me — French, and I should say from the country — were horrified and ashamed at the behavior, and rightly so.[3]

It wasn't until 1932 that the Olympics embraced the now-accepted pattern of a separate medal ceremony for each event, together with a three-step podium and the raising of flags while the anthem of the victor's nation is played. The podium first appeared at the Lake Placid Winter Games that year. The protocol for the Games stated that "each victory is recorded by the hoisting of the national flag of the winner. The national anthem of the nation is then played during which time the spectators remain standing."[4]

The modern era of anthem ceremonies had arrived. But the Olympic movement knew almost immediately that it had created a monster that could not be controlled. Nationalism had become inseparable from sporting achievement. The Olympic Games was the perfect vehicle for nations to strut on the world stage. It took just forty years to kill the naive idealism of the modern Olympic movement. The first modern Games were held in 1896, based on the idea of promoting peace through creating understanding across cultures. But the reason the Olympics caught on and became so popular was for exactly the opposite reason. The participating nations and the fans knew what was going on in the stadiums: the athletes were proving the superiority of their nation, race, morals, culture, and political system by winning.

The Berlin Games of 1936 was the moment when the Olympic movement as we know it today truly came of age. The thin veneer of amateur athletes competing for the joy of sport was cast aside to reveal the true nature of international competition: the real sport is politics, and the weapons are state-sponsored athletes and propaganda. And the Nazi propaganda message was crafted around the medal ceremony introduced just four years earlier. It was a perfect stage for presenting the superiority of the German nation.

When people today think of the 1936 Olympics, they tend to remember the magnificent achievements of Black American sprinter Jesse Owens, whose four gold medals were seen as a major blow to the Nazi message of Aryan superiority. But at the time, the Games — despite Jesse Owens — were seen as a triumph for the Nazi regime. German athletes dominated, winning thirty-three gold medals — nine more than the Americans, who finished second in the medal table. And the Germans made sure those medals were presented in front of vast crowds. German athletes on the podium gave the Nazi salute even when they weren't the gold medallists. Germans won 101 medals — almost a quarter of the total — so a lot of Nazi salutes were shown around the world.

And German anthems were played constantly — not just the familiar tune that is still used by Germany today, but also the Nazi anthem, "Horst Wessel Lied," a stormtrooper fighting song written by a Nazi Brownshirt commander killed by Communists in 1930. The Nazis knew the power of anthems and flags and symbolism mixed in with military might and propaganda.

Everyone knew the Olympics had been co-opted by the Fascist regime years before the opening ceremony. There had been calls for a boycott over Germany's persecution of Jews. The calls were so powerful and so persuasive that the head of the American Olympic Committee went to Germany in 1934 on a fact-finding mission — at the invitation of the Nazi government — and was convinced by his hosts that Jewish athletes would be treated fairly. On his return, he told reporters, "I was given positive assurance in writing ... that there will be no discrimination against Jews. You can't ask more than that and I think the guarantee will be fulfilled."[5]

The American Olympic Committee voted to attend the Games. The head of the committee justified the stance in a special pamphlet called *Fair Play for American Athletes*, in which he wrote, "The Olympic Games belong to the athletes and not to the politicians." He went on to say that "Jewry suffers from the radicalism and self-seeking of a few in its ranks who put personal advantages before the welfare of the race."

In the end, no country boycotted the Berlin Olympic Games. Without leadership from the United States, no other nation was interested in taking a stand. Fifty-one countries were represented in Berlin, making them the biggest Games up to that point. The man largely responsible for that — the man who claimed the calls for a boycott were part of a "Jewish-Communist conspiracy" — was future IOC president Avery Brundage.

We saw at the opening of this chapter how Brundage grew to regret the role of nationalism in the Olympic Games. But he never apologized for his position on the 1936 Games. Or for other controversial decisions during his twenty years at the helm of the Olympic movement.

While he ruled with an iron fist, he didn't get his own way every time. He couldn't get the support he needed to eliminate anthems, losing a vote on the issue in 1963. However, he wasn't the only person who wanted to get rid of anthems and flag ceremonies. When the matter was brought up again at an IOC meeting during the 1968 Mexico City Games, it almost passed.

At that time, the charge was led by another IOC member — Germany's Prince George of Hanover, who was also the president of the International Olympic Academy, which seeks to educate students, teachers, athletes, and journalists about the goals of the Olympic movement.

Prince George belonged to that peculiar class of elite people making up the royal families of Europe. They have spent generations intermarrying. They are a mixture of German, Scandinavian, Russian, Greek, and English, and all seem to be descended from Queen Victoria. They drift along in a rarefied world where they are all related to each other, and national boundaries don't seem to matter as much as bloodlines.

Georg Wilhelm Ernst August Friedrich Axel Prinz von Hannover was, amongst many other things, a grandson of the last German emperor, Wilhelm II, and — of course — a descendant of Queen Victoria, which meant that he also inherited British royal titles. His wife was Princess Sophie of Greece and Denmark, the sister of Prince Philip — which made him Queen Elizabeth's brother-in-law.

Despite being a German national — and serving for a time in the German army during the Second World War — he was obliged because of his British titles to seek permission from King George VI for his marriage. The king replied that "in view of the fact that a state of war still exists between Great Britain and Germany, His Majesty is advised that the case is not one in which it is practicable for His consent to be given."[6] Prince George got married anyway. The royal refusal didn't sour relations with his British cousins: Prince Philip attended the wedding (which happened after the war).

With connections like that, it's not surprising that he was able to live a comfortable and somewhat idealistic life. In his case, he was devoted to the ideas of education and athleticism. Becoming a member of the International Olympic Committee was an easy step for someone so well connected. And it was his idealistic attachment to the idea of purity in sports that led him to make a proposal for consideration by the IOC: "I propose that during the Victory Ceremony at the Olympic Games neither the national flags of the winners be hoisted, nor the national anthem of the champion be played. I propose, on the contrary, that just like in ancient Greece, each winner be saluted by the same flourish of trumpets."[7]

Prince George made a passionate case, arguing that the "Olympic Games are in great danger of losing their soothing and uniting effect on humanity through the growing interference of political trends."

While Prince George may have been idealistic, he wasn't blind to the importance of medal ceremonies to athletes like Rosie MacLennan. "It can not be denied that the hoisting of the national flag and the playing of the national anthem may have great significance for the individual athlete. It is, however, against good sense to impart the honour of victory to the winner's country by playing the anthem and hoisting its flag, thus distracting public attention from the personality of the athlete, which is done formally by the fact that all eyes are diverted from the athlete to the flag."

Prince George argued that the IOC should work to prevent the Olympic Games from becoming an event where "athletes merely fulfill the role of collecting points for their country."

While obviously sympathetic to the idea, IOC president Brundage pointed out that most national Olympic committees — in other words, most countries — were opposed. He seemed resigned to the fact that anthems and flags were there to stay. But the rules demanded a vote. You already know the outcome, because any human being with access to a television or streaming video service has almost certainly seen at least one Olympic victory ceremony. And flags and anthems are very much front and centre.

But Prince George's proposal actually received overwhelming support. The minutes of the Mexico City meeting record that a secret ballot was held. There were fifty-six members of the IOC present and thirty-four voted in favour and twenty-two against. So, what happened? Because the proposal required a change in rules, it needed a two-thirds majority in order to pass. It fell short of that mark by three votes. And that was the last realistic attempt to get anthems out of the Olympics, although supporters of the idea never quite let go of the idea, even though they knew it was dead.

Among the anti-anthemers was Lord Killanin, Brundage's successor, who served as IOC president from 1972 to 1980. In 1984 he wrote: "I am opposed to nationalism and I would be happier if national anthems were not used at the Games, but I realize that my view is not that of the majority. There is no doubt that some of the larger powers wish to retain the present medal ceremony and many of the newer nations, although it may be some years before their anthem is played or national flag raised, eagerly await their day."[8]

You just need to look at the reaction in Bermuda to Flora Duffy's victory to see the truth of Killanin's statement about nations eagerly awaiting their day. The government declared a national holiday called Flora Duffy Day. A street in the capital, Hamilton, and part of the national stadium were renamed in her honour. The Bermuda Post Office issued commemorative stamps and a statue was commissioned.

Many athletes say that hearing their country's anthem during a medal ceremony is one of the greatest moments of their lives. That's one of the reasons why many major events do their best to make sure that what they hear is the right tune and that it's well played. You'll remember IOC president Avery Brundage's complaint in 1964 about badly played anthems. He had good reason to say that, because back then the anthems were played live by an Olympic band. And it didn't always go well. The bands focused on learning the anthems most likely to be played, for the very pragmatic reason that most countries won't produce a gold medal–winning athlete. In fact, there are more than seventy countries that have never won any kind of Olympic medal. So, what's the point of learning a bunch of anthems that will never be played?

At the 1952 Helsinki Games, sixty-nine countries were represented and athletes from twenty-seven nations won gold. Among them was Josy Barthel of Luxembourg, who was the surprise winner of the 1,500-metre race. It was one of the biggest upsets of the Games. It was particularly upsetting for the band tasked with playing the live anthem. Not only had they never played it, they didn't have even the sheet music for Luxembourg's "Ons Heemecht." But the show had to go on, so the band improvised, playing something that sounded nothing like the Luxembourg anthem. Barthel stood on the podium in tears — although he was probably more moved by winning Luxembourg's first-ever Olympic gold than by the mangled music.*

Of course, badly played national anthems aren't just the preserve of sporting events. We'll leave aside the long list of individual singers who have spectacularly imploded while performing anthems live — usually they're Americans. That is probably because "The

* Almost half a century later, a researcher discovered that a Luxembourg athlete had won the men's marathon at the 1900 Paris Olympics. Michel Théato competed for France, although he apparently never became a French citizen. In 2021, at the request of Luxembourg, the IOC changed the nationality of the winner on the official Olympic record. Technically, Josy Barthel won his country's second gold medal, but no one knew that at the time.

Star-Spangled Banner" is performed at so many more events than are the anthems of other countries; indeed, outside the United States, anthems tend to be sung only at major national occasions and not at every high-school game. American performers also seem to take delight in introducing challenging changes to the anthem, which only increases the likelihood of a horrible outcome.

If you had to pick a winner for the World's Worst Anthem Band, then Egypt's army orchestra has to be a serious contender. You'd think that the visit of a foreign head of state would be the time to shine for a military band. It's not like the need to play the foreign anthem would come as a surprise. The band would have weeks to practise; they'd know exactly what they have to do, and they are professional musicians. So, it's hard to understand how the band has self-destructed so spectacularly on numerous high-profile occasions. It's easy to find YouTube videos of the Egyptian army band playing (and that's too generous a word) some of the world's most famous anthems while the leaders of the visiting nations stare straight ahead, presumably wondering just what was going on — or if this was a deliberate insult, worthy of a declaration of war.

When France's president François Hollande visited Cairo in 2016, he had to endure a performance of "La Marseillaise" that would have been considered monumentally embarrassing if delivered by a grade two school band sight-reading the music for the very first time. The French newsmagazine *Le Point* accused the band of "massacring" the anthem. But that wasn't the first time the band had dropped the ball so badly. When Russia's president visited a year earlier, the same thing happened. Vladimir Putin appears to wince during the off-key rendering of what news organizations called a "mangled" performance. And German chancellor Angela Merkel was also treated to a version of her country's anthem that sounded like it was played on kazoos.

While the Egyptian band may be a strong contender for Consistently Bad Performance, even it would have a hard time matching the noise that greeted then British foreign secretary Boris Johnson when he visited Libya in 2017. A BBC camera operator was there and shared a video that the kindest of commentators could only describe as "unique." It is staggeringly, hilariously bad and well worth the effort of finding on YouTube. As the BBC says in its tweet about the performance, "The UK's national anthem as you've never heard it before."

There are so many cringe-worthy performances of national anthems from bands around the world — Venezuela's greeting of China's president Xi Jinping is another classic — that we can't get to them all. But they all prove the point that it can be a bad idea to ask a third-party band to play your national anthem. If a head of state really thinks it's important to mark their arrival on foreign soil with a national song, perhaps they should bring their own band — just as some bring their own bulletproof vehicles. Or maybe it would be better to just have a good sound system and a digital file of the anthem recording so there are no surprises.

That was the solution adopted by most international sporting events after it became clear that the growing number of participating countries made it impractical for a live band to do the job. There are almost three times as many countries competing at the Olympics today as there were in 1952 when the unfortunate Luxembourg incident occurred. At the 2021 Olympics, sixty-three nations won gold medals, but there were 205 countries competing.* That's a lot of anthems to play perfectly. Which is why today's anthems are approved in advance, recorded, and played over speakers.

* There are 206 countries recognized by the International Olympic Committee. North Korea was the only country that didn't send athletes in 2021, citing concerns over the Covid-19 pandemic.

And making that happen is a huge undertaking. You could ask the office intern to go online and download a bunch of anthems. But that kind of approach can result in the disaster of the Borat anthem incident. It's also potentially illegal; just because you can find a song on the internet doesn't mean you can simply broadcast it over loudspeakers and around the world. Someone arranged and recorded that song, and while they might be thrilled that the Olympics is playing it, they'll also expect to be paid.

There's also a question of standards. The anthems should be consistent so that one isn't played by a military band and another by a symphony orchestra or a rock group. And that means getting someone to record all the anthems — even the ones that will never be played at a medal ceremony.

The organizers of the 1956 Melbourne Olympics wanted to make sure they would not be caught out by a surprise victory of an athlete from an unexpected country. It was decided two years ahead of the Games to ask every participating country to supply the sheet music of their national anthems scored for military bands. They specified that the music should last no longer than a minute. The request was timely, precise, and polite, but in many cases, it was ignored, forgotten, or misinterpreted. The official report of the Melbourne Games notes that a further letter had to be sent as a reminder. "Eventually," it states, "all anthems were received but in many different forms — symphonic score, piano score, gramophone record or tape recording."

So, instead of getting sixty-seven musical scores all arranged for a military band and lasting less than a minute, the Melbourne organizers got a messy mix of arrangements and recordings that had to be whipped into shape. The task of sorting it all out was dumped on Squadron Leader L.H. Hicks, director of music of the Royal Australian Air Force. It took him six months to prepare and record the anthems with the air force band. In many cases, he had to decide which bits to cut in order to make the music fit the time available. He achieved this either by stopping them halfway through or by lifting a chunk out of the middle in order to include the final bars.

The recordings were transferred onto discs and provided to all indoor venues, where they were used in place of live bands at medal ceremonies. When medals were awarded outdoors, a live military band was still used, and the organizers made sure that every band had a copy of every anthem. They were determined that no one was going to mess up the music on their watch.

However, even all that planning didn't guarantee everything would go smoothly. When it came time to hand out the medals for the cycling road race, the promised band was nowhere to be found. Nor was there time to get a recording of the Italian national anthem delivered to the venue. But the crowd didn't want to spoil winner Ercole Baldini's golden moment, so Italian spectators and officials joined together for an a cappella performance of the anthem while the flags were raised. Which actually seems like a nice ceremony, if the point is to get everyone emotionally involved in the experience.

Recorded national anthems are now the norm at the Olympics. That at least takes care of the badly played concern raised by Avery Brundage back in 1964. It's also interesting to note the move away from military band performances to orchestral ones, which softens the martial tones of some of the more triumphal songs (although, as we'll see in Chapter 10, some Americans complain that recent Olympic recordings of their anthem are too "Europe-friendly" — and that's definitely not meant as a compliment).

The Olympic movement has now chosen to embrace the anthems it once thought of as divisive. In retrospect, it seems quaint that it was ever really considered possible to remove anthems and flags — and therefore nationalism — from the Games. They have been a nationalistic contest from the very beginning. Athletes are there as representatives of their nations. Pierre de Coubertin believed "the Olympic Games will be a potent, if indirect factor in securing universal peace."[9] But from the very start, they were all about which country won the most medals.

The winner of the very first modern Olympic marathon was Spyridon Louis of Greece. The race was the last event of the 1896 Athens Games — and the marathon has since become the traditional closing race of all Olympic Games. When Louis entered the Olympic stadium on April 10, 1896, he was greeted by a passionate crowd of home supporters. One commentator wrote, "The atmosphere resounded on every side with unending cries of victory. Women waved their handkerchiefs, the men their hats; little Greek flags, carefully concealed until now, were unfurled; quite beside themselves, the people demanded that the band play the national hymn."[10]

This exuberant display of national fervour was not what de Coubertin had in mind for his new Olympic movement. One of his companions watching the final moments of the marathon was the French author and right-wing politician Charles Maurras, who turned to his compatriot and observed rather dryly: "I see your internationalism does not kill national spirit — it strengthens it!"[11]

There is a solution to this, one the Olympic movement itself has created — or has at least laid the groundwork for. The International Olympic Committee allows athletes to compete as independent Olympians under certain circumstances. At the 2020 Tokyo Olympics, twenty-nine athletes from eighteen countries took part in the IOC Refugee Olympic Team — marching under the Olympic flag. They didn't win any events, but if they had, the Olympic flag would have flown, and the Olympic anthem would have been played. At the same Games, the Russian team wasn't allowed to compete as "Russia" because of doping scandals, but they were allowed to take part as the "Russian Olympic Committee."

The flag used at medal ceremonies was the ROC flag, and the anthem was taken from Tchaikovsky's *First Piano Concerto.*

However, the Olympic Charter states that "only National Olympic Committees can enter athletes to the Olympic Games." So, while some exceptions have been made because of political turmoil, no athlete is allowed to compete on their own behalf. But changing that part of the charter might be a better way of dealing with the anthem issue than just trying to ban them. If an athlete qualifies for the Games under his or her country's rules, then why not let them opt to compete as an individual under the Olympic rings? Of course, the reality is that most athletes — like most of the spectators — want to see their flag and hear their anthem, but the Russian example shows another way is possible.

Three days before the closing ceremony at the 1956 Melbourne Olympics, the head of the organizing committee got a letter from a seventeen-year-old schoolboy. John Ian Wing had a suggestion for how the Games should end. Instead of each nation's athletes marching in separately, he proposed something different:

> During the march there will be only 1 NATION. War, politics, and nationality will all be forgotten. What more could anybody want, if the whole world could be made as one nation? This is how I think it can be done. No team is to keep together and there should be no more than two teammates together, and they must be spread out evenly and they MUST NOT MARCH, but walk freely and wave to the public.*[12]

---

* Wing didn't sign his letter, and despite a search for the author, he never came forward. A researcher figured it out thirty years later. When Wing was asked why he didn't tell anyone about his idea, he said, "I had done my job. I didn't win any gold medals. I wasn't entitled to anything."

It seems unimaginable today that with just hours to go before the closing ceremony of an Olympic Games, the whole plan would be changed. But it was. Wing's idea arrived at exactly the right time. The Games were stumbling toward a chaotic closure due to international tensions. A water polo match between the Soviet Union and Hungary had to be abandoned after fighting broke out. Several players were injured. It was just a few months after the Soviet Union invaded Hungary to crush a national uprising. That invasion led to some countries boycotting the Games. Others refused to attend because of the Suez Crisis, when Britain, France, and Israel invaded Egypt to try and seize control of the Suez Canal. And some of the countries that did attend told their athletes not to mingle with other delegations.

The proposal to get everyone to march together was immediately seized on as the perfect solution to mending the broken Olympic spirit. And it was all made to happen in less than a day. The athletes were told to wander into the stadium however they wanted. Everyone recognized the symbolism of showing the Games were about the athletes, not the nations. The idea still retains its power today. The protocol for the closing ceremony of the Tokyo Olympics called for the athletes to enter the stadium "en masse and in no particular order."

So maybe that's how to deal with anthems at the Olympics: let the athletes decide. Sure, most — maybe all — will want that moment with their national flag and music. But perhaps a few will see an opportunity to do something more unifying and settle for the purity of personal victory over the triumph of national will.

5

GOD LOVES LOTS OF COUNTRIES

The congregation of about two thousand filled London's St. Paul's Cathedral, which was an unusual event for a Tuesday morning in September. It was an invited audience, heavy on military uniforms, and including royalty and top politicians. The day was cloudy but warm enough for those walking to the church to dispense with overcoats. This meant the colourful medal ribbons on the soldiers, sailors, and aviators were on full display. A handful of decorated veterans, accompanied by attentive minders, were escorted slowly to their seats. They were the last of "The Few," the 2,936 Royal Air Force pilots who flew the Spitfires and Hurricanes that beat back Hitler's Luftwaffe to win the Battle of Britain and end the threat of a Nazi invasion.

"Never was so much owed by so many to so few," said wartime prime minister Winston Churchill in 1940 when he honoured the heroic exploits of the pilots. That victory is marked every year on September 15. It's usually a predictable, low-key, and non-controversial occasion. But on this particular Battle of Britain Day — in 2015 — the celebrations were more elaborate than usual.

It was the seventy-fifth anniversary of the battle and almost certainly the last significant date that would be attended by surviving veterans, all of them at that point well into their nineties. As well as the service, there was an aerial display featuring wartime aircraft, and as usually happens on major anniversaries, there was a lot of media attention focused on the veterans, whose stories were retold to an audience of people far too young to have experienced the war.

There was another reason for the media to pay particular attention to the St. Paul's service: it was the first formal event attended by the new leader of the British Labour Party. Jeremy Corbyn had been elected just three days earlier. He was a controversial choice to head up the country's main opposition party, with left-wing views that signalled a new direction for Labour. The country's right-wing newspapers and commentators were looking for any excuse to attack him personally or politically. Corbyn was about to deliver them a great gift without even opening his mouth.

Given that Corbyn was a republican and dubious about the existence of God, it shouldn't have come as much of a surprise to anyone who had been paying attention to him that he would have some issues with a national anthem that celebrates both God and the monarchy in its very first line. When the St. Paul's congregation was asked to stand for "God Save the Queen," everyone joined in except for Jeremy Corbyn, who stood in silence, head bowed, while everyone around him sang.

The storm of criticism was inevitable and entirely predictable. "Corb Snubs The Queen," declared the right-wing *Sun*. "Shameful: Corbyn Refuses to Sing National Anthem," complained the equally right-wing *Daily Express*. Of course, the "gotcha" British tabloids would have gone after him whatever he did: if he was seen singing, he'd have been accused of hypocrisy. But the damage was done. His leadership was off to a terrible start; his later commitment to sing the anthem in future didn't make things better. The British public never took to Corbyn, and he was replaced as Labour leader five years later.[1]

Disrespecting the monarch and God is a recipe for disaster for a politician. But Britain isn't alone in calling on a deity to give them special treatment. God, in his or her or its or their various forms, appears to have lots of favourite countries and is determined to protect, bless, or defend all of them — or at least the person or people who rule them.

I've listened to the anthems of all 218 countries recognized by the UN, the Olympics, and FIFA. Sixty percent of them have religious references. Sometimes, they are buried deep in rarely sung extra verses (like verse four of the American national anthem*). Sometimes, the references are subtle — as in Sierra Leone's anthem, with its heavenly metaphor right off the top: "High we exalt thee." God isn't directly mentioned, but who else is being called on when the singers "pray that no harm on thy children may fall"?

Sierra Leone's anthem, with a few minor changes, would fit perfectly into a Christian hymnal. It shares the same kind of phrases that hymns use, like "exalt thee" and "singing thy praise." In today's world, archaic terms such as "thee," "thy," "thou," and "thine" are reserved almost exclusively for Christian songs — but these words can also be found in many national anthems, even ones written recently. In a hymn, those otherwise-obsolete pronouns are attached to God; many anthem writers very consciously adopt the same religious tone to glorify the nation.

Here's a quick test. Which of these lines comes from an anthem, and which from a Christian hymn:

---

* Here it is:
Then conquer we must, when our cause it is just,
And this be our motto: "In God is our trust."
And the star-spangled banner in triumph shall wave
O'er the land of the free and the home of the brave!

Ever we seek to honour thy name
Fill every heart with thanksgiving
Fill our hearts with true humility
Hear our voices, we entreat
We stand on guard for thee
Marching as to war*

Only the last of those lines comes from a Christian hymn.

In many anthems, religion is upfront and centre — often in the first line; think of "God Save the King," "God Defend New Zealand,"† "God Bless Our Homeland Ghana," and "God Bless Latvia." And those are just some of the anthems that have God as their first word. The deity usually pops up a little later in the lyrics.

In some countries, there is no difference between the state and religion. This was common in many European countries until well into the twentieth century. Even today, the British monarch is also the head of the Church of England. The United Kingdom is one of the few countries in the world to have an official state religion, although it is one that is no longer imposed on the people.‡ Most of the countries that nowadays use state power to enforce religious rules are majority-Muslim ones, like Saudi Arabia and Iran. That is reflected in their national anthems, which, in the case of Saudi Arabia, praises both Allah and the king, while Iran's anthem honours the ruling imam or ayatollah as well as the believers in truth (truth, in this case, meaning what Allah wants, as defined by his servants on earth).

---

* The lines are from the anthems of Sierra Leone, Kenya, Ghana, New Zealand, and Canada, and the hymn "Onward Christian Soldiers."

† New Zealand actually gets a double dose of God. It has two official national anthems. Guess what the other one is.

‡ The Church of England is officially known as the established church of England. Over the years there have been efforts to separate church and state by disestablishing the religion. Opposition to that campaign is known as antidisestablishmentarianism, which, at twenty-eight letters, is one of the longest non-scientific words in the English language and hard to work into a casual conversation.

Most Western countries — the United States being a significant outlier — have largely removed religion from everyday life. Church attendance and the number of people who identify as Christians have been steadily falling in most Western countries since the Second World War. The Church of England — like all denominations — keeps a good track of bums in pews on Sundays. And it's getting easier with each passing year to count the congregation. In 2019 attendance at Sunday Church of England services averaged 854,000, and more than a third of the worshippers were aged seventy or over. The total number of churchgoers in England on any given Sunday and across all denominations is now less than 5 percent of the population.[2]

Canadians seem to be more interested in religion. Statistics Canada data from 2021 reports that just under two-thirds of Canadians claim some kind of religious affiliation, although only 16 percent attend any kind of weekly service. As in England, people who regularly attend religious services tend to be older. And almost 20 percent of Canadians who report a religious affiliation don't actually identify with any organized religion and don't consider their spiritual beliefs to have any bearing on how they live their lives. This growing group represents people who don't participate in organized religious activities but believe in some kind of spiritual power in the universe. They are occasionally referred to as "nones," from the option "none of the above" on surveys about religious affiliation. However, this term can be misleading, as it may include people with no religious beliefs at all.

When it comes to the United States, God is a bigger deal. Almost half of all Americans belong to a church, synagogue, or mosque — this might seem like a lot, but it is actually a big drop from the 70 percent who said they attended a house of worship as recently as 1999.[3] The number of people who say they have no religion has been rising steadily in the United States and in other

Western countries, most of which have entered what is known as the post-Christian era; people may still claim some kind of religious affiliation, probably inherited from their parents, but in their daily lives they give the concept little or no thought and generally only ever attend a religious service if there is a wedding or a funeral.

The increasing indifference toward religion can be seen in its treatment in everyday life. Religious leaders in most Western countries have lost their power to influence public policy. For example, Roman Catholic bishops in Ireland kept a tight grip on social issues until the late twentieth century, holding an effective veto on any legislation dealing with divorce, contraception, abortion, and a wide range of other matters falling under the umbrella of "family values." Outside of the United States, no one in any of the major Western nations expects their political leaders to be churchgoers.

Where we do see religion in public life is at state funerals and events like Remembrance Day ceremonies, where prayers — as non-denominational as possible — are recited. It also lingers in some institutions. In Canada, each sitting of the House of Commons begins with the following prayer:

> Almighty God, we give thanks for the great blessings which have been bestowed on Canada and its citizens, including the gifts of freedom, opportunity, and peace that we enjoy. We pray for our Sovereign, King Charles, and the Governor General. Guide us in our deliberations as Members of Parliament, and strengthen us in our awareness of our duties and responsibilities as Members. Grant us wisdom, knowledge, and understanding to preserve the blessings of this country for the benefit of all and to make good laws and wise decisions. Amen.

The British House of Commons and the U.S. Congress also start their days with prayer. And there doesn't seem to be any serious attempt to stop this. But change is possible. Nova Scotia's House of Assembly abandoned its daily prayer in 2021 and replaced it with a moment of quiet reflection, ending a tradition that dated back to the legislature's first sitting in 1758.

Refusing to swear an oath on the Bible or other holy book no longer causes raised eyebrows in courts. A simple promise to "tell the truth" is sufficient. The Covid-19 pandemic may have helped the low-key campaign to rid courts of religious symbols; some courts decided they didn't want multiple people handling the same book, so they were removed in favour of an affirmation.

Dropping God from a court oath or eliminating prayer from a legislative assembly can be done quickly, quietly, and without most people noticing or caring. The only people likely to object are some of the very religious — although it should be noted that when prayer was eliminated from the Nova Scotia legislature, the move was welcomed by the New Democratic Party leader Gary Burrill, an ordained United Church minister.

♫

Removing God from a national anthem is a whole different can of worms. It's pretty much a non-starter for countries like the United Kingdom or New Zealand, where doing so would really require the creation of a whole new national anthem. When the very first word of your country's song is "God," then you can't really remove it or write around it. You have to start again. That's not to say people haven't suggested the idea. It just doesn't get much traction.

In Britain's case, it seems the only sure way of dumping the anthem — and God — would be to remove the monarchy. Not having a queen or king would make the whole song redundant. But as Jeremy Corbyn found out, republican tendencies in the United Kingdom don't garner much support — although a massive constitutional upheaval, such as Scotland voting for independence, might kickstart calls for change. The trouble is, the songs waiting in the wings — ones that have been sung at various sporting events and gatherings over the years in place of "God Save the King" — aren't really much of an improvement.

William Blake's "Jerusalem" is a magnificent hymn, set to music by the English composer Sir Hubert Parry* and used as the anthem for England at the Commonwealth Games (although much of the world uses "England" as a synonym for "Britain," England is not technically a country, in the same way that Scotland and Wales are not legally nations as defined by membership in the UN). But while "Jerusalem" might seem perfect as an English anthem, with its closing lines, "Till we have built Jerusalem, / In England's green and pleasant land," the entire song is imbued with Christian symbolism. It would probably be the single most religious anthem in the world if it was adopted, and that includes the anthem for Vatican City.

The other spectacularly rousing song that's been tipped as a potential English or British anthem is "Land of Hope and Glory," with words by A.C. Benson and music by Edward Elgar. North American audiences will immediately recognize the tune, "Pomp and Circumstance March No.1." It's the music played at graduation ceremonies for schools and universities across Canada and the United States. Anyone who has witnessed its performance at

---

* Sir Hubert Parry is credited with composing an actual national anthem. He wrote the music for "Ode to Newfoundland," which served as the national anthem of Newfoundland from 1904 to 1949, when the Dominion of Newfoundland surrendered its independence to become a province of Canada. The song is now the official provincial anthem of Newfoundland and Labrador.

the Last Night of the Proms in London's Albert Hall will know what a great national song it is — but once again, God makes a big appearance with the repeated line, "God, who made thee mighty, make thee mightier yet."

And then of course there's "Rule, Britannia!" It was composed by Thomas Arne — the man who helped kickstart the whole national anthem craze with his arrangement of "God Save the King" back in 1745. "Rule Britannia" is a terrific song, and while God isn't exactly front and centre, He's definitely watching over the whole thing — who else made Britain arise "at heaven's command"? And while the English might be happy singing it, I can't really see it catching on with the Scots and Welsh.

New Zealand has adopted the practice of singing the first verse of its anthem twice, first in Māori and then in English, which satisfies the need for inclusion. As long as you don't feel excluded by the God stuff. But there's no real demand for change. New Zealand sports journalist Jamie Wall had this to say about his country's anthem after watching a singer's spectacularly bad performance before a rugby league game in 2018:

> Maybe [she] did get a copy of the anthem lyrics, took one look at it, and thought that it wasn't worth taking seriously. I wouldn't blame her, the English verse is an objectively terrible song that makes no sense. For those who don't know, our national anthem is based on a piece of doggerel poetry written by an Irishman, with the turgid melody composed by an Australian in one sitting. "God Defend New Zealand" didn't even officially become the anthem until 1977, and has four other awful verses that, thankfully, no one knows.[4]

Ouch. When it came to adopting the song as the anthem, it probably helped that the New Zealand government had bought the copyright in 1940, so at least it didn't cost anything to make it official. Mind you, Prime Minister Jacinda Ardern did seem to open the door to some changes in 2020, when she responded to suggestions that some arcane language be removed from the English lyrics, including "shafts of strife and war" and "entreat." Ardern agreed that the language was outdated and said that the anthem could evolve if enough people supported it. Which is a politician's way of saying when hell freezes over.[5]

Ardern had good reason to be cautious. New Zealand's last attempt to change a national symbol didn't go well. A proposal for a new flag that didn't feature the Union Jack resulted in a national debate that extended for ten months, the holding of two referendums, and a government outlay of over $30 million — and in the end the people decided to keep the old flag with its British colonial connections.

For those who like the idea of consulting the people on that kind of important issue, just remember what happened when a British government agency asked the public for suggestions on what to name a new polar research vessel. The runaway winner was "Boaty McBoatface." The boat was named after the natural history broadcaster Sir David Attenborough.

It looks like God will keep on defending New Zealand for some time yet.

Like New Zealand, Canada also has a national anthem that's sung in two languages. Surprisingly, that's not as common as you might think, given all the countries in the world with more than one official language. South Africa is unique in having a single national anthem that uses five of the country's eleven official languages. Most countries opt for one anthem and one language. Those with more than one official language usually have several versions of their anthem — four in Switzerland and three in Belgium, for example — while some countries, like India, with hundreds of languages, just take the simplest route and pick the most widely spoken one for the official anthem.

Canada has two official languages — English and French — and it has three different versions of its anthem, "O Canada." It has official lyrics for English and for French, and it has bilingual renditions. While the music for all three is the same, the lyrics are different. The French version came first, in 1880, and then many English versions followed, using the same music but completely different words. The most popular proved to be the 1908 one by Robert Stanley Weir, which form the basis of the anthem we know today. But there are differences.

> O Canada! Our home, our native land.
> True patriot love thou dost in us command.
> We see thee rising fair, dear land,
> The True North strong and free;
> And stand on guard, O Canada,
> We stand on guard for thee.
> O Canada! O Canada!
> O Canada, we stand on guard for thee!
> O Canada, we stand on guard for thee!

Note that while there is no mention of God, the use of archaic words like "thou," "dost," and "thee" would have nevertheless been familiar to an early twentieth-century audience used to the King James Bible and church hymnals. And God does eventually make a personal appearance in verse four.

Weir kept working on the lyrics and eventually came up with a final version that is much closer to the modern anthem.

O Canada! Our home and native land.
True patriot love in all thy sons command.
With glowing hearts we see thee rise,
The True North strong and free!
And stand on guard, O Canada!
We stand on guard for thee.
O Canada, glorious and free.
We stand on guard, we stand on guard for thee!
O Canada! We stand on guard for thee!

Nobody mourned the disappearance of "dost," but God still remained absent. So how did God become a part of Canada's anthem? The version we know today has "God keep our land glorious and free" as the third-last line. We can thank a committee.

Although "O Canada" slowly became the de facto national song, it wasn't official. In fact, the rights to the lyrics were owned by a music publishing firm until 1970. In the 1960s, a parliamentary committee was established to come up with an official national anthem in both French and English. "O Canada" was the obvious choice.

The French version proved easy. This was, after all, the original song written to the music composed by Calixa Lavallée. Those words were adopted without change. Associate Parliamentary Librarian J.G. Sylvestre told the committee that given the song's familiarity to most Quebecers, "an attempt to change those words would be a somewhat risky business." That's a polite Canadian way of saying don't provoke Quebec nationalist feelings, even though many Quebecers don't feel much attachment to the Canadian anthem in either language. A 2013 survey by Statistics Canada found that just 38 percent of Quebecers considered the anthem a very important national symbol, compared to 64 percent for the country as a whole. The best way of boosting support for the French-language version of "O Canada" would be to get a bunch of English-speaking politicians to insist on rewriting it.

But there was no shortage of opinions on how to improve the English anthem. The parliamentary committee was flooded with suggestions. More than six hundred changes were proposed, including brand new lyrics in English and versions that used both English and French. But the vast majority of submissions were based on amending the Robert Weir song. Most people seemed to agree there was far too much "standing on guard."

It's not clear from the minutes of the Special Joint Committee on the National Anthem exactly who suggested that God needed to be added to the words. But when the final recommendation came out in 1968, the deity was right there. It certainly helped with the standing on guard problem, which was reduced from five mentions to three. The committee's report — like a lot of government reports — gathered dust for more than a decade before it was adopted. The National Anthem Act became law in 1980, and Canada finally had an official anthem, with two sets of lyrics: the unchanged French words and the tweaked version of the English song.

O Canada!
Our home and native land!
True patriot love in all thy sons command.
With glowing hearts we see thee rise,
The True North strong and free!
From far and wide,
O Canada, we stand on guard for thee.
God keep our land glorious and free!

Ô Canada!
Terre de nos aïeux,
Ton front est ceint de fleurons glorieux!
Car ton bras sait porter l'épée,
Il sait porter la croix!
Ton histoire est une épopée
Des plus brillants exploits.
Et ta valeur, de foi trempée,

O Canada, we stand on guard for thee.	Protégera nos foyers et nos droits.
O Canada, we stand on guard for thee.	Protégera nos foyers et nos droits.*

The French version of the anthem celebrates a muscular Christianity typical of the time in which it was written. Think of it as an "Onward Christian Soldiers" kind of song, creating a vision of Canada as a hero wearing a garland of glorious deeds with one arm wielding a sword and the other carrying a cross. With valour steeped in faith, this mythical figure of Canada protects homes and rights. It all seems a little too martial and religious, not in line with the tolerant and peace-loving image that Canada likes to present to the world.†

Just sticking the word "God" into your anthem doesn't guarantee that all believers will buy into the idea that you are living in God's favourite country. Some religions refuse to have anything to do with national anthems, whether God is included or not.

---

* "The Government of Canada's Translation Bureau provides this translation of the French version of "O Canada":

O Canada
Land of our ancestors
Glorious deeds circle your brow
For your arm knows how to wield the sword
Your arm knows how to carry the cross;
Your history is an epic
Of brilliant deeds
And your valour steeped in faith
Will protect our homes and our rights

† The third official version of "O Canada" is, as mentioned above, the bilingual song, which mashes together these two completely different sets of lyrics to create a strange mongrel version familiar to anyone who has watched a professional hockey game in Canada. It uses the French lines about wielding the sword, carrying the cross, and a history of brilliant deeds.

Jehovah's Witnesses decline to take part in patriotic ceremonies. They don't salute flags. And they don't sing anthems. You have to admire the principle they follow in this, because it applies equally to all nations. It's explained on the Jehovah's Witnesses website, and it's hard to disagree with the logic: "Since there is no Scriptural basis for the nationalistic pride that has so divided our world, we do not join in singing songs that extol any earthly nation."

You don't have to be a Jehovah's Witness or a member of any religion to support the idea that national anthems can be horribly divisive and we would be better off without them. The Jehovah's Witness sanction against anthem-singing applies to any song that serves the same kind of purpose — like a school or regional song. In a guide for teachers and school administrators, the Jehovah's Witness website states, "They are often sung with religious fervor and with cheers. Our youths do not share the sentiments of such songs."

Taking that position comes with a cost. Principles are rarely free and almost never easy. Sticking by them can infuriate angry nationalists. Jehovah's Witnesses were among the early targets of Nazi Germany because of their refusal to use the Nazi salute or fly the swastika flag. Thousands were sent to concentration camps. More recently, their position on national symbols has put them in conflict with authorities in many countries around the world — children have been expelled from schools and adults arrested for refusing to sing national anthems. In the United States, their position is seen by some as a sign of disrespect or as a protest, particularly after sports figures started taking a knee during pre-game anthems as a gesture against racism.*

---

* The "taking a knee" protest began in 2016, when National Football League player Colin Kaepernick of the San Francisco 49ers refused to stand during the playing of the national anthem to draw attention to racial inequality and police brutality. Other NFL players soon joined in, and "taking a knee" spread to other sports and other countries. The practice angered some fans and politicians, most notably Donald Trump, who called for the protesting players to be fired. Kaepernick left the team the following year and hasn't played in the NFL since.

Other religious groups take a different approach: they believe that God is very much on the side of their country and take pains to remind people of that. Australia's national anthem is one of only a handful that is not sexist, religious, or violent. But in 2011 some Christian schools weren't happy about that and started singing a new version of the anthem with the lyrics "With Christ our head and cornerstone, we'll build our nation's might / Whose way and truth and light alone, can guide our path aright."

Not everyone is thrilled about the rewrite of the anthem and have pointed out that once people start using their own words, they're not actually singing the Australian anthem at all. But there's no real way of stopping Christians from singing the song.

This is the exact opposite of what happens in China, where the state can very much force you to sing what it wants. Churches there have been ordered to play the Chinese anthem, raise the national flag, and pray for the Communist Party. If they don't, the churches can be shut down and congregations and priests can be arrested and imprisoned.

A pastor at a Seventh-day Adventist church told the online magazine *Bitter Winter*, which reports on religion and human rights in China, that the state's "ultimate goal is to make all people believe in communism only, to 'sinicize' Christianity."[6] It's the ultimate state religion: where the state *is* the religion and the number one song in the hymnal is the national anthem.

The links between church and state remain strong in even the most de-Christianized of countries. Churches are frequently recognized as charities and given special tax status. Many church hymnals in countries like the United States, Canada, and the United Kingdom include the national anthem, and it is regularly sung by congregations on national holidays.

The words "anthem" and "hymn" are not synonymous in English. They have different origins and different meanings, although there is clearly some crossover in usage, and both have strong religious roots. But in virtually every European language, from Albanian to Ukrainian, the word "anthem" translates directly as "hymn," and the national songs of countries using those languages are often referred to as hymns. For example, Austria's anthem is officially titled "Bundeshymne der Republik Österreich." Hungary's song is simply titled "Himnusz." Paraguay's is called "Himno Nacional Paraguayo." Malta has "L-Innu Malti." And so on. The Swiss, just to be different, call their anthem a psalm, but that's really just a synonym for hymn.

Removing God from anthems is no simple matter. The strands of religion, nationalism, and military prowess are woven very tightly together in national songs. Military bands are the major players of the songs. Military jets zoom over stadiums spreading smoke in national colours as part of anthem and flag-waving ceremonies. Priests, ministers, rabbis, and other religious leaders are on hand to add God's blessing to whatever undertaking is being considered — from the launch of a warship to the playing of a baseball game. And these threads cannot be easily unravelled.

The official motto of the United States is "In God We Trust."* It appears on the currency. It is carved into the wall of the chamber of the U.S. House of Representatives. And yes, it pops up, in an amended version, in the American national anthem: the fourth verse, rarely sung today, contains the line, "And this be our motto: 'In God is our trust.'"

Given these close links, you can see why it is so hard to suggest changing an anthem. What may seem like a reasonable and

---

* It is also the city motto of New Westminster in British Columbia, where the phrase "In God We Trust" is included in the city's coat of arms.

inclusive suggestion to some can be interpreted as an attack on the entire structure of the state by others. This is particularly true of countries where patriotism is closely associated with the love of symbols (flag, motto, anthem), national history, and the military. Try to dump God, and you will likely be accused, very loudly and probably aggressively, of attacking the country's soldiers, dead and alive, its past, its beliefs and maybe even the entire image of the country.

In a way, the great tragedy of most national anthems is that they are written to paint a picture of how a country sees itself and how everyone else should view it — but no one outside the country cares. The most you can expect from a non-citizen on hearing your national anthem is "great tune." They don't listen to the lyrics. They probably don't understand them. Do you think anyone in Spain gets upset today at listening to South American anthems that hurl abuse at their former overlords? National anthems are largely for internal nation-building purposes, even if many are sung in a "don't mess with us" way. We sing them to boost national pride, to let our sports teams know that the crowd stands behind them, and to intimidate opponents. "Look!" we cry. "Our people stand as one! And not only that, we have God on our side."

6
CHANGING TIMES

The surprise announcement came in a New Year's Eve tweet on the last day of 2020.

"Happy New Year, Australia," wrote then prime minister Scott Morrison, "because we are one and free!"

What Morrison was announcing was a change to Australia's national anthem. A change of precisely one word, but a word that carried a lot of weight. What the government was trying to do was address the glaring absence of any reference to the people who were the original inhabitants of the country.

"Advance Australia Fair" became the official anthem in 1984 (replacing that old colonial standard "God Save the Queen"). The song itself was written in the late nineteenth century and quickly become a national favourite. When the Australian government decided in the 1970s that a home-grown national anthem was needed, "Advance Australia Fair" emerged as the people's choice, beating out that other well-known antipodean song, "Waltzing Matilda," in a referendum.

The lyrics were adjusted for the official version of the anthem. Three of the original four verses were deemed unsuitable, as they contained references to Britannia ruling the waves and founding peoples from England, Scotland, and Ireland. The first verse worked, after the opening line, "Australia's sons, let us rejoice," was changed to "Australians all let us rejoice." And the second verse was taken from a rewritten version first performed in 1901.

God wasn't an issue in the anthem, but the lack of any recognition of Indigenous Australians was a problem. They weren't just ignored: the anthem's second line, "for we are young and free," dismissed tens of thousands of years of Aboriginal history. Among the many people who objected to that exclusion was soprano, composer, and playwright Deborah Cheetham. She is an Aboriginal Australian and in 2015 was invited to sing the anthem at the country's largest sporting event: the Australian rules football Grand Final. She refused, saying, "I simply can no longer sing the words 'we are young and free.'" Cheetham also issued a call for change: "Australia, it's time to sing a new song."[1]

Cheetham had a song in mind, one she had sung several times and which she was backing as a new national anthem. The song was written by Australian music legend Judith Durham of The Seekers in conjunction with Indigenous singer Kutcha Edwards and others. It uses the same tune, but very different words. In urging the government to adopt her version, Durham said, "I do so hope you like the proposed new lyric, with its potential as an inspiring unifying force."

The rewritten anthem contains the lines, "Australians let us stand as one, upon this sacred land / A new day dawns, we're moving on to trust and understand."[2]

Durham's anthem proposal didn't go anywhere. But she wasn't the only person offering an alternative anthem. The Recognition in Anthem Project was inspired by Deborah Cheetham's refusal to sing at the Grand Final. It came up with a three-verse version called "Advance Australia Fair 2.0." One of the verses recognizes the sixty-thousand-year history of the First Peoples of Australia with a call to "unite our cultures from afar, in peace with those first here." But the first verse — in the case of most anthems, that is the only verse that's ever sung — was exactly the same as the existing anthem, with one small change: the words "we are young and free" were replaced by "we are one and free."

That's what Prime Minister Morrison was tweeting about at the end of 2020. His government adopted the one-word change, a move he said "recognizes the distance we have travelled as a nation. It recognizes that our national story is drawn from more than 300 national ancestries and language groups."

Morrison's announcement was largely welcomed by many Australians. However, Deborah Cheetham said much more change was needed. "The next step is not just replacing a word. It's saying, 'Who are we? What have we achieved? Where are we going?' We can't capture the spirit of this nation one word at a time."

The Recognition in Anthem Project continues to lobby for its entire song to be adopted. "Our quest is simple," the group states, "to make the song whole. To finish the job."

Sometimes, just tweaking the lyrics isn't enough. The whole song becomes so tainted by history that it has to go. But if you've got one of the world's great tunes, it seems a pity to sacrifice the song if the lyrics are the only problem.

There's basically only one national anthem with a big-name composer, and he didn't even come from the country that eventually adopted his tune. Joseph Haydn was an eighteenth-century Austrian who set himself the task of writing a local equivalent of "God Save the King" to honour Emperor Francis II. The music, with changing lyrics, continued to be used as an Austrian anthem until the country was annexed by Nazi Germany in 1938.

Meanwhile, Germany had adopted the same music for its anthem after the First World War, taking its lyrics from a nineteenth-century poem, "Das Lied der Deutschen" (The Song of the Germans). The opening lines of the poem are famous: "*Deutschland, Deutschland über alles, Über alles in der Welt*" (Germany, Germany above all, above all else in the world). Those lines became so indelibly associated with Nazi Germany that the post-war state of West Germany decided to adopt just the third verse of the original poem, with starts out with a call for "unity, justice and freedom." But the music stayed the same.

That remains the anthem today. But not everyone got the memo about the lyric change. Occasionally, the old version pops up, much to everyone's embarrassment. It was delivered with particular gusto at a tennis match between the United States and Germany in Hawaii in 2017. The male soloist gave it his a capella all. The entire performance is available on YouTube, where you can see the German players and many in the stands doing their best to belt out the correct lyrics.

The German coach, Barbara Ritter, said the mistake was "an absolute scandal, a disrespectful incident and inexcusable." And the head of the German Tennis Association, Ulrich Klaus, released a statement saying, "The fact that in the year 2017 a wrong anthem can be played that is associated with the horror of the past was for players and staff and the officials present both shocking and disturbing."[3]

The U.S. Tennis Association apologized profusely. But of course, that wasn't the first or last time the mistake was made. Another apology had to be issued by Dutch TV station NPO in 2021 when it wrongly subtitled the German anthem before a football match between Germany and England.[4] You can be sure this will happen again.

There's another thing about the German anthem — something that maybe you've already wondered about. The poem "Das Lied der Deutschen" has three verses. So why did the modern German state skip over verse number two when it was looking for new words? Easily answered. Where the first verse is all "Germany over everything" and the third verse is the more sober and reasonable call for "unity, justice and freedom," verse number two is the awesome party in between.

It starts and finishes with the lines "German women, German loyalty, German wine and German song." It sounds like a great drinking song, but you can see why the committee set up to review the anthem probably didn't think it was the better choice of the two remaining verses. This means that Germany's go-to anthem poem is now used up, so the current one better stick or it's back to the drawing board.

The music for the German anthem has also caused some issues over the years. It shares with "God Save the King" the distinction of being used as the tune for a well-known Christian hymn:* in this case, "Glorious Things of Thee Are Spoken."† That proved awkward during the Second World War. British congregations were understandably reluctant to sing along to their enemy's anthem. A new tune was composed. That music, "Abbot's Leigh," is still used today, but it never completely supplanted Haydn's composition, which remains the standard in many hymnals, where the tune is called "Austria."

It took several years after the Second World War for Germany to once again re-enter the global community of nations. West Germany — created from the parts of the country occupied postwar by the Western allies — was established in 1949. But it didn't

---

* "America" ("My Country 'Tis of Thee") is obviously a uniquely American song. It features in many Christian hymnals in that country.

† The hymn was written by eighteenth-century Anglican cleric and former slave trader John Newton, who in later life embraced Christianity and became a fierce abolitionist, which provided the material for his other greatest hit, "Amazing Grace."

adopt a national anthem until three years later, when it was decided to keep the old tune but use the third verse of the poem. It's been claimed occasionally that the original Nazi-era lyrics are banned in Germany, but that's not the case. It's just viewed as staggeringly bad taste to use them.

What's really interesting is that for three years — between 1949 and 1952 — West Germany was able to function as a nation-state without a national anthem. When national music was called for — at official receptions or sporting events — the bands played popular German carnival tunes, including some that showed a sense of dark comedy that belies the stereotype of the humourless German. One of those songs was "Wir sind die Eingeborenen von Trizonesien" (We Are the Natives of Trizonesia), which referred to the three zones of West Germany occupied by the Americans, British, and French. It was undoubtedly appreciated by the Germans, with lyrics that included:

> We're the natives of Trizonesia
> Our women are wild and passionate
> We may not be cannibals
> But we sure know how to kiss.

You can still hear the songs that briefly stood in for the German anthem at the numerous carnivals in cities like Cologne, Dusseldorf, and Mainz. It's a shame the country didn't stick with the practice. With so many songs to choose from, it would have been a great way to promote German culture, and as most Germans already know the words, there would have been no problem in getting a crowd to sing along.

Germany wasn't the only country forced into an anthem change by political events. The collapse of the Soviet Union left Russia without an anthem. It initially adopted a lyric-free tune by nineteenth-century Russian composer Mikhail Glinka. It never really caught on. Athletes complained about not being able to sing along during sporting events and medal ceremonies (although that doesn't seem to bother the other countries with lyric-less anthems). The anthem was even blamed for Russia's failure to win more gold medals at the 2000 Sydney Olympics.

Players on Russia's most successful football club, Spartak Moscow, wrote to President Vladimir Putin in 2000 demanding an anthem with lyrics. "We don't want to hang our heads any longer when our country's anthem is played in domestic and international arenas. This is the best way to lose a match before it even starts."[5]

Putin agreed. But the Russian strongman didn't just want lyrics; he wanted a reminder to the world that Russia was still a superpower. And what better way to do that than to bring back the tune that everyone already knew? The old Soviet anthem was dusted off, provided with new lyrics, and Russians were back to singing along. However, it didn't seem to do much to boost their athletic prowess: the Russian gold medal tally at the 2004 Olympics was even lower than the disappointing total in 2000, and the Russian national football team still struggles to make an impact internationally.

♫

Not all efforts to change an anthem are successful, no matter how well-intentioned. In 1997 a Colombian man filed a lawsuit in the country's Constitutional Court, claiming that ten of the eleven verses of the anthem were unconstitutional because they "subliminally induce violence, intolerance and racism." Alexandre Sochandamandou espoused a philosophy of happiness and pacifism, which he explored in his self-published books *La filosofía del mestizo* (*The Philosophy of the Mestizo*) and *La llave de la felicidad* (*The Key to Happiness*). He also liked to file constitutional lawsuits. Lots of them. In the four years before he took on the anthem,

Sochandamandou filed twenty cases, dealing with topics as diverse as abortion, decriminalizing drugs, and national holidays.

He seemed to accept that his case was a longshot, saying that "my purpose is to make the country that sings it like an automaton think about the true meaning of the anthem's messages." And Sochandamandou thought those messages were the wrong kind for a country that promoted secular and pluralistic views. He said the anthem's author — future Colombian president Rafael Núñez — was a devout Catholic who infused his poem with his religious beliefs. That's hard to deny when you look at lines like "the whole world understands the words of the one who died on the cross."

And the thing is, you really have to agree with Sochandamandou. Colombia's anthem is violent, sectarian, and sexist. Even his critics concede its flaws. Commenting on the lawsuit, an editorial in the weekly newsmagazine *Semana* described the Colombian anthem as "incomprehensible, cheesy, lengthy, and flowery," but it also predicted the court's verdict when it noted that despite its flaws, the anthem was "never unconstitutional."[6]

In its ruling, the court said, "The national anthem is a poetic-musical composition whose point is to honour historical figures and events that contributed to the emergence of the Colombian nation." But it also said that a song isn't a legal document, and its meaning is purely philosophical, historical, and patriotic. "No one is forced by its stanzas, and to pretend otherwise is to fall into the absurd."[7]

The Colombian anthem remains unchanged. But that doesn't make it a good anthem; it just means that any change will only come about through public pressure. As we saw in Canada, that can take decades. But almost every country has a group of people like Alexandre Sochandamandou who have taken on that mission, though usually without much success. Let's face it, in a world with many problems, reviewing national anthems rates pretty low on the list of priorities.

The Finnish national anthem has some baggage associated with it that has led to calls over the years for a new song, but it's been hard to generate any passionate support for change. Those raising objections worry that "Maamme" (Our Land) isn't terribly Finnish. Finland has two official languages: Finnish and Swedish. Only about 5 percent of the population are native Swedish speakers, although about two-thirds of Finns can speak both languages. But it wasn't always that way. Finland was conquered by Sweden and ruled as part of the Swedish Empire for centuries. Swedish was the language of the ruling class. Even when Finland was seized by Russia at the start of the nineteenth century, Swedish remained the only official language until 1863. The rise of Finnish nationalism was closely tied to the use of Finnish, and by the time Finland finally became an independent nation in 1917, Finnish had taken over as the language of government.

So, what has all that to do with the national anthem? Well, the anthem was written in 1846 by Finland's national poet, Johan Ludvig Runeberg, who only wrote in Swedish. "Vårt land" (Our Land) was part of an epic poem designed to promote patriotic feelings among the Finns during Russian rule. It was first sung in 1848 to music written by Fredrik Pacius, a German immigrant to Finland. It wasn't translated into Finnish until twenty years later.

And that's what makes the Finnish anti-anthemers unhappy: it is a national song originally written in Swedish to a tune composed by a German. Its tune is also used by neighbouring Estonia for its national anthem, so it's not even unique. Not only that, but there is a truly world-class all-Finnish option just waiting there to be grabbed: "Finlandia Hymn" by Jean Sibelius. It is a gorgeous tune, certainly worthy of anthem status. And there's another thing: "Maamme" isn't even an official anthem. While the country's flag and coat of arms are legally defined, the anthem has just come to be accepted through tradition.

All those arguments have been used over the years — most recently in 2016, when members of the National Coalition Party, then the second-largest party in the coalition government, supported the calls for change. But the campaign fizzled out when it became clear that most Finns seem quite happy with the song they've been singing for more than a century. At least for now.

No anthem is safe from domestic critics, not even one as iconic and recognizable as "La Marseillaise." There are good reasons to criticize it, which we've gone over in Chapter 2, and they are quickly summarized by noted French actor Lambert Wilson,* who described the lyrics as "terrible, bloody, racist, and xenophobic." In a 2014 interview with RTL Radio, Wilson said, "When I hear the line, 'Let impure blood water our furrows,' I am amazed that we continue to sing it."[8]

He was speaking during one of the more recent calls for the anthem to be rewritten. It was prompted by the failure of then Justice Minister Christiane Taubira to sing "La Marseillaise" during a ceremony to mark the abolition of slavery. Taubira, who is Black, was criticized for staying silent (even though other senior politicians present, all white, did not sing either). Taubira defended herself in a Facebook post, pointing out that the anthem was performed by a soloist and it wouldn't have been appropriate to join in. But what really sent her critics over the edge was her comment that "some occasions are more suitable for contemplation … than stage karaoke."[9]

You can imagine the racist and sexist attacks that followed. But many people spoke up to defend Taubira — and to say the

* English-speaking audiences will likely know him best from his role as the Merovingian in the *Matrix* movies.

real problem was with the words of the anthem. Lambert Wilson wasn't the first person to call for them to be changed. Author Victor Hugo had proposed a new version. Musician Serge Gainsbourg* recorded a reggae take of the song in 1979, which he called "Aux armes et cætera," which led to death threats and protests at his concerts. The organization La Nouvelle Marseillaise is campaigning for new lyrics, saying they're needed for a modern democracy. On its website, it says, "this discrepancy between the words of a national anthem, which is supposed to represent the state of mind of the nation that sings it and the reality of today, is no longer acceptable." Its alternative anthem still calls on the French to "*marchons, marchons*" — but instead of watering the fields with impure blood, they would now march toward a peaceful future.

Despite support from many leading citizens over the years — including Danielle Mitterrand while her husband was serving as president — there doesn't seem to be much appetite for an anthem change among the French population. It's hard to mess with success, and there's no argument about the success of "La Marseillaise"; it's one of the most stirring and recognizable songs in the world.

Opponents of changes to national anthems often call on the past to support their position: don't rewrite history, they say. *It's political correctness gone mad. Why do you hate your country?* These kinds of ad hominem attacks are used to deflect attention from legitimate concerns. It's not unreasonable to believe that a revolutionary song from the eighteenth century no longer has the same relevance to a modern nation. We update our laws to reflect our evolving society, so why should a national anthem be immune from change? Simply repeating "but that's how it's always been" doesn't really work (particularly when "always" is measured in relatively short periods of time).

---

* Probably best known outside France for his 1969 duet "Je t'aime," with Jane Birkin.

But not all calls for change are because a song has outlived its usefulness. Sometimes, the objections are based on artistic merit: there are better songs available. That's the case with America's "The Star-Spangled Banner."

One of the most prominent activists for replacing the U.S. anthem was former senator Tom Harkin. The Democratic senator from Iowa argued for a new song for decades. His last act before he retired in 2014 after forty years in Congress was to introduce a bill to make "America the Beautiful" the national anthem.[10] He was by no means the first person to propose this; the song has long been considered by many as equally patriotic. And it has, in Tom Harkin's view, one major advantage: the current anthem doesn't even mention the name of the country. Of course, that's not unique to the United States. Although most anthems do include their country's name in the lyrics, there are many that don't.* And it's not like anyone is going to mistake "The Star-Spangled Banner" for another country's anthem just because it doesn't include the word "America."

Harkin also had another, more practical reason for wanting to make the change: he believed the current song was too hard for most people to sing. Given the number of truly horrendous and off-key performances that have been endured over the years, he certainly had a point. And while the Senate didn't seriously consider his proposal, he's not alone in wanting to dump "The Star-Spangled Banner."

We met UCLA Voice Performance professor Michael Dean in Chapter 1. He's a classically trained singer who has performed in many of the world's leading opera houses and concert halls. He knows about singing — and he specifically knows a lot about singing the U.S. anthem. Dean has taken it upon himself to save U.S.

* By my reckoning, 147 of 193 UN members have anthems that include their country's name, although some of the rest — like Belize's — include unique geographical references and others — like "La Marseillaise" — do mention the country, but only in later verses that aren't usually sung.

anthem singers from themselves. He coaches pop stars who've been asked to perform the anthem and worry about embarrassing themselves. Because here's the thing about the American anthem: unlike other anthems, it's rarely sung by crowds, mainly because it's too hard.

"There's almost no key you can put 'The Star-Spangled Banner' into that all people can sing comfortably," Dean says. "Everyone is going to scream the high notes."

So, the U.S. anthem is usually performed as a solo and often without accompaniment. And that can be a challenge. Dean says the anthem's octave-and-a-half range is no problem for a classically trained musician like himself. He sings me a little of it to prove his point. But for a pop singer — even a hugely talented one — it can prove problematic.

"The reason we hear so many people crash and burn on that piece is because they're not trained singers, and the upper range in pop music, if things get really high, generally gets to be more of a yelling."

That bothers Dean. He thinks the anthem should be taken more seriously and treated with more respect. He notes that when pop stars and other celebrities tackle the anthem, the audience holds its breath, waiting for the big notes — the ones the singer hits on "rocket's RED GLARE" and again at "land of the FREE" — and cheering if they make it.

"I hate the cheering that happens when they hit the high note. It's as if this person is doing some kind of athletic event," he says. "The singer has a responsibility to deliver this song in an inspiring way, because it's actually about the song, as opposed to being about the singer."

Dean is frustrated by the fact that, although pop singers so often deliver poor performances of the anthem, classically trained singers are so rarely asked to deliver it on major occasions like the Super

Bowl.* "Over time, it's become an opportunity for a pop singer to perform, and to show off their own voice and their pop music style. And the reason that it is so ineffective and doesn't work is because this isn't a pop song."

I assumed that because Dean spends so much time working with singers to improve their anthem performance, he was a fan of "The Star-Spangled Banner." But he surprises me.

"I think 'America the Beautiful' would actually be my choice for a much better national anthem. It is more easily sung by a group, the range is much easier for most people to sing. And it's frankly a better song."

So, Dean and former senator Tom Harkin are in agreement about the best song for a U.S. anthem. Dean does recognize the problematic issue of God in the lyrics but doesn't think people will mind. "It's so brief, and it goes by so quickly, that I think it would probably fly for most people."

And there are other high-profile endorsements of the need for change — including from Frank Sinatra, who frequently performed "America the Beautiful" and loved the song. But he didn't think much of "The Star-Spangled Banner."

"It's a terrible piece of music," he said in 1969. "If you took a poll among singers, it would lose a hundred to nothing."[11]

Among singers perhaps, but not among the public. An opinion poll in 2020 found that only 15 percent supported selecting a new song. Another 12 percent wanted it gone — and replaced with nothing.

One of the big objections to the U.S. anthem comes from supporters of the Black Lives Matter movement. They point to a

* Soprano Renée Fleming is the only classically trained singer to perform the anthem at a Super Bowl, in 2014. Not surprisingly, she nailed it with almost effortless professionalism. Perhaps out of a desire to not appear elitist, the stadium announcer didn't mention the word "opera" when introducing Fleming, describing her as "Grammy Award winner and soprano superstar."

controversial slavery reference in the rarely sung third verse and to the fact the author was a slave owner who certainly didn't include them among those living "in the land of the free."

A statue of Francis Scott Key in San Francisco's Golden Gate Park was toppled during protests after the murder of George Floyd by a white police officer in 2020. A year later, 350 sculptures were installed on the site, representing the first Africans who were kidnapped and shipped across the Atlantic in 1619 to be sold in America as slaves. During the unveiling of the *Monumental Reckoning* sculptures, a choir sang what is widely described in the United States as the Black national anthem. "Lift Every Voice and Sing" was a poem written by teacher, writer, and civil rights activist James Weldon Johnson* in 1900 to commemorate Abraham Lincoln's birthday. His brother, J. Rosamond Johnson, later supplied the music.

There are three verses to the song, but when it is sung as an anthem, usually only the first verse is performed.

> Lift every voice and sing,
> 'til earth and heaven ring,
> Ring with the harmonies of Liberty;
> Let our rejoicing rise
> High as the listening skies,
> Let it resound loud as the rolling sea.
> Sing a song full of the faith that the dark past has
> taught us,
> Sing a song full of the hope that the present has brought us;
> Facing the rising sun of our new day begun,
> Let us march on 'til victory is won.

---

* Johnson went on to head the National Association for the Advancement of Colored People (NAACP). The organization began promoting the song as a Black national anthem more than a hundred years ago.

If you are not familiar with the song or doubt its anthemic qualities, I suggest you seek out the performance given by the contemporary gospel duo Mary Mary at the 2022 Super Bowl. It's remarkable.

While the song has been identified with the Black community since its creation, there are moves to widen its appeal — and even to suggest it as a replacement for "The Star-Spangled Banner." A leading U.S. politician thinks there's room for both songs. James Clyburn, a South Carolina member of the House of Representatives, wants to have "Lift Every Voice and Sing" declared a national hymn, which could be sung alongside the existing anthem by everyone, not just African-Americans.

"I believe its appeal is much more universal and its words applicable to nearly every ethnic background in America," he wrote in 2021. "Enshrining 'Lift Every Voice and Sing' as our national hymn will be a substantive step toward 'liberty and justice for all.'"[12]

Of course, there is strong resistance to such a change. But there are still people alive today who were born before "The Star-Spangled Banner" became the official American anthem in 1931. It's not a founding symbol of the country. The important piece of writing that represents the United States is not its anthem, but its Constitution, which has been amended twenty-seven times to reflect the changing realities of the nation. As other countries have realized, change can be for the better.

7

MAKING ROOM FOR WOMEN

It probably doesn't come as much of a surprise that women don't tend to feature heavily in the world's national anthems. Where they have a role, it tends to be as the mothers of present and future (male) soldiers or as people to be protected or fought for. Remember, many national anthems are all about revolution and fighting and nation-building, and as so many have been taught at school, that's purely a guy thing. Just as women have been ignored in our histories or reduced to a minor supporting role, so too have they been pushed aside in our anthems. And it's surprising how that isn't more of an issue.

Trying to adopt gender-neutral language is a prickly matter, and over the years, there has been a great deal of fractious debate on the subject. The lengthy list of titles, jobs, and even products that contain the word "man" has been slowly whittled away over the years, though always with a furious rearguard action fought by people whose reasons for opposition can often be hard to fathom. The idea that the word "man" actually includes both sexes has been widely argued, particularly when it's used in words like "mankind" or "manhunt," but that discussion quickly spirals out of control with the suggestion that what's sauce for the goose is also sauce for the gander, and perhaps we should just replace all "man" words with "woman." Somehow, supporters of a universal mankind don't seem to think that womankind can also include men.

Despite those arguments, our daily language constantly changes. We no longer have firemen, policemen, mailmen, or salesmen. Remember the thunder of verbal cannons sounded over the suggestion that we stop using "chairman" and instead use "chairperson" or even just "chair"? All those people who angrily refused to be referred to as a piece of furniture? The battle is largely over, but there are still skirmishes being fought. As recently as 2014, the first woman to be appointed as head of the BBC Trust was described as the chairman — or somewhat bizarrely as the "female chairman" by London's *Daily Mail*,[1] which is a thoroughly and unapologetic right-wing publication. The *Daily Telegraph*, which shares the same trench as the *Mail* in the culture wars, clearly didn't see anything odd in reporting that a leading businesswoman was named as the BBC's chairman.[*2] But what you have to know is that Rona Fairhead chose that title herself. She never asked to be called chair or even chairwoman.[3] Sometimes, opposition to change comes from places you don't expect.

At the turn of the century, the Canadian Broadcasting Corporation instructed its writers and reporters to describe people who catch fish for a living as "fishers." The word "fisherman" was one of the few remaining job descriptions that hadn't been made

---

* The print edition of the *Daily Telegraph* headlined its story "Mother of Three Poised to Lead the BBC," which seems an odd way to describe a woman with a resume that includes a law degree from Cambridge, an MBA from Harvard, serving as a boss of the Financial Times Group, as a director of HSBC and PepsiCo, and as a British business ambassador appointed by the U.K. prime minister. The headline was widely mocked online and compared to a 1963 story in the *San Diego Tribune* when Maria Goeppert Mayer, a professor at the University of California at San Diego, became the second woman to win the Nobel Prize in physics. The headline read: "S.D Mother Wins Nobel Physics Prize."

gender-neutral, so it probably seemed like an overdue and uncontroversial change by the language police at the CBC. Did they ever misread the room!

The decision was widely ridiculed both inside and outside the organization. Some CBC journalists flat-out refused to use the word. And it wasn't because they were sexist throwbacks; the biggest pushback came from women who worked on the ocean.[4] While the number of women putting to sea on fishing boats is growing, it's still only around 10 percent of the total fishing population. But those women were quite clear about what they called themselves: fishermen. This wasn't a fight that the CBC could win, so eventually it backed down, and people who catch our fish from boats are still mostly referred to as fishermen by CBC News. I suspect that when the number of women in the fishing industry increases, we'll hear calls from many of those women for a gender-neutral term. I don't think any police officers are arguing for a return to the days of "lady policemen."

It was women who led the charge to change Canada's national anthem. There were proposals to change just two words, but you'd think they were proposing to undermine the entire history and culture of the country and make Canadians look like illiterate fools in the eyes of the world. The two words were in the line, "True patriot love in all thy sons command." You can see the problem. Half the country's population is left out. Supporters of change wanted the line to read, "... in all *of us* command." But the parliamentary committee that approved the official words of the anthem was made up entirely of men. The problem with the lack of female representation in the song was pointed out at the time, but no one on the committee was paying much attention. The campaign to fix the anthem began almost immediately.

In 1991 Toronto City Council passed a motion recommending the federal government change the words of the anthem to "in all of us command." As well, the council suggested replacing the phrase "our home and native land" with the less-charged phrase "our home and cherished land." The proposal went exactly nowhere. But it did show there was appetite for change.

And some federal politicians were listening. Several private member's bills were introduced in the House of Commons in favour of "all of us," but they all failed. Things really started to change in the early 2000s. Senator Vivienne Poy took up the campaign and introduced two bills. They both died. But this time, there was a feeling that momentum was on the side of the forces of change.

Senator Nancy Ruth became the next standard-bearer for "all of us." She encouraged the Conservative government to back the idea as part of a series of reforms intended to benefit Canadian women in time for the fortieth anniversary of the Royal Commission on the Status of Women in 2010. And her suggestion was adopted when the government set out its agenda in the throne speech delivered in March 2010. The speech, delivered by Governor General Michaëlle Jean, said Parliament would be asked to review the "original gender-neutral wording of the national anthem."

No one was expecting that commitment. And the reaction was swift and angry. It took just two days for the government to back down. A statement from Prime Minister Stephen Harper's office said, "We offered to hear from Canadians on this issue and they have already spoken loud and clear. They overwhelmingly do not want to open the issue. The Government will not proceed any further to change our national anthem."[5]

That, it seemed, was that. But of course, it wasn't. Senator Ruth was initially elated at the government's apparent support and then disappointed at the speedy flip-flop. However, she wasn't a woman to give up after a setback. As someone who had spent much of her life campaigning for women's rights, she was used to people pushing back against change they didn't like. And she knew how to mobilize and build support for a cause. The Sing "All of Us" campaign was founded, with an impressive list of backers — Ruth herself; former Senator Vivienne Poy, who was also chancellor emerita of the University of Toronto; Kim Campbell, Canada's first female prime minister; Sally Goddard, whose daughter Captain Nichola Goddard was the first female Canadian soldier to be killed in combat; and one of Canada's most distinguished writers, Margaret Atwood. These were not the kind of people who accepted "no" for an answer.

With the government now firmly opposed to changing the anthem, the pressure had to come from the bottom up. The grassroots campaign to win support included persuading people to sing the gender-neutral words and posting videos online for others to see. In the lead-up to Canada Day in 2014, Ruth encouraged people to sing the new line and to persuade their friends, families, and colleagues to do the same. And she also found a new ally in Ottawa. Liberal MP Mauril Bélanger told Ruth that he planned to introduce yet another private member's bill to change the anthem and asked for her support. Of course, he got it. But the governing Conservatives defeated the bill, which was hardly a surprise.

Then there was an election, and the Liberals led by Justin Trudeau became the new government. And Trudeau wanted to show his feminist credentials. His new Cabinet was a Canadian first: gender-balanced, with fifteen female and fifteen male Cabinet ministers. When asked why he had done that, Trudeau famously replied, "Because it's 2015." So, when Mauril Bélanger reintroduced his bill on a gender-neutral anthem a year later, the House of Commons finally voted in favour. But it still required approval in the Senate, where the opponents of change fought a desperate rearguard action.

Some claimed that removing the word "sons" would be an insult to Canada's war dead, an argument that obviously did not find favour with Sally Goddard, whose daughter died fighting in Afghanistan. In a news release, Goddard said, "I believe that restoring the anthem celebrates the role that all Canadians play in the modern era."

Others were passionately upset about grammar. Senator Michael MacDonald spoke at length about the grammatical integrity of the anthem: "'Thy sons command' is a plural and possessive phrase. I argued, when I spoke in the Senate — and I still believe this firmly to be true from the people I have spoken to who have degrees in literature — that the proper replacement for 'thy sons command' would not be 'all of us command' but would be, in fact, 'all of our command.'"[*6]

I see. Senator Joan Fraser also worried about the new language (remember that we're talking about precisely two words here), calling it "clunky, leaden and pedestrian." She also said it was "a fine example of what happens when you let politicians meddle. Politicians are not usually poets."[7]

Interestingly, Fraser pointed out one of the other big issues with Canada's anthem: the inclusion of God. "What about people who are not Christian?" she asked. "What about people who do not believe in any god or perhaps believe in many gods? How do they feel when they're obliged to stand and sing 'God keep our land glorious and free'?"

Fraser was speaking against the desire for change, but her argument seemed to be making the opposition's case. She attempted to clarify. "National anthems all over the world have a marked tendency to be bloodthirsty, ethnocentric, focused on a single religion, and otherwise not inclusive.... The value of those national anthems does not lie in the specific words they use. It lies in the fact that they

* You don't need a degree in literature to know that "Thy sons command" is not a possessive phrase; otherwise it would read "Thy sons' command," which has a very different meaning and would make no sense in the context of the anthem.

have been sung by generations of the citizens of those countries." In other words, we've always done it that way, so why stop now?

My own personal favourite argument against "in all of us" was made in a column on the Inquinte news site for the Quinte region of southern Ontario.

> The new song replaces the words "thy sons" with "of us." In the old song, the "s" at the end of "sons" is crisp, whereas the "s" at the end of "us" is stretched, and when it connects with the syllable "com" in the word "command," the sound "scum" is vocalized. When the words "of us" are respectively aligned with the music notation to replace "thy sons," the following is what will be heard … true patriot love, in all of us scum, and with glowing hearts …[8]

That is now the only way that I can imagine myself singing that line.

Other opponents of the change appear to have time-travelled back to the 1950s to find their arguments, presumably because nothing newer was available. Before you read on, remember what you are about to absorb was written in the twenty-first century.

Peter Goldring was a Conservative MP in Edmonton, Alberta. He wrote a brief essay to his constituents in August 2013 about why removing "sons" from the anthem was completely unnecessary. It's still available on his website. He explained his position very clearly:

> The word "son" has more than one definition; it does not necessarily refer to a male offspring. This is particularly true when referencing nationhood.
>
> Take *Merriam Webster's Collegiate Dictionary*, tenth edition. A son is defined as: "a person closely

> associated with or deriving from a formative agent (as a nation, school, or race)." Or the *Concise Oxford*, ninth edition, which includes in its definition: "a person regarded as inheriting an occupation, quality, etc. or associated with a particular attribute (sons of freedom, sons of the soil)." Hence, sons in this context can be seen as persons.
>
> Therefore, if sons are persons in the national context, then the word "sons" in our national anthem "O Canada" is gender neutral and indeed means both male and female persons.
>
> I see no reason to change the anthem's lyrics. The current anthem wording is politically correct and is gender neutral.

I don't think there's much I can add to that argument, except to mansplain to the little ladies out there that apparently mankind refers to you too! Daughters are sons and women are men and gaslighting is just a way to make a dark room brighter. I'm guessing that it doesn't work the other round: so "womankind" doesn't seem to include men (even though the word "man" is literally included in the word).

By that point, however, it did seem that most of the opponents finally knew that the jig was up. They did what they could by way of a delaying action — preventing the hoped-for change in time for Canada's 150th anniversary in 2017. When the amendment to the National Anthem Act finally became law in February 2018, it was too late for Mauril Bélanger. The man whose private member's bill led to the change died in August 2016 from ALS.

♫

The sky has not fallen in Canada since the new words were introduced. But many other anthems remain proudly sexist and resistant to change. And even when change happens, some people refuse to go along with it. There are Canadians who still insist they'll stick with singing the old words.

The same thing happened in Austria in 2012, when its anthem was altered to become gender-neutral. The case of the Austrian anthem is especially interesting because the lyrics were written by a woman — a rarity in the world of national anthems.* Paula von Preradović, an Austrian poet, was asked to come up with words for a new anthem after the Second World War. The music had already been selected — it was taken from a melody thought at the time to have been composed by Mozart but now considered to be the work of another composer. The new anthem was necessary because the old one was banned after the war. Austria had used the same Haydn tune as Germany for its anthem since the eighteenth century. After Austria was absorbed into the Nazi state, the lyrics were changed to the ones used in the rest of the Reich. West Germany kept the tune after the war, but Austria wanted a fresh start. A national competition was held in 1946, but the judges weren't impressed with the entries, and it was decided to ask some prominent poets to submit their ideas.

The government selected a three-verse poem by von Preradović as the new anthem. It was first performed officially in 1947. But despite being one of the few anthems in the world to be written by a woman, it wasn't gender inclusive. It declared that Austria was

* It is always dangerous to make definitive claims, such as stating just how many of the world's anthems have lyrics written by women. Because despite careful research, it's always possible to make mistakes. With that qualification, the very short list of female-written anthems (drawn from the UN list of countries) includes the Federated States of Micronesia, Nauru, Saint Vincent and the Grenadines, and Sao Tome & Principe. The anthem for the Solomon Islands was co-written by a husband-and-wife team. Some other anthems — such as South Africa's — are collective works that include contributions by women.

home to great sons and had fraternal choirs singing in unity to pledge allegiance to the Fatherland.

The campaign to change those words gathered steam in the early twenty-first century, with opponents making much the same arguments used in Canada. In 2010 the government commissioned Austrian singer Christina Stürmer to record a pop version of the anthem that included a line about both sons and daughters. This was obviously a trial balloon, to see how people actually felt about changing the lyrics. What they presumably didn't expect was a copyright suit brought by the heirs of the original author.

The heirs claimed to have the right to reject any changes to the original text and stated that recording an altered version for a government campaign or commercial use required their consent. The court didn't buy the argument, noting the work belonged to the state and anyone could use it without copyright restrictions. It also said the state had the right to adjust the lyrics in response to changes in social conditions, such as enshrining equality between men and women.

The way was open for a formal change, which happened in 2012. But the government couldn't force people to sing the new words. Folksinger Andreas Gabalier caused a minor controversy two years later when he was asked to perform the anthem before the start of the Austrian Grand Prix. He used the old lyrics and defended his decision by saying the anthem was a piece of history and tradition that shouldn't be changed, and that 99 percent of Austrians agreed with him.

He's probably wrong about the 99 percent — but he wasn't the only one to reject the changes. Among the opponents was Paula von Preradović's daughter-in-law. Hanna Molden said in a 2019 interview that she thought the idea was "ridiculous" and stated that when the national anthem is sung, "I stubbornly stick to 'sons.'"[9]

One thing that wasn't changed in Austria's anthem is the use of "Fatherland."* And that word also poses a problem for neighbouring Germany. In 2018 the country's Equal Opportunities Commissioner suggested replacing the word "Fatherland" in its anthem with "Homeland" and the phrase "brotherly with heart and hand" with "courageously with heart and hand." In a letter to staff at Germany's family ministry, Kristin Rose-Möhrin wrote, "Why don't we make our national anthem ... gender-sensitive? It wouldn't hurt, would it?"

Perhaps not. But the idea was quickly rejected by then Chancellor Angela Merkel. Her spokesperson told a news conference, "The chancellor is very happy with our nice national anthem as it is in its traditional form and doesn't see any need for change."[10]

And that pretty much ended that debate. Until the next time. Because you can be certain that supporters of gender-neutral language won't give up, and if the Canadian lesson is an example to follow, they know it can be a decades-long journey.

There's a running joke in Lebanon about people not knowing the words to their national anthem. It's one of those "You Know You're Lebanese When ..." things, but like a lot of clichés based on humour, there is some truth to the joke. A survey released in 2011 found that only 5 percent of the respondents knew all the words to the anthem. In 2017 a student organization at the Lebanese American University in Beirut decided to test that theory by asking students on campus to sing the anthem. Most struggled to get through more than a few lines. Two years later, a Lebanese bank

* The word "father" is an ancient one that shares a common root with the words "patriot" and "patriarchy." Languages have a lot of daddy issues.

launched a tongue-in-cheek marketing campaign aimed at rebranding its image as a national bank by encouraging people to learn the anthem and sing it.

But there is a serious side to the lack of awareness of the anthem. Lebanon is a country that's been devastated by civil war and divided into sectarian factions. It's a fragile nation that struggles with finding a common national identity. There are four recognized Muslim sects, twelve Christian groupings, a Jewish community, and the Druze. It's asking a lot of an anthem to try and unite those diverse groups. To be fair, the song does try, with its opening line "All of us for the nation, for glory and the flag" but it's an uphill battle and most people just didn't seem interested.

And then something different happened. In October 2019 Lebanese citizens began holding anti-government protests. It's a sign of the times that one of the triggers that brought people onto the streets was a proposed tax on internet calls using applications like WhatsApp. But the demonstrations quickly changed into demands for political and economic change. People were tired of corruption, their sectarian and ineffectual government, and its failure to provide basic services like water and electricity. And what's the best way to show nervous rulers that the citizens are united against them? Waving the flag and singing the anthem. All of sudden, Lebanese from all backgrounds and traditions were in the same place at the same time singing the same song. The anthem was finally becoming a unifying force.

Sadly, many of the changes the people sought didn't happen. Lebanon's economic and constitutional crises continued. But people finally started paying attention to the anthem — and they noticed a problem. Women were at the front and centre of the 17 October Revolution but sadly missing from the anthem they were singing so passionately in the streets and squares of the country's cities. The anthem praises Lebanon's mountains and valleys that "bring forth stalwart men."

On October 31, 2019, the Beirut newspaper *An-Nahar* published a special edition dedicated to the women of the revolution. It included an altered version of the anthem: "our mountain and our valley, they bring forth stalwart women and men."[11] The adjusted words were quickly taken up by protesters — and predictably attacked on social media.

"A change in rhythm and melody just for the sake of feminism," sniffed one offended Twitter user.

"Women ruin everything they're part of," said another.

"Changing the lyrics is so stupid. Is changing the country's name next?"

But there was also massive support from the people who sang the new lyrics as the protests continued. So far, though, the government hasn't moved to change the official wording — but as we've seen, women can play a long game, and betting against their campaign for both radical social change and a minor tweaking of Lebanon's anthem would be foolish.

Not everyone wants to take the long and tortuous route of winning over public opinion when it comes to eliminating sexism from a national song. One woman in Costa Rica tried to do it through the courts. Oriette Zonta is a trade union leader who got fed up with singing parts of the Costa Rican anthem. In particular, she objected to the line about "fruitful toil that brings a glow to men's faces" as well as the phrases "your sons" and "brave and virile." She filed a complaint with the country's Constitutional Court in 2010, arguing that because the anthem favoured men over women it breached the constitutional requirement of equality. In her submission to the court, Zonta said the anthem ignored women's participation in the fight for Costa Rica's freedom. She wanted the anthem declared unconstitutional and asked the court to order a rewrite.

It didn't take the court long to respond. The court ruled the anthem was not a law, but a literary work, and it wasn't their job to carry out an analysis of the constitutionality of a literary work — much less to edit it. And as there didn't seem to be any popular uprising in favour of change, Costa Ricans still enjoy their manly anthem.[12]

You do have to feel a little sympathy for the Costa Rican judges who considered the case. I should note that the judge who wrote the decision was a woman, so this wasn't a simple matter of a bunch of crusty old men dismissing the application out of hand. But the judges must have been quite frankly terrified at the request they should rewrite the anthem to make it gender-neutral. That's a task very few people would volunteer for, and it's certainly far outside the expected duties of a judge.

♫

Part of the problem with many anthems is the actual language they are written in — not the words, but the language that is used: English, French, Spanish, and so on. Most languages are not gender-neutral. Nouns in Romance languages are gendered, with male and female versions. But when it comes to using them collectively, the male version takes precedence. So, a group of one male and nine female French students is referred to as *étudiants* (the male plural) rather than the all-female *étudiantes*. The same thing happens in Spanish: an inhabitant of Latin America is called a Latino — unless you're a woman, when you're a Latina. But the plural is always Latinos. That led to the creation of the gender-neutral word "Latinx" (pronounced Latin-ex), which is used in some liberal universities and colleges and media outlets. But it's struggling to catch on with Latinos themselves; a 2020 survey by the U.S. think-tank the Pew Research Center found that 76 percent of them had never heard of the term and only 3 percent use it to describe themselves.[13]

English may not assign male and female genders to nouns, but that doesn't make the language gender-neutral. Think of all those people who still persist in arguing that words ending in -man also include women. And English-speakers also struggle with pronouns. The default position when we don't actually know the gender of the subject is to use "he" or "his." For example, Canada's Citizenship Act states that a person is a citizen if at "the time of his birth one of his parents, other than a parent who adopted him, was a citizen." More recent laws use the clunky "his or her." But while there is no current official gender-neutral pronoun in English, there's actually a long history of using "they" as a singular pronoun. It's not a recent usage created to enrage social conservatives, unless you consider William Shakespeare and Jane Austen* to be woke liberals. It's slowly being readopted as a solution to the problem of writing an elegant sentence without resorting to "he or she" or the humanity-depriving "it."

A gender-neutral pronoun would certainly help New Zealand's national anthem, which features "her" as well as "men." But what's interesting here is the Māori version of the anthem. The Māori language uses gender-neutral pronouns. While the Māori anthem is not a literal translation, it does seek to capture the intent of the original English version. For example, the lines "Guide her in the nation's van / Preaching love and truth to man"† become "Let it never be ashamed / But rather let its name be known" in Māori.

---

* I'm not sure if Austen would go so far as to nominate "they/them" as her preferred pronouns, but she certainly used them a lot in her novels. One of the many examples is: "To be sure, you knew no actual good of me — but nobody thinks of that when they fall in love," from *Pride and Prejudice.*

† It would be wonderful if this lyric was about asking for God's help as a heavenly GPS to guide people around the country in one of the ubiquitous campervans so popular with tourists, but it's sadly more prosaic. "Van" in this context means at the forefront.

And "men" is turned into "all people." There are no gender-specific references in the Māori song.

Perhaps the strangest thing of all is that we're still talking about this. National anthems are constantly being changed, rewritten, dumped, restored, tweaked, and replaced. So why is it apparently such a big deal to even ask for an anthem that recognizes the equality of a nation's citizens? You'd think most countries would just go, "Oops. Missed that. My apologies. Quick stroke of the pen — problem solved." That's what happened with every other part of national life that discriminated against women. And where politicians baulked at making the inevitable change, they were forced into action by the courts. So, yes, I can understand why Costa Rica's Constitutional Court wanted nothing to do with rewriting a sexist anthem — but couldn't they at least have issued a gentle rebuke to encourage the government to do the right thing?

Traditions are important to a society, but just because something has been around for a long time doesn't mean that it should stay around forever. It seems that every major societal change has taken place far later than it probably should have because of furious resistance led by so-called traditionalists. Abolish slavery? It would lead to economic collapse; slaves would be unable to support themselves. Give women votes? Women lack the mental capacity and emotional detachment to make important governing decisions. Equal pay for women? Women will take jobs away from men and shouldn't be encouraged to leave the home. Abortion. Gay marriage. Racial discrimination. Divorce. Social welfare. Public health care. The list goes on and on. We are only now tearing down the statues of men who fought for and profited from slavery.

National anthems are just another changeable part of our past. It doesn't seem unreasonable to expect that if they are to win our respect then they should reflect the nation they represent. And that includes making room for women.

8

THE VERSES WE DON'T SING

We need to be clear about something: nothing stays the same. Nor should it. Our culture changes. Even our history changes. If it didn't, we would only need one everlasting history book. Looking back on our past gives us perspective and allows us to see how things that we once accepted as the norm — like women not having the vote or gay people not being allowed to marry — are now unacceptable. So, we fix that and move on to a hopefully better future.

National anthems are no different. In some countries, they are so new that the people who wrote them are still alive. And the idea of a national anthem itself is less than three hundred years old. Not living memory, I'll grant you, but hardly ancient history. The songs that some countries adopted were creatures of their time. They reflected the nationalist fervour that drove that particular country at the time of writing. And most of them had a lot more to say than we realize today. Because some of the original songs weren't designed to fit into a ninety-second limit set by a sports organization; they were much longer, with several verses that are now rarely performed or were not adopted as part of the official anthem either for reasons of length or just sheer embarrassment.

For example, the original "O Canada" song had another three verses that speak of "stalwart sons and gentle maidens" and "our own beloved native land," and there's a whole lot more stuff about God. No one appears to be actively campaigning for those stanzas to be reattached to the anthem.

The song with the most to lose through editing for time is Greece's national anthem. "Hymn to Liberty" was written in the nineteenth century after the Greek War of Independence, waged against the Ottoman Empire, which had ruled Greece for hundreds of years. The poem has 158 verses, but only the first two are commonly used for the national anthem — generally a good thing, because the full version, which is performed occasionally, takes almost an hour to sing. The anthem's tune is one of the world's most recognizable because it is played at the closing ceremonies of the Olympic Games to honour the fact that Greece was where the Games began.

The stanzas that aren't sung describe in blood-soaked detail the history of the war against Turkey, with a few swipes at other countries for failing to come to Greece's aid. There's lots of detail about enemies being slaughtered, their heads and bodies split open, and guts and brains spilling out. Powerful stuff, but you can see why the more aspirational and less violent opening stanzas were selected for the official anthem rather than the graphic descriptions of battle. The Christian God, not surprisingly, also makes an appearance and is very much on the side of the Greeks. The country's ancient glories are recalled, including a reference to the three hundred men led by Leonidas who fought to the death against the invading army of Persia's King Xerxes at the Battle of Thermopylae.

While all of that may be missing from the official anthem, it's well known to the Greeks who sing the abridged version. They may not work through all 158 verses, but they haven't forgotten the story that the full poem tells.

The same can't be said for other countries. In fact, citizens of many nations aren't always aware that there's more to their anthems than what they learned at school. You'd be hard-pressed to find an American who knows all the words to "The Star-Spangled Banner." The version of Francis Scott Key's poem officially adopted as the U.S. national anthem in 1931 contains four verses. If you haven't heard them, you're not missing much. Except for the third verse. That's a problem.

The third stanza of the U.S. anthem includes the lines, "No refuge could save the hireling and slave / From the terror of flight or the gloom of the grave." Quite what Key meant by that is open to interpretation, but there's no disputing the fact that it contains one of the most loaded words in U.S. history: "slave." In the end, arguing over what Key may have meant — or not meant (and, as was noted earlier, he was a slave owner) — doesn't really matter. What's important is how it is viewed today. There are Black people in the United States who believe it to be racist.

The California chapter of the National Association for the Advancement of Colored People passed a resolution in 2017 calling for the anthem to be replaced. Chapter president Alice Huffman said in an interview with Sacramento TV station KOVR, "This song is wrong. It should never have been there, and just like we didn't have it until 1931, it won't kill us if it goes away." She had no doubt about the meaning of the controversial line. She said, "It's racist. It doesn't represent our community. It's anti-Black people."[1]

The resolution didn't go anywhere, and most Americans remain unfamiliar with the three verses of their anthem that are rarely performed.

Other countries, too, have national anthems their citizens believe have only one verse, because the extra stanzas have been quietly dropped over the years. The British national anthem has had several iterations. The royal family's official web page does include a second verse:

> Thy choicest gifts in store,
> On him be pleased to pour;
> Long may he reign:
> May he defend our laws,
> And ever give us cause
> To sing with heart and voice
> God save the King.

But there's actually yet another verse, one that the royals skip over: the standard version of the U.K. anthem includes this appeal:

> O Lord our God arise,
> Scatter his enemies,
> And make them fall:
> Confound their politics,
> Frustrate their knavish tricks,
> On Thee our hopes we fix:
> God save us all.

I rather like the last line of that usually unsung stanza. It has a world-weary quality that I think many people can relate to.

There have been other verses added to and dropped from the U.K. anthem depending on the political climate of the day. As we've seen, the 1745 Jacobite Rising prompted the addition of a verse calling for the crushing of the rebellious Scots. And there was an impromptu composition of a celebratory verse after an assassination attempt on King George III during a visit to the Drury Lane Theatre on May 15, 1800.

Before the play began, a former soldier in the audience fired a pistol at the monarch. A newspaper report noted that the slug from the pistol was found "in the cornice of the royal box, not more than 18 inches above the place where his Majesty stood."[2]

The shot was fired by James Hadfield, who had received serious head injuries in a battle against the French during the Napoleonic Wars. He apparently believed if he attempted to assassinate the king, he would be executed and that would, for some unclear reason, hasten the Second Coming of Jesus Christ. Not surprisingly, his defence lawyer argued Hadfield was not guilty due to insanity. The judge agreed. Hadfield was detained in the notorious Bethlem Royal Hospital, an asylum for the mentally ill. He remained there (apart from a brief period when he escaped) until he died in 1841.[3]

The king appeared to be largely unshaken by the assassination attempt. When the queen asked if they should leave, he replied, "We will not stir, but stay the entertainment out."

The owner of the theatre was the playwright Richard Brinsley Sheridan, author of such enduring works as *The Rivals* and *The School for Scandal.* He was with the king when the shot was fired and immediately composed an extra verse for the national anthem to mark the occasion.

The theatre's musical director, Michael Kelly, recounted in his memoirs that Sheridan's handwritten lyrics were delivered while the audience was singing "God Save the King" at the end of the play. Kelly, who was also a singer of some renown, then delivered the additional verse as a solo, repeating it three times.

From every latent foe
From the assassin's blow
God save the King
O'er him Thine arm extend
For Britain's sake defend
Our father, king, and friend
God save the King!

Kelly wrote that the audience received the new verse "with the most rapturous approbation."[4] The lyrics were printed in the *Times* the following day, along with the comment that it was "needless to observe that it was received with enthusiastic applause."

Sadly, the idea of updating a national anthem based on current events hasn't endured into our times. It seems like a fun way to make the song contemporary — and if you don't like it, it will be different tomorrow.

♫

Countries that were born from revolution do tend to favour national songs that glorify violence and extol the joy of dying for one's country — and that take subtle and not-so-subtle digs at their former enemies. The U.S. anthem, for example, celebrates a battle in the War of 1812 against Britain, its former colonial ruler. Other countries have their own national myths to feed, even if the rest of the world doesn't fully understand what they're saying.

Italy's anthem was written in 1847, at a time when Europe was seething with national fervour. Republicanism was on the rise. The following year would see popular revolutions against monarchies right across the continent. Italy in those days was not a unified country, but the local revolutionaries rallied around the idea of one Italian state. This inspired twenty-year-old poet Goffredo Mameli to write "Il Canto degli Italiani" (The Song of the Italians).*

Italy was eventually unified as a single nation in 1871, but as a monarchy, and while Mameli's poem was popular, it was seen as too republican for the new state. It wasn't until after the Second World War and the abolition of the monarchy that "Il Canto degli

* Mameli wasn't just a theoretical nationalist: he joined the armed campaign to unite Italy and died from wounds during a battle with French troops in Rome in 1849 at the age of twenty-one.

Italiani" was adopted as the national anthem — although it wasn't officially declared the national song until 2017.

Given the time of its writing, it's hardly surprising the six verses of the poem contain references to events that are pretty much forgotten today by everyone outside of Italy. Fortunately, most of those events are recorded in verses that aren't usually sung. The reasons behind the Battle of Legnano in 1176 require a much deeper understanding of European medieval history than any of us have time for here, but you can take it on trust that it was a significant event in Italy's long military history. Significant enough that it merits a reference in verse four, along with the confident assertion that every Italian man has the heart and hands of fifteenth-century Florentine military hero Francesco Ferruccio.

The fifth stanza makes it clear who the real enemy is: the Austrian Empire, which, at the time of the poem's composition, controlled large chunks of northern Italy, along with much of central Europe. The Italians weren't the only people pushing back against the emperor. The song notes that the eagle of Austria may have drunk the blood of Italians, Poles, and Cossacks, but the blood burned its heart.

We don't usually get to hear all of that. The more common condensed version of the anthem consists of the first verse sung twice, followed by the chorus, also repeated, in which the singers promise they are ready for death and then confirm that promise with a shouted "*Sì!*" to end the song. It's generally sung with more delighted passion than you'd expect from people who are basically saying they're ready right now to lay down their lives, but that's national anthems for you.

Italy is not, of course, the only country to record its campaign for independence in its national anthem. And its message, even in the shortened anthem we hear at sporting events, is pretty clear. But if you have a complicated story to tell, cutting off your anthem can leave the listeners wondering exactly what is going on.

The Dutch national anthem is, very unusually, written in the first person.* It describes how its narrator, William of Nassau, struggled to maintain his loyalty to the king of Spain, who ruled the Netherlands at the time of the anthem's composition in the sixteenth century. That makes it one of the oldest anthems in the world, although it wasn't adopted as the official national song until 1932. It's also long, at fifteen verses, and has a unique characteristic, one that will be familiar to fans of Rick Astley and the phenomenon of "rickrolling."

Both the Dutch anthem and "rickrolling" involve acrostics. That's when the first letter or word of each line spells out a message. In the case of rickrolling, the idea is to write a composition where the chorus of Astley's hit "Never Gonna to Give You Up" is hidden in the first words of each line or sentence. Before you realize it, you have the words "never going to give you up, never going to let you down" planted in your mind. You've been rickrolled.

The Dutch anthem, "Wilhelmus," isn't trying to have some light-hearted fun at our expense. It's all about the politics of the time. If you take the first letter of each verse, they spell out "Willem van Nassov." So, if you don't sing the whole thing, you miss part of the message. Mind you, if you do sing it all, you'll be standing to attention for a while; it takes about fifteen minutes. Usually, people just sing the first verse. This means the rest of us are left wondering why a lot of Dutch people are singing:

> William of Nassau, scion
> Of a Dutch and ancient line,
> I dedicate undying
> Faith to this land of mine.
> A prince I am, undaunted,

* Andorra's anthem is also written in the first person, referring to the nation as a princess — "I am the only remaining daughter of the Carolingian empire." That empire ruled much of western and central Europe in the early Middle Ages.

Of Orange, ever free,
To the king of Spain I've granted
A lifelong loyalty.

The first-person stuff is strange enough (imagine if the British anthem was called "God Save Me" and sung from the perspective of the monarch), but why are you pledging lifelong loyalty to the king of Spain?

It's complicated, because it's all tied up with the strange way that royal families around Europe intermarried and exchanged thrones and property, which for them basically meant the places where most people lived. So, what is now the Netherlands ended up being part of a parcel of land belonging to the Habsburg dynasty that, at the time, ran large chunks of Europe, including Austria and Spain. So, the king of Spain ruled the Netherlands.

William of Nassau started out as a loyal Spanish subject, which was pretty much a requirement if he wanted to hang onto his ancestral estates. But he grew disillusioned with Spanish rule and helped kick off the eighty-year-long Dutch War of Independence. That's all covered in the other fourteen verses of the anthem as he recounts his conversion to the cause of Dutch freedom. It's a very long story for a man who was famously known as William the Silent.

William didn't live to see independence from Spain; he was declared an outlaw by the Spanish king, who offered cash, land, and a peerage to anyone who killed him. William of Nassau was assassinated in 1584, but his killer didn't get to claim his reward: he was captured, brutally tortured, and executed. The king of Spain gave the promised land to his parents instead. The War of Independence ended with Spanish recognition of the Dutch Republic in 1648. Today's Dutch royal family is descended from William the Silent. His great-grandson William of Orange became William III of England; that's the William still revered by sash-wearing Northern Ireland Unionists, who named the Orange Order in his honour.

Many of the countries in Spain's former empire left on very bad terms and adopted long and bloody anthems to remind their citizens of the battles that led to their hard-won independence.

Mexico's anthem was written in the mid-nineteenth century, thirty years after the country gained its independence. The author was a poet celebrated for his romantic works. When Mexico's president launched a competition for a national anthem, Francisco González Bocanegra wasn't interested in entering. Patriotic themes weren't his thing. But his fiancée insisted that he take part in the competition. She locked him in a room and wouldn't let him out until he wrote an entry. It took him just four hours to write the ten-verse epic that would become Mexico's anthem.

It was eventually decided that ten verses — each followed by a chorus — was too long, and in 1943 the anthem was edited down to the chorus and four of the original verses. Most of what was cut was actually less bloody than what remained, which retains a focus on war, the roar of cannons, shedding blood (lots of it), and calls on Mexicans to fight to their last breaths. But even the shortened version is too long for these impatient times. It runs for almost five minutes. The abridged anthem that we mostly hear today is the chorus, the first verse and the chorus again. We lose the verse that begins with "War! War!" as well as all references to blood, including the lines about drenching the flag in waves of the stuff, as well as the one about watering the fields with blood (an echo there of a similar line in "La Marseillaise").

The longest anthem of them all belongs to Uruguay. I'm excluding Greece's anthem and its 158 verses because each verse is sung to the same tune. What makes Uruguay's anthem the champion is that it is one piece of music that can take more than five minutes to perform, depending on the speed of the orchestra. And that's just for the chorus, the first verse, and the repeated chorus. There are eleven verses in the original lyrics, plus choruses. It would take a while to get through them all. Those forgotten verses contain the traditional stuff about blood, war, tyrants, and battles, which probably isn't really missed, but there are a couple of nice touches that might be worth resurrecting.

There's an entire verse about the Incas, which is a rare and welcome nod to Indigenous people in an anthem. It tells of the roar when the tomb of the last Inca emperor is opened and Atahualpa's skeleton cries out for revenge. It's understandable that the emperor would call for revenge. After all, he was executed by the Spanish, and the Inca Empire was destroyed. But he probably wouldn't have seen much difference between the original Spanish invaders and their rebel descendants.

There are also some nice classical references — to Olympus, the home of the Greek gods — and a warning that the enemies of the people could expect the spear of Mars, while the tyrants would get the dagger of Brutus. But you're unlikely to ever hear about that. Those verses don't get much airplay anymore.

However, the Uruguayan anthem is definitely worth a listen. It sounds more like a condensed light opera than a traditional national anthem. It comes with an overture, key changes, an aria with an answering chorus, and a grand finale. It almost seems sacrilegious to condense it down to the standard sixty seconds that we're used to hearing.

Strangely, the author of Uruguay's anthem was no passionate rebel, despite the fiery language of his lyrics. Francisco Esteban Acuña de Figueroa was a poet and the son of a member of the colonial administration in Uruguay. He left the country during the independence struggle, although he eventually returned and worked for the new Uruguayan government. His words were adopted as the anthem in 1833. And you might think that was a pretty good legacy for a poet. But Acuña is something of an overachiever in the world of national anthems. His work so impressed the president of Paraguay that Acuña was asked to write that country's anthem as well.

The Paraguayans got a seven-verse anthem, plus chorus, which incorporated the usual themes of freedom or death, overthrowing tyranny, and martial glory. It comes as a pleasant surprise to find that there are no torrents of blood to be found. Perhaps Acuña de Figueroa had mellowed somewhat now that the fighting was over. Of course, it's far too long to perform in full, so the standard practice is to use just the first verse and chorus.

The unsung lyrics also draw on classical references, describing Paraguay both as Eden and as a new Rome, comparing its founders to Romulus and Remus. Acuña also pulls in the Greek sun god, Apollo. But he does lay it on a bit thick when he writes about the entire world acclaiming Paraguay as an invincible bastion of heroism. Then, as now, it seems unlikely that people would have known much about the country and would struggle to find it on the map. But when you're commissioned to write a song, you give the buyer what they want to hear.

♫

We already know the French national anthem is thoroughly violent. But we usually only hear the first verse. So, what don't we hear? Can the unsung verses be even more bloodthirsty?

The song was written in 1792 by Claude-Joseph Rouget de Lisle, an army officer stationed in Strasbourg after France went to war against Austria. He called it "Chant de guerre pour l'armée du Rhin" (Battle Song for the Army of the Rhine). It was later adopted as the anthem of the French Revolution and got the name we know today after it was used as a marching song by revolutionary volunteers from Marseilles. It became so popular that it was chosen as the French anthem by the first republican government in 1795. Rouget de Lisle is credited with writing six verses. The other five are rarely sung today — but they don't contain much that's surprising. Verse three does introduce God, which doesn't really work with the anti-clerical fervour of the revolution, but it's more of an idiom than a statement of faith; in the context of the song, *Grand Dieu!* is a bit like a non-religious speaker saying "My God!" just because it's such a part of the language, not as a genuine appeal to the supernatural.

The rest of the verses are standard revolutionary stuff, though not quite as nasty as the familiar opening stanza. But right at the end of the anthem comes a twist. There is a seventh verse, which the website of the French president notes was added by an unknown author shortly after the song's composition. It's called "Couplet des enfants" (Children's Verse).

Based on the title, you might expect this to be a more age-appropriate verse suitable for young singers who might otherwise be frightened by the talk of slaughter and blood. You'd be wrong. This is a verse aimed at making sure the next generation of revolutionaries is ready to take the place of their parents at the battlefront — sharing their coffins if necessary, because it is better to die in glory than to merely survive. We shall have the sublime pride, the children sing, of avenging or following our elders. Given the coffin-sharing reference, it's reasonable to assume the children are expected to follow them into an early grave.[5]

You expect the anthems of countries born from revolution to reflect that violent birth, but you might be surprised at the bloody background of a country that is seen today as peaceful, democratic, and inclusive. When it comes to glorifying death or glory you probably wouldn't think of Norway's anthem. And to be fair, the version sung today does leave out most of that stuff. A call to arms certainly doesn't fit with the modern image of Norway as a progressive country, but when you think about it, we are talking about the home of the Vikings, who weren't exactly known for their peaceful negotiating strategy when it came to visiting new places.

Norway has used several songs as de facto national anthems over the past couple of centuries, but the one that eventually came to be adopted (although not until 2019)* was written in the mid-nineteenth century by Bjørnstjerne Bjørnson, one Norway's most famous poets. Bjørnson went on to win the Nobel Prize for Literature in 1903. The poem that came to be the anthem was called "Ja, vi elsker dette landet" (Yes, We Love This Country).

The poem has eight verses, but usually only the first and last two verses are played, and for sporting events, it's just the first verse. So, if that's all you hear (assuming that you look up the translated lyrics), it all sounds terribly nice and Norwegian. There's a lot about love and about the rugged land rising from the ocean and the retelling of the nation's sagas. No violence, no nastiness. But the lyrics of the verses no longer sung tell a different story. They tell of a nation of farmers with sharpened axes ready to fight any advancing army — for Norway, this is pretty much limited to any advancing Swedish army. As you might expect from a Scandinavian country, women have an equal role in all of this: "Even women stood up and fought as if they were men."

The Norwegians may not have the numbers, but "we were enough," and they didn't give up — "we would rather burn our land than declare defeat." And the fight for freedom gave them the strength to cope with famine and war and was well worth the price of a glorious death. The Norwegians may sing nice, but clearly their Viking legacy is hidden just below the surface.

---

* There were calls for another song to be selected as national anthem following the domestic terror attacks of July 22, 2011, when a Norwegian right-wing extremist murdered seventy people, including sixty-nine people at a youth camp. As the nation mourned, one song in particular helped people deal with their grief. "Mitt lille land" (My Little Country), by Ole Paus, is a gentle description of Norway as a land of peace, beauty, and dreams. It was described in the media as the country's unofficial anthem and featured prominently in the memorial ceremonies following the attacks.

It is generally true that the world's older anthems — those composed prior to the twentieth century — tend to be the longest. There was no public pressure to have short anthems, and they were in any case only played on special occasions. The need for shorter anthems, created largely by sporting organizations, led to officially approved abridged songs, which are the versions that most people outside the country get to hear. But at least one anthem was created with that timescale in mind.

When the apartheid regime in South Africa ended in the 1990s, Nelson Mandela became the first president elected by the entire nation. He recognized that a new and inclusive national anthem was needed. A committee was established to do the job. Mandela directed that the new anthem should be shorter than two minutes. That's not much time for a song to carry the weight of uniting a country so divided by race and language.

The song they came up with is unique among the world's anthems. It uses five languages and incorporates parts of the old Afrikaner anthem, "Die Stem," and the song "Nkosi Sikelel' iAfrika" — the anthem of the African National Congress, which led the fight against apartheid. Most compromises produce results that leave everyone equally unsatisfied. But occasionally, bringing people together can produce a spark of genius. And that seems to have happened with the South African anthem. In 2017 the *Economist* magazine declared it the best anthem in the world, although that selection doesn't seem to have much statistical or scientific credibility. However, it's hard to disagree with the magazine's conclusion that the song performs an act of musical healing.[6]

In September 2011 I was in New Zealand for the Rugby World Cup. I listened as the South African rugby team and its travelling fans — the vast majority of both being white — belted out lyrics written in Xhosa, Zulu, Sesotho, and the more familiar (to them) Afrikaans and English. It was hard not to feel that this was a Very

Good Thing. Of course, there are critics. Not everyone is happy with the inclusion of the Afrikaans section, because of its link to the apartheid state, but Nelson Mandela's mandate to the committee wasn't just to get the timing right: he knew that he had to win the support of old enemies. Sometimes, that means dumping words that no longer work. And sometimes, it means including them.

9
ABANDONED ANTHEMS

The crowd cheered and sang as the statue of their former ruler was toppled from its plinth. The sight of the noose tightening around the statue's neck was a particularly appreciated touch and prompted applause. One observer noted that only a band was missing to complete the party atmosphere. Then the statue was gone, carted off to a government storage site to be dumped and forgotten alongside other monuments no longer suited for public display.

It's a scene that's been played out many times, in many places and eras, when one regime falls and another takes its place. The first things to go are the old symbols of the unwanted state. Statues. Flags. National anthems. But sometimes, those symbols can make a comeback.

The statue described above was of Britain's Queen Victoria. It was erected in Dublin in 1908 outside the building that would later become the Irish Parliament. The presence of the queen's statue was a daily irritant to the politicians who were forced to work in the shadow of their former ruler. Victoria was popularly known in Ireland as the "Famine Queen" due to her apparent indifference to the deaths of a million people when the potato harvest failed in the mid-nineteenth century, and the continuing presence of her statue after independence in 1922 was described in the *Irish Times* as "repugnant to national feeling." However, mainly because of the cost of dismantling the elaborate pedestal on which it stood, the bronze figure wasn't taken down until 1948.

Victoria's final moments overlooking Dublin were described in the *Irish Times*: "As I watched, another workman appeared, clambering over her head, gripping her sometimes by the nose and occasionally sticking a finger into her disdainful eye. Perhaps it was just the effect of the glistening rain on the bright, green copper, but it seemed to me that the old lady — never exactly pleasant-looking at the best of times — was glaring about with loathing and disgust."[1]

While the statue was gone, it was not entirely forgotten.

In the 1980s, the company renovating the iconic Queen Victoria Building in Sydney, Australia, decided it would be nice to have a statue of the actual queen in front of the newly created shopping centre. They reached out to other former British colonies, seeking an appropriate and unwanted effigy of the British queen. When they got to Ireland, someone finally remembered the abandoned Victoria (by this stage, it had been dumped in an overgrown yard at the back of a former reform school in County Offaly).

Queen Victoria was packed up and transported to Sydney. The irony of the queen being shipped off to Australia as so many Irish convicts had been during her reign was much appreciated domestically. It seemed an appropriate way of getting rid of the statue. And she still sits there today, in front of one of Sydney's most prominent buildings, awaiting the next twist in the long tradition of reassessing which statues are best displayed and which should be removed.

Statues are not the only things that are toppled when old rulers are discarded. There is also a dumping ground for unwanted, unappreciated, unloved, and unmissed anthems. Not a real dumping ground — a virtual one. History is littered with anthems that have been cast aside, never to be heard from again. For some, that's a good thing. But for others, it seems a shame. Stacks of perfectly good anthems, slowly rotting away when they could be restored, polished up, and given new homes — just like Queen Victoria.

♫

As we wander through the grounds of this virtual anthem necropolis, we find plenty of examples of songs that are the equivalent of toppled Saddam Hussein or Confederate army general statues: best removed from public spaces and only remembered as cautionary tales.

High on that list is the brief reign of Rhodesia's national anthem, which lasted five years. Rhodesia was a former British colony that resisted British attempts to shed itself of its African possessions in the 1960s. It had been assumed that Rhodesia would transition to independence under Black-majority rule like other colonies on the continent. But the white minority that ruled and owned most of the country didn't want to give up their privileged lifestyle. They staged a constitutional coup and unilaterally declared independence in 1965. The new nation was ostracized internationally, with sanctions imposed on the racist government. A long and vicious guerrilla war began, which lasted until negotiations led to the creation of Zimbabwe in 1980.

The Rhodesian government didn't get around to adopting a national anthem until 1974. It probably wasn't a big deal — it's not like there were many opportunities to play one. Rhodesia wasn't recognized by the United Nations and was kicked out of the Olympic movement. Other than the apartheid state of neighbouring South Africa, it didn't have many friends in the world. And the vast majority of its citizens certainly didn't feel any national pride in being Rhodesian. However, the illusion of being a real country had to be maintained, so an anthem was required.

You get the impression that not much effort was put into the selection process, even though a committee to find an anthem was appointed in 1969. When they did finally pick a tune, the London *Times* noted dryly that the Rhodesian government "after five years' search for something catchy, has settled for Beethoven as a replacement for 'God Save the Queen.'"[2]

The music Rhodesia went with was "Ode to Joy," the choral theme from the last movement of Beethoven's *Ninth Symphony*. Although the Rhodesian government decided to use the melody from that movement, the *Times* noted that it decided not to go with the actual poem used by Beethoven, pointing out that the words of Friedrich Schiller might be an "embarrassment," with its "remarks about all men becoming brothers and the breaking down of the barriers erected by stern society."

Instead, a competition was held for the anthem's lyrics. It was won by Mary Bloom, whom Reuters news agency recorded as being "an avid contestant in competitions who recently won a prize for naming a cocktail bar."[3]

Mary Bloom's lyrics are surprisingly uncontroversial, assuming you don't know the backstory. The two-verse anthem is a traditional hymn-style poem featuring the predictable appearances by God (one assumes this God is white) and sprinkled with the requisite number of "thys." If anyone saw the jaw-dropping irony in the opening lines, "Rise, O voices of Rhodesia, / God may we Thy bounty share," they kept their thoughts to themselves. There was definitely no bounty-sharing going on in Rhodesia in the 1970s.

No one really cared about the lyrics. But plenty of people were upset about the appropriation of music that had already been selected as Europe's anthem. The European Confederation of Veterans, which advocates for peace and human rights, complained that "the European anthem has become the anthem of apartheid."

The Council of Europe was also concerned, although it seemed more fixated on the issue of possible copyright infringement than the broader question of ousting Rhodesia's racist rulers. The concern was whether Rhodesia would use the arrangement created for Europe by Herbert von Karajan, the principal conductor of the Berlin Philharmonic. The council discussed the possibility of legal action, until the absurdity of trying to launch a copyright case against a government that no European nation actually recognized was pointed out.

In any event, the Europeans needn't have worried. The Rhodesians came up with their own arrangement. It was first played at the opening of the Rhodesian parliament in August 1974. The only long-term consequence of using the tune was to ruin Beethoven's *Ninth Symphony* for those Zimbabweans who couldn't shake the connection between the music and the racist state of Rhodesia.

But if you're looking for an off-the-shelf, ready-to-go anthem in the style of Western, Christian triumphalism and aren't too worried about the provenance, why not grab this one? Change the title from "Rise, O Voices of Rhodesia" to whatever country name you need (it works best with a three-syllable name with the emphasis on the second syllable), add a new tune, and away you go. See if anyone notices what you've done. It's the anthem equivalent of cutting the head off an unsuitable statue, sticking on a new, more acceptable one, and saluting your shiny new leader.

If recycling the anthem of a racist state isn't your thing, there are other options. One of the best of the abandoned anthems belonged to East Germany. The Soviet Union created the German

Democratic Republic in the part of Germany it occupied after the Second World War. The new state opted for a new anthem, unlike West Germany, which stuck with the old pre-war tune and just picked a different verse from the same poem. And the East Germans chose not to shy away from what had happened between 1939 and 1945. Its anthem was called "Auferstanden aus Ruinen" (Risen from Ruins). It's all about building a new and better future in a world that longs for peace.

The lyrics also make it clear that Germans should be united again so that "the sun, more beautifully than ever before, shines over Germany." Too bad the country it represented was a secret police state that collapsed almost overnight in 1990. But words are powerful things, and even the Communist government seemed embarrassed by the disparity between the anthem's message of happiness, peace, and unity, and the reality of fear, oppression, and despair that marked daily life in East Germany. The words were rarely sung after 1970.

When German reunification did happen, it was made clear it wasn't an equal merger of consenting countries but a one-sided takeover by West Germany. The East German anthem was unceremoniously dumped. And that's a pity, because it's a great tune and would have been a good choice for a unified Germany.

However, the East German anthem has acquired new life in a virtual world. The online game *Cyber Nations* allows participants to create and run their own countries with alternative histories and an amazing level of detail about these imaginary nations. One of the created countries is called Gross Germania, formed — in the online world — after Germany seceded from the European Union. In this alternative universe, the new German Empire adopted "Auferstanden aus Ruinen" as its anthem, with some changes to the words. It seems appropriate that the anthem for a state based mainly on illusions should end up as the symbol for a pretend country.

Germany has also contributed to the pile of almost-anthems: songs promoted as national symbols that didn't quite make the cut. Before deciding to stick with the pre-war anthem tune, the new West German state tried out some other songs as national anthems. One of the post-war contenders was a folk song from the early nineteenth century, "Ich hab mich ergeben" (I Have Surrendered Myself). The surrendering in the song isn't a military term: it's about the singer giving in to their love for Germany.

> I surrendered
> with heart and hand,
> You land full of love and life
> My German fatherland!

It may not have made it as the German anthem, but another country saw the potential of the song. The Federated States of Micronesia is a tiny nation spread over a huge area of the western Pacific. It is made up of more than six hundred islands that came under the influence of various European powers, including the Spanish, British, and German empires. The Japanese administered the islands after the First World War, and the United States took over that task after the Second World War. Independence was granted in 1979. Its first anthem was called "Preamble" because it largely consisted of the words of the preamble to the country's constitution.[4] It didn't prove popular and was replaced in 1991 by a new song, "Patriots of Micronesia," with lyrics loosely based on "Ich hab mich ergeben" and using the same tune. Germany's missed opportunity was Micronesia's gain.

There's another tune left behind by Germany that's worth mentioning. Not everyone favoured bringing back the pre-war anthem, even using different words. Advocates for a new start included West Germany's first president, Theodor Heuss. President Heuss commissioned a new anthem, "Hymne an Deutschland" (Hymn to

Germany), but it received a lukewarm response. More importantly, it failed to win the support of Chancellor Konrad Adenauer, who wanted the Haydn tune back. There was no contest in that power struggle: the position of president in Germany is mainly ceremonial; real political power rests with the chancellor.

The song promoted by the president is rather wistful and sad. It speaks of waves sweeping over the nation, fires that have burned it, sorrow, and remembrance of death. Given its composition in the immediate aftermath of the worst conflict in human history, that's not surprising. It's unlikely that anyone else would be interested in adopting it. But the tune, by distinguished composer Hermann Reutter, is worth another listen. While it doesn't have the same power as the current German anthem, it's certainly worth considering by any country that's looking for a change.

♫

One of the most popular BBC television dramas of the 1970s was *The Onedin Line*, which told the story of a fictional Liverpool shipping company in the latter part of the nineteenth century. The opening credits feature stirring music, which perfectly matches the shots of a tall ship pushing through the waves. The music was from the 1956 ballet *Spartacus*, composed by Aram Khachaturian — an Armenian who became one of the Soviet Union's leading composers. His most famous work — one you've probably heard — is the "Sabre Dance" from his ballet *Gayane*. It's a staple of classical pops orchestras around the world and has been covered by an eclectic range of artists, including the Pretenders and several punk rock and heavy metal bands.

Khachaturian is very much on the list of top twentieth-century composers and a national hero in Armenia, where he is celebrated as the country's leading composer and honoured with a statue outside the opera house in the capital, Yerevan. So, when a heavyweight like him agreed to write their national anthem, Armenians thought that they had hit the musical jackpot. There was just one problem. Khachaturian was a composer — not a lyricist. His anthem music was matched with words from an Armenian poet who knew what he had to deliver in the world of 1944, where Soviet Russia was in the ascendancy. The priority wasn't poetry, but politics.

The lyrics praise "great Stalin" and "immortal Lenin" for giving Armenia a "new, free, glorious life." And then the Soviet Union collapsed, and Armenia became a truly independent country in 1991. No one wanted to praise Russia, Stalin, and Lenin anymore. Those were tumultuous times, so dumping the Soviet-era song was inevitable. There was also an alternative waiting in the wings: in 1918, taking advantage of the turmoil caused by the Russian Revolution, Armenia had declared independence. It adopted a nineteenth-century poem for its anthem, but it didn't get much playtime.

As soon as the Communists controlled Russia, they started re-occupying the former parts of the old empire. Armenia was invaded by the Red Army in 1920. The short-lived republic was destroyed, and the anthem, with its anti-Soviet message of freedom and independence, was banned. It sat on the abandoned anthem shelf for seventy years until it was reembraced by the reinvigorated nation.

Except not everyone was thrilled by the old anthem's reemergence. While no one wanted a return to the Soviet-era words, people did miss the tune. There have been several attempts to bring it back with new lyrics. The problem is that good lyrics are hard to find, and so far, no one has come up with the right words to win over the Armenian people. So, Khachaturian's great music sits there, waiting for the day when it can be matched to a worthy poem.

♫

Not all anthems are destined to get another day in the sun; they are just too toxic to be played again. "God Save the South" was the unofficial anthem of the Confederate States of America. Sheet music published in Virginia described the song on the cover as "Our National Confederate Anthem." It was written in the early years of the American Civil War as a counter to the powerful "Battle Hymn of the Republic." It follows the drearily predictable model of revolutionary-type songs with its promise of victory or the grave, "chanting our battle cry, 'Freedom or death!'" It also makes it clear who was responsible for the war — and what it was all about:

> War to the hilt, theirs be the guilt,
> Who fetter the free man to ransom the slave.

This is one song that needs to be left to gather dust on the shelves of the abandoned anthem warehouse.

The Confederate States never adopted an official anthem — the claim in the sheet music mentioned above was just good marketing — and there were two other songs that also vied for the title. The song "Dixie" predated the war and was originally written for the popular minstrel shows of the time that featured white singers in blackface. Both sides in the war used the song. It was a favourite of President Abraham Lincoln and was played at the inauguration of Confederate president Jefferson Davis in 1861. On hearing that, the author, who supported the Union in the war, is reported to have said, "If I had known to what use they were going to put my song, I'll be damned if I'd have written it."[5]

President Lincoln called for the song to be played when he announced the surrender of the southern states. "I have always thought 'Dixie' one of the best tunes I have ever heard," he told a crowd outside the White House on April 10, 1865. "Our adversaries over the way attempted to appropriate it, but I insisted yesterday that we fairly captured it. I presented the question to the Attorney General, and he gave it as his legal opinion that it is our lawful prize."*[6]

The song remains popular, so we can't really call it abandoned. At least, not yet. African-Americans and civil rights campaigners have long criticized it for its racist roots and appropriation by supporters of the Confederate cause. Their opposition is having an impact. In 2016 the University of Mississippi told its marching band to stop playing the song at athletic events. A statement from the university explained the decision: "Because [the band] is such a large part of our overall experience and tradition, the Athletics Department asked them to create a new and modern pregame show that does not include 'Dixie' and is more inclusive for all fans."[7]

There is one other song that shares the title of unofficial Confederate anthem and, like "God Save the South," it remains largely forgotten — at least, as far as the lyrics are concerned. "The Bonnie Blue Flag" celebrated the first flag of the Confederacy, which featured a single white star on a blue background. The words are irredeemable, which probably explains why it hasn't survived as a song outside Civil War groups, although it was hugely popular at the time. Several verses are just lists of the states that seceded from the Union, which of course is blamed on "Northern treachery." It concludes:

> Then here's to our Confederacy,
> Strong are we and brave;
> Like patriots of old we'll fight
> Our heritage to save.
> And rather than submit to shame,
> To die we would prefer;
> So cheer for the Bonnie Blue Flag
> That bears a single star.

---

* This was one of Lincoln's last speeches. He was assassinated five days later.

The lyrics may have been abandoned, but the tune is still around. The words were written by Harry McCarthy, an Irish immigrant to the south, who set it to the tune of an Irish folk song, "The Irish Jaunting Car," which is still performed today.

Wandering through the warehouse of unwanted and discarded anthems is a journey through history. You can find all sorts of things that you probably never knew about countries that briefly existed and then disappeared — but not before taking the time to adopt an anthem.

The apartheid state of South Africa came up with an ingenious and ethically appalling way of dealing with the undeniable fact that the country's white population was vastly outnumbered by its Black citizens. In 1970 the government passed the Bantu Homelands Citizenship Act, which created four "independent" nations within South Africa. Ten Bantustans, including Bophuthatswana,* Ciskei, Transkei, and Venda, were set up as ethnic homelands for different tribal groups. The Black majority population of South Africa was declared to be citizens of these "nations."

This piece of legal trickery allowed the whites-only government to state, presumably with a straight face, that South Africa was actually a white-majority country. Needless to say, very few Black South Africans ever set foot in the new countries to which they had been assigned. But the Bantustans were given all the trappings of nationhood: parliaments, heads of state, armies, flags — and anthems.

* Bophuthatswana was home to the notorious Sun City resort, which used its "independent" status as well as bags of cash to persuade major international entertainers to perform there despite the international cultural boycott of South Africa. Among the artists who took the money were Elton John, Queen, The Beach Boys, Frank Sinatra, and Rod Stewart.

Two of the statelets adopted the pan-African liberation song "Nkosi Sikelel' iAfrika" (Lord Bless Africa) as their anthem, a tune that was later incorporated into the post-apartheid anthem of South Africa. Bophuthatswana and Venda had their own anthems. The Bophuthatswana anthem, "Lefatshe leno la bo-rrarona" (Land of Our Forefathers), is pretty good and worth a listen if you're in the market for a lightly used national song.

The rest of the world wasn't fooled by the South African chicanery, and the Bantustans were never recognized as independent countries. They were dissolved and reintegrated into South Africa in the 1990s.

Other parts of Africa also lost their anthems when they ceased to exist as states. The island of Zanzibar was an early victim of European colonization. It was first occupied by the Portuguese in the early sixteenth century. They ruled the island until they were driven out by the locals with the help of the Sultan of Oman. Zanzibar was then ruled by the sultan until the British took over. Never a formal colony, it was listed as a "protectorate," which meant that when the British finally stopped protecting it in 1963, it became a separate country. That didn't last long; almost immediately, the sultan was overthrown, a republic was declared, and the new government agreed to merge with neighbouring Tanganyika to form the new country of Tanzania.

Until then, Zanzibar had a flag and an anthem. "The National March for the Sultan of Zanzibar" was adopted in 1911. It was one of those anthem rarities: it had no words. But a tune dedicated to a deposed sultan was clearly not going to cut it as an anthem for a new republic. After more than half a century of use, the music was unceremoniously consigned to the dustbin of history.

There are also tragic tales to be found in the vaults of forgotten anthems. As a child, I remember seeing disturbing pictures of large-eyed children with distended bellies accompanied by appeals for aid. The children were from Biafra, a region of Nigeria that declared independence in 1967. That started a terrible civil war. The new republic was recognized by a handful of African states and received aid from many European countries. But it was not enough to hold back the Nigerian military, which blockaded the breakaway region, causing mass starvation. We will likely never know how many people died from hunger. Estimates go as high as two million — 15 percent of the Biafran population. Most of the dead were children. The people were starved into submission, and the Biafran government surrendered in 1970.

Despite its short existence, Biafra had time to adopt an anthem, "Land of the Rising Sun," sung to a heartbreakingly beautiful tune adapted from "Finlandia" by the Finnish composer Jean Sibelius. The words are eerily prophetic. It seemed as if the writer could see the tragedy to come:

> We must defend our lives or we shall perish,
> We shall protect our lives from all our foes;
> But if the price is death for all we hold dear,
> Then let us die without a shred of fear.

Like so many human conflicts, the horror of the Biafran War was quickly forgotten outside of its homeland. For much of the world, it only exists in memories occasionally triggered by old photographs of emaciated children who truly gave their lives for their country without ever understanding the sacrifice imposed on them. For that reason, the anthem of the Republic of Biafra is an important testament that must be remembered.[8]

♫

The Ottoman Empire ruled much of southeastern Europe, western Asia, and northern Africa between the fourteenth and early twentieth centuries. Of course, it didn't have or need a national anthem for most of its existence — a reminder that anthems are neither essential nor particularly useful to a nation. But like everyone else, once the sultans saw other monarchs adopting songs about themselves, they wanted one as well. But they did it differently. And I have to say, I like their approach.

Remember that the first modern anthem was a tribute to Britain's King George II — its original lyrics mentioned him by name. The intent was obviously to praise George. There wasn't any long-term thought given about how this song would come to represent a nation. When the song proved popular, it was easy to just tweak the words to apply to all monarchs still to come (as the next two kings were also called George, no real change was required until William IV in 1830). The sultans of the Ottoman Empire liked the idea of the personal touch. The first to order up a song was Mahmud II. In 1829 he commissioned his court musician to write an anthem.

Giuseppe Donizetti* was an Italian musician who ended up in Istanbul after a long career as a military bandmaster, which included service under Napoleon at the Battle of Waterloo. Donizetti was hired to introduce European-style military music to the sultan's armies. When he was asked to write an anthem, he came up with "March of Mahmud," which served as the sultan's song until his death in 1839. But instead of just renaming the anthem in honour of the next sultan, it was decided a new ruler needed a new tune. So. Donizetti composed "March of Abdülmecid." That served until 1861, when Abdülaziz took the throne and got his own march — this pattern continued all the way down to the collapse of the Ottoman Empire after the First World War.

---

* He was the older brother of the famous opera composer Gaetano Donizetti, whose major works include *Lucia di Lammermoor*.

If your anthem is going to be a song about your ruler, then it makes perfect sense to commission a new one every time there's a change at the top. That's what happens with currencies: the new monarch's face appears on notes and coins. So why not a new song? Changing up the anthem would be an opportunity to get rid of all that nasty stuff about marching over the bodies of your foes, cutting throats, and celebrating ancient battles.

The downside of an anthem that's tied to a ruler is that it doesn't have much of a future if the monarchy is overthrown. So, the shelves of our virtual anthem warehouse are lined with songs honouring royal families dumped by republican successors.

Vietnam was an early anthem adopter. Emperor Gia Long ordered an anthem in 1802. "The Emperor Mounts His Throne" remained Vietnam's anthem until the end of the Second World War and the end of the monarchy.

It must be hard to be a monarch and have thousands of people singing you a song about how great you are. After a while, you'll start to believe it's true. So, the king of Afghanistan probably felt pretty comfortable on his throne when his people sang about being his faithful followers, ready to sacrifice themselves for their brave and noble king. Turns out, the song wasn't a true reflection of the people's wishes: the king was overthrown in 1973.

The emperor of Ethiopia didn't last much longer; Haile Selassie was kicked out in 1974, along with the anthem that called for his long life and glorious rule. The shah of Iran's enforced departure in 1979 meant an end to his anthem and its rather forlorn appeal to God to protect him "now and evermore." And Romania's "Long Live the King" was added to the pile of unwanted songs in 1948. Romania has managed to churn through quite a few anthems; it's currently on its seventh song since 1862.

We have saved the best for last. Right at the back of our warehouse, under a pile of long-forgotten and little-missed anthems, lies a true gem. I do not understand why Norway abandoned this anthem — but it's not too late: it doesn't really work for any other country without a big rewrite, so it's not likely to be top of the list for any nation browsing the racks looking for a new song. But you never know. My advice to Norway: bring back "Norges Skaal" (Toast to Norway).

First of all, it has to be said that this was never an official Norwegian anthem, but that's because Norway was the junior partner in a union with Denmark when it became popular. The Danish authorities didn't like the song — calling it anti-Danish — and banned it, which, of course, only increased its popularity and led to its identification with the burgeoning Norwegian nationalist movement. Norway eventually separated from its Danish union, only to be forced into a similar partnership with Sweden that lasted until 1905. There was a lot going on, and somewhere along the way, "Norges Skaal" lost its position as a potential official anthem. It's time to bring it back.

"Norges Skaal" is a drinking song. It reminds me of the traditional Scottish song "The Parting Glass." Each verse starts with a toast, beginning with a raise of the glass to Norway, "birthplace of warriors." Singers then drink to honour and "each honest Norwegian, among cliffs born." The third verse kicks off with "a toast to you, my handsome friend and to the Norwegian girls!" and calls down shame on those who hate "girls, wine, and song." By the time we get to the fourth and final verse, several drinks in, things are getting a little maudlin and conclude with a toast to Norway's mountains and its "cliffs, snows, and hills."

Sure, it needs a little rewriting to make it more twenty-first-century gender-friendly, but who could object to an anthem that's about friends sitting around a table, sharing wine and stories?

Anthems can be revived, even after sitting unused for decades — just as Queen Victoria's statue was recovered from apparent oblivion in an Irish storage yard. It has happened. The Baltic states of Latvia, Estonia, and Lithuania seized the opportunity created by the turmoil following the Russian Revolution and the end of the First World War to declare independence. They all adopted anthems, but their independence was short-lived, ending with the Second World War and their absorption into the Soviet Union. The independence-era anthems were banned.

There was one brief moment of vocal rebellion during the 1980 Moscow Olympics. The sailing events were based in the Estonian capital, Tallinn. The Finn class event was won — appropriately — by a Finnish sailor. When Finland's anthem was played at the medal ceremony, many Estonians burst into song. They knew the anthem very well. It is sung to the same tune as the Estonian anthem and was played at the end of the broadcast day on Finnish television, which many Estonians could watch despite Soviet attempts to block the signal. It was a rare opportunity to publicly express love for their country without fear of imprisonment.

All three Baltic states regained their independence after the collapse of the Soviet Union and readopted the same anthems they had used before. National symbols rise and fall with history.

Outside a museum in Tallinn, there is a park filled with old statues from the Soviet era. Huge monuments of Lenin, Stalin, and Red Army soldiers were taken down from prominent positions around the city and dumped at the museum, where they now fill a statue graveyard. They are a reminder of the nation's past. But it's also possible they will have a future. Like Queen Victoria, yesterday's torn-down statues may reemerge in another country in a place of honour. And abandoned national songs may just be resting in silence until a moment of change allows them to burst back into life. Nothing is forever.

10

DON'T MESS WITH MY MUSIC!

The opening scene in the classic 1980s horror movie *Poltergeist* was very familiar to the audience at the time but likely makes little sense to generations who have grown up in a world of twenty-four-hour television and streaming services. Television and radio stations did not always broadcast around the clock. They used to sign off, figuring there wasn't much of an audience after midnight. So, they would just … stop. And in many countries, they stopped in the same way as the TV station in *Poltergeist* did. It would play the national anthem, usually accompanied by an inspirational video of gorgeous scenery, the nation's powerful military, waving flags, and happy and smiling citizens. When the music ended, the transmitters were turned off and the TV screen just showed static.

It was a key plot point in the movie. And just as in the movie, those of us who were adults in the '80s know what it's like to fall asleep during the late show, wake up to a screen of black and white static, then turn off the TV and go to bed. Less familiar is getting sucked into the screen by a demonic presence, but to see how that turned out you'll have to watch the movie yourself.

Many countries adopted the practice of playing their anthem at the start or end of the broadcast day. Some made it mandatory; most did not. It was just one of those things that lots of people did, so no one really questioned it. The practice predated broadcast technology; it began in theatres, then moved to cinemas, then radio, and finally television. And of course, it wasn't done because of popular demand. As with many things related to national anthems, it was all about politics. If there's one thing you can be sure of, there's a direct link between public performances of anthems and the desire of the state to create or enforce nationalism.

It became standard practice to play national anthems in theatres, music halls, and cinemas during the rise in passionate nationalism that preceded and followed the First World War. It was rarely required by law, but the power of convention up until the social revolutions of the 1960s was every bit as controlling as state legislation. Cinemas in the United Kingdom continued to play the anthem at the end of movies into the 1970s, but the tradition had been dwindling since the end of the Second World War. And the idea that the playing of the song somehow helped to create a feeling of patriotism and pride was always suspect: audiences never thought much of the idea, and there was always a rush to the exit when the movie ended to avoid having to stand for the anthem.

That post-movie rush was so commonplace it was mocked in a 1972 episode of the BBC sitcom *Dad's Army*, about a Home Guard unit of volunteers who were ineligible for active military service during the Second World War. The unit, in their army uniforms, went to the local cinema. As soon as the words "The End" appeared on the screen, the entire audience stampeded for the exit, leaving the pompous commanding officer standing to attention for "God Save the King" in the empty theatre.

"I've never seen anything so disgraceful in my life. Everybody charging out like that during the national anthem," the character complains afterwards on the bus ride home.[1]

The joke was instantly recognizable to the audience, many of whom had lived through the war and would have witnessed similar post-movie rushes to the exit. It showed that when you try to force people to listen to an anthem, most will vote with their feet. Quickly. And it confirms that most people fully understand that forcing them to participate in a national anthem ceremony will not make them love their country more (and may in fact make them love it less). But that doesn't mean that people will stop trying.

One of the more recent attempts at enforced patriotism took place in India in 2016 when the country's Supreme Court ordered all cinemas to play the Indian anthem before the film was screened. The justices had obviously learned from the British experience and recognized that playing "Jana Gana Mana" after the movie could lead to an unseemly charge to the doors.

The person who started this whole process spent years fighting for more public respect for the Indian anthem. Shyam Narayan Chouksey, a social activist and retired engineer in Bhopal, began his battle in 2003 after going to see the popular movie *Kabhi Khushi Kabhie Gham* (Sometimes There Is Happiness, Sometimes There Is Sorrow). The film featured a scene where the anthem was played as part of the plot. When that happened, Chouksey stood up in the cinema out of respect. Hardly anyone else followed his example, and several people behind him complained that he was blocking their view.

Chouksey was upset that so few people seemed to care about the anthem. He took his concerns to the theatre manager, then to the police, then he mounted public protests, and when none of that produced any action, he went to the courts, demanding that the scene featuring the national anthem be deleted from the film.

The High Court in the state of Madhya Pradesh agreed with his argument that the law did not allow the commercial use of the national anthem, and it directed that the movie should not be shown unless the offending scene was deleted. The ruling was later stayed, but Chouksey did not give up his fight. He kept recording examples of what he saw as insults to the national anthem and petitioned India's Supreme Court to take action.

Chouksey has denied any links to political groups, but his passionate support for the anthem has been welcomed by members of the Bharatiya Janata Party, which represents Hindu nationalist interests. And it certainly played well among right-wing groups with notions of nationalism that view non-Hindus (and Muslims in particular) as not-fully Indian.[2]

The Supreme Court directed that "all the cinema halls in India shall play the National Anthem before the feature film starts and all present in the hall are obliged to stand up to show respect to the National Anthem." This action, the court found, would instill "a sense of committed patriotism and nationalism." And the court wasn't above lecturing Indians about their national duty: "The citizens of the country must realize that they live in a nation and are duty bound to show respect to National Anthem."[3]

The ruling, predictably, led to conflict, with reports of confrontations in movie theatres over patrons refusing to stand for the anthem. One of those confrontations was widely shared on social media after four people were heckled in a movie theatre in Bengaluru for not standing during the anthem. A man on the video can be heard shouting, in English, "Not able to spare fifty-two seconds for the country, but you have the audacity to sit here and watch a three-hour movie? Are you Pakistani terrorists?"[4]

The court order mandating that all cinemas play the anthem was rescinded in 2018 at the request of the national government, which said it was working on new guidelines around where and when the anthem should be played. It's the traditional way that governments deal with controversial issues: bury them in a committee. The playing of India's anthem remains optional in the country's cinemas, and the question of whether or not patrons should stand when that happens isn't clear — although it remains a convenient tool for nationalists who equate love of national symbols with love of country.

♫

Fervid nationalists in any country share a common belief that true citizenship is best judged by tying it to symbols like flags, anthems, national leaders, and a narrow interpretation of the country's history. Questioning any of the above can be seen as a direct attack on the state. If you want to check the truth of that statement, try posting something on social media with appropriate hashtags challenging some aspect of nationalist orthodoxy in your country of choice. Perhaps suggest the removal of a statue. Or the renaming of a public building that honours a prominent figure with a sketchy past. Or changing the words of an anthem.

In some countries, knowledge of national symbols is a patriotic test. You'd think that knowing the words to your own national anthem wouldn't be much of a challenge, but it can be trickier than it appears, particularly in multilingual countries. Belgium is a nation that struggles with cultural and linguistic divisions. It has three official languages — French, Flemish (Dutch), and German — and some people are super-sensitive to perceived slights against their ethnic groups. Most of the nation's political parties are either Dutch-speaking or French-speaking and are focused on those communities, so politicians are used to being asked loaded questions to test their knowledge of the country as a whole. Still, when one of Belgium's top politicians was asked by a reporter to sing the national anthem, it seemed like he'd been lobbed a very soft question.

Yves Leterme was the head of the Christian Democratic and Flemish Party and trying to form a coalition government with himself as prime minister when he was asked on Belgium's National Day, July 21, 2007, to demonstrate his knowledge of the country. He was interviewed, in French, by a television reporter while on his way to a church service commemorating the holiday.

"Belgians don't know their country very well," the reporter said. "Do you know what we celebrate today?"

"I think it is the proclamation of the constitution," Leterme replied.

The reporter seemed a little taken aback and told him that the National Day actually marked the date in 1831 when Leopold I became the first king of the Belgians. The reporter tried another question, asking him if he knew the national anthem, "La Brabançonne." Leterme was walking away at this point. He should have kept going. But he didn't. He turned back and sang, "*Allons enfants de la Patrie, / Le jour de gloire est arrivé*," which are the opening lines of "La Marseillaise." Given that Leterme had already earned the animosity of French-speaking Belgians by saying they were too stupid to learn Dutch, this anthem gaffe merely confirmed what they already knew: the leader of the majority–Flemish speaking party didn't care about them and probably didn't care much about Belgium either. They had a point: Leterme had already described Belgium as an "accident of history" united only by its king, its football team, and some brands of beer. He did manage to serve two short terms as Belgian prime minister but did little to unite the nation.[5]

Yves Leterme's disdain for the symbols of a country he clearly didn't much care for is unusual. People usually run into trouble when they care too much. The passionately nationalist are often in favour of mandated love of country, supporting laws that protect national institutions and symbols. It seems like a very insecure sort of nationalism if it feels threatened by the burning of a flag or the ignoring of an anthem, but it's not hard to find examples of national outrage over messing with the music.

Flags tend to be more protected by countries than anthems. Flag protocol is written into many laws and constitutions, whereas anthems generally don't rate much of a mention — probably because most countries didn't even officially adopt an anthem until relatively recently, and also because it's harder to burn an anthem, disfigure it, or wear it as a hat, all of which would get you in trouble under India's Prevention of Insults to National Honour Act. The only reference to the anthem in that law is a clause making it illegal to intentionally prevent or disrupt the singing of "Jana Gana Mana."

Compare that to the rules in Canada, where there is etiquette for treating the flag — but no laws* — and when it comes to the anthem, the government states simply that "there is no law or behaviour governing the playing of the national anthem; it is left to the good citizenship of individuals." What people want to do or say about the anthem comes under the heading of free speech, which in both Canada and the United States has strong legal protection.

Of course, just because the law says you can do something doesn't mean that people will shrug their shoulders and ignore you when you actually do it. There is a long history of anthem-related protests in the United States, and while such protests may be protected by law, they don't always go over well with the public.

Perhaps the most famous anthem protest isn't often viewed as a protest today because the context has been forgotten. When

* The National Flag of Canada Act is one of the shortest acts on record. It has only two articles, both of which set forth directions that are purely aspirational. The first encourages all Canadians "to proudly display the National Flag of Canada in accordance with flag protocol." The second encourages people who own or control apartment or condo buildings to allow residents to display the flag (presumably on their balconies). My condo building does not allow me to hang a flag on the balcony railing or as a window covering.

guitarist Jimi Hendrix took to the stage as the final act of the legendary 1969 Woodstock festival, few expected to hear him play the American national anthem. By then, most of the crowd — immortalized by Joni Mitchell as "half a million strong" — had left. Only a few thousand remained to hear what became one of the most extraordinary performances of "The Star-Spangled Banner" ever played by anyone. Fortunately, the moment was captured on film — otherwise, we might never have known about it. And because this was before the days of live streaming and camera phones, most people weren't aware of it until weeks or months later.

Hendrix had played the American anthem many times before at live shows. There are other recordings. But the Woodstock performance is the one that broke out and was seen by people who weren't necessarily Hendrix fans.

The Woodstock concert took place at the height of the Vietnam War. Opposition to the war was too loud to ignore. And since a disproportionate number of African-Americans were being drafted to serve in combat — something that many quite unsurprisingly saw as racist — the demand for civil rights that was raging through American society became mixed up in the anti-war protests. Hendrix — he had served in the army but not in Vietnam — drew on the war for his interpretation of the anthem. At one point, where the words "and the rocket's red glare" would be sung, Hendrix makes his guitar sound like bombs falling from the sky and exploding. He then segues into the bugle call "Taps," which is traditionally played at American military funerals. At other times, his guitar sounds like an air raid siren and ricocheting bullets. It was seen as an anti-war statement. Predictably, some people were offended, even (or possibly especially) people who hadn't actually heard it.

A few weeks after Woodstock, Jimi Hendrix appeared on *The Dick Cavett Show* on ABC television. By that time, people had become aware of his anthem performance but would not have seen it. The documentary movie about the festival was not released until 1970. Anticipating some audience pushback, Dick Cavett reminded people that Hendrix had served as a paratrooper.

> CAVETT: This man was in the 101st Airborne so when you write your nasty letters in —
> HENDRIX: Nasty letters? Why would you — ?
> CAVETT: When you mention the national anthem and talk about playing it in any unorthodox way, you immediately get a guaranteed percentage of hate mail.[6]

Cavett knew the nasty letters were inevitable because of what had happened a year earlier during Game 5 of baseball's World Series. Puerto Rican singing star José Feliciano walked out to deliver the national anthem. And it changed his life. The version he delivered was slowed down and sung like a folk ballad. It's fair to say that no one in the audience had heard anything like it before. The game was televised, so lots of people were also watching at home. And many of them didn't like what they heard. The broadcaster, NBC, received hundreds of calls from people, who weren't placated by the explanation that the TV station was just showing the game — and hadn't picked the singer. In the absence of social media, outrage had to be passed on either by telephone or by the Twitter of its day, the Letter to the Editor.

One unhappy fan wrote to the *Detroit Free Press* (the game, between the Detroit Tigers and the St. Louis Cardinals, was played in Detroit): "What screwball gave permission to have the National Anthem desecrated by singing it in the jazzy, hippy manner that it was sung? It was disgraceful and I sincerely hope such a travesty will never be permitted again."[7]

That comment wouldn't be out of place in a Twitter thread today. It's kind of reassuring to be reminded that caustic comments, like death and taxes, have always been with us.

Feliciano's career was hurt by the controversy. Radio stations stopped playing his records. He lost bookings. He's since said that he didn't perform the song as a protest — he just wanted people to hear a different way of singing it. But it's clear that for all the noise that opponents made, plenty of people did like Feliciano's interpretation: a few weeks after the game, RCA Records released his live performance as a single, and it cracked the Top 50 — the first time the U.S. anthem made the charts.*

Both Hendrix and Feliciano obviously read the state of the nation more accurately than their critics, because many other singers followed their examples and stepped up to put their own stamp on the anthem. It's interesting to note that Marvin Gaye was also invited to sing the anthem at the same 1968 World Series. He sang at Game 4 — the one before Feliciano's appearance — and delivered a straight-up traditional performance. Fifteen years later, Gaye sang the anthem at the 1983 NBA All-Star Game. It's a completely different rendition, featuring a synthesizer and drum machine. His soul-infused delivery is cheered throughout by the crowd, with applause punctuating each line of the song. It's now become expected that a star singer will deliver their own interpretation of the anthem. The reception is never a given, and the singers who have attempted it have met with varying degrees of success or disaster.

♫

* We get to hear José Feliciano every Christmas. His most enduring hit is "Feliz Navidad," one of the most-played Christmas songs of all time.

The American anthem is perhaps unique in being sung in so many ways. Most countries don't tend to play their anthems as often as Americans do — elsewhere, it's rarely featured, apart from at formal state occasions or international sporting events, whereas in the United States, almost every event, from local festivals to high-school sports matches, has an anthem performance, usually delivered by a solo singer. That ubiquity — and the ground-breaking performances that broke the mould of tradition — encourages personal expression and unique versions.

When it comes to the American anthem, there's no law preventing good, bad, or ugly performances of the song. The federal law relating to the anthem lays out the behaviour to be followed while the anthem is played, but there are no penalties. Given that the U.S. Supreme Court has ruled that flag-burning is allowed as an expression of free speech, it seems unlikely that any attempt to regulate anthem performance would succeed.

Other countries have taken robust action in connection with the performance of their anthems, even when there are no actual laws in place. In 1977 the English punk rock band the Sex Pistols released their second single to immediate controversy. It was called "God Save the Queen" and featured a picture of Queen Elizabeth on the cover, her eyes and mouth hidden by the song's title and the band's name.

The song isn't actually a version of the British anthem, but it does begin with the same first line, "God Save the Queen," before adding, "the fascist regime." With its closing sequence of a repeated "no future," the song captures the anger that drove much of the early punk rock movement. It's hard to imagine anything more anti-establishment than this song, particularly as it was released while the nation was celebrating the queen's Silver Jubilee. I remember as a teenager being blown away by the song and wearing out the single, which (sadly) I no longer have. Early pressings are worth thousands of dollars.

The British anthem doesn't lend itself to the kind of spectacular performances that "The Star-Spangled Banner" has inspired. It's not that kind of a song. But just calling a pop song "God Save the Queen" was enough to send official Britain into conniptions. A fairly typical institutional reaction came from Bernard Brook-Partridge, a Conservative member of the Greater London Council, who described the Sex Pistols as "unbelievably nauseating. They are the antithesis of humankind. I would like to see somebody dig a very, very large, exceedingly deep hole, and drop the whole bloody lot down it. I think the whole world would be vastly improved by their total and utter non-existence."[8]

The BBC and other broadcasters refused to air the single. Major retailers refused to stock the record. Such bans would normally be enough to bury a song, but the late 1970s were a time of youthful anger against what was seen as the stultifying traditions of the state. Being ordered what to do — or what to listen to — no longer worked.

The song soared up the charts, despite not getting much airplay. It reached Number 1 in the *New Musical Express* (NME) chart. But the Official U.K. Singles Chart — the one used by the BBC for its hugely popular show *Top of the Pops* — placed the song at Number 2, leading to widespread rumours the chart had been fixed to stop the Sex Pistols from reaching the top spot. That would have put the BBC in the embarrassing position of not being able to play the Number 1 song. Instead, the top song that week was the much more inoffensive "I Don't Want to Talk About It" by Rod Stewart. I didn't buy that single.[9]

The only rules around the British anthem are those of convention. In some countries, the anthem is protected by law. France has one of the world's toughest anthem laws, at least on paper. And it seems to be at least partially the product of an infamous football match between France and Algeria in October 2001. We can't escape the history here: Algeria was a French colony until it won independence in 1962 after a long and brutal war. France's rule is not remembered with affection by Algerians, whose entire national anthem is about the fight for freedom. You may remember that it also includes a line about "the sound of machine guns as our melody." And it's one of the few anthems to actually name another country — it promises France a day of reckoning.

There have been efforts over the years to improve relations between the two countries. The first-ever football match between France and Algeria was billed as an act of reconciliation. The idea that a football match could somehow heal those divisions seems hopelessly naive, but the French and Algerian governments seemed to think it was worth a shot. After all, the superstar of the French team — reigning world and European champions — was Zinedine "Zizou" Zidane, born in Marseille to Algerian Muslim parents. He was hailed as a French national hero after scoring twice in the 1998 World Cup Final and winning the Man of the Match award. On the night of that victory, his picture was projected onto the Arc de Triomphe while crowds chanted "Zizou président!" Who better to show how France was changing?

It all started to go wrong when the French national anthem was played. There was a huge contingent of Algerian fans in the crowd at Paris's Stade de France. They booed "La Marseillaise." Then things didn't go well for Algeria's footballers. They were losing 4–1 with just a few minutes left in the game when hundreds of Algerian fans stormed the pitch. Riot police were deployed. Bottles and seats were thrown from the stands. The match was abandoned, along with hopes of reconciliation.

French player Frank LeBoeuf, in a 2018 interview with French television, said, "We didn't play a soccer game. We played a political game for people who wanted to tell a story. I was afraid for myself and my teammates."[10]

The booing of the anthem angered not only many French people but their political leaders as well. It helped win support for an amendment to a security law, making it an offence to show disrespect to the anthem at public events. A conviction carries a fine of up to €7,500 and six months in jail. While the law has been used against people who have insulted the French flag, it's proved tougher to find someone guilty of jeering the anthem. How do you convict an entire crowd? And what do you do when the booing happens abroad? Since the law was passed in 2003, football games against Morocco and Tunisia — both also former French colonies — have been disrupted by booing.

It's not surprising that people don't like the idea of their national song being booed or sung badly. But fortunately, most countries recognize that you can't enforce patriotism. Most countries ... but not all. Generally, the more repressive the regime, the more likely it is to have strict rules around symbols like flags and anthems. And when those rules are aimed at its own citizens, it's clear that what's really demanded is total allegiance to the state.

One country where you definitely don't want to mess around with the anthem is China. The ruling Communist Party sees no difference between the party and the state; you can't love China without loving the party, and criticism of one is criticism of the other. And you certainly can't protest against the government without severe consequences. So, it's no surprise that in 2017 the National People's Congress — essentially a rubber-stamp legislature for laws submitted by the party — approved a statute that carries a penalty of up to three years in jail for insulting the national anthem. The law also forbids any distortion of the lyrics or music of the anthem or the singing of it in a derogatory fashion. So, there's no possibility of a Chinese José Feliciano or Jimi Hendrix delivering a new take on "March of the Volunteers." The law also makes it illegal to play the anthem at funerals, weddings, or other "inappropriate" occasions.

The reasons behind the tough law were explained by Zhang Haiyang, deputy head of the legislature's Law Committee, in a release from the state-owned Xinhua News Agency: "The legislation governing the use of the national anthem is feasible, necessary, and of great significance to foster and practice socialist core values and to promote the patriotism-centred spirit of the nation."[11]

It's hard to believe that the law was inspired by multiple occasions of the Chinese anthem being insulted domestically. That would have earned the protesters a quick trip to a re-education camp. But there was one place where "March of the Volunteers" did suffer indignity. Hong Kong was allowed liberties denied to people elsewhere in China as part of the agreement returning the former British colony to Chinese rule. The "One Country, Two Systems" approach was designed to allow a measure of democracy in Hong Kong, and many people took advantage of that to protest against China's strengthening control over the territory. Among those protests were several at football matches where the Chinese national anthem was played.* Many fans booed the song. Beijing's response was to insist the Hong Kong legislature pass the National Anthem Ordinance with its harsh penalties. The first arrest under the new law took place in 2021 during the Olympics, when a man booed the anthem while watching a medal ceremony at a public viewing site in a shopping mall.

Most anthem laws are aimed at protecting the dignity of a country's national song. But when legislators in Slovakia's parliament voted in 2019 to protect state symbols, they also unwittingly voted for a clause that made it illegal to sing any other country's national anthem at public events unless a delegation from that country is present. The law was proposed by the right-wing Slovak

* Hong Kong may be part of China, but it is recognized as a separate country by FIFA and competes in international football tournaments under its own flag. However, the anthem that's played is "March of the Volunteers."

National Party, a junior coalition partner in Slovakia's government. It seemed relatively innocuous until people actually read what Parliament had passed.

The anthem amendment appears to have been slipped in without anyone noticing to deliberately target ethnic Hungarians — there are about 450,000 Hungarians in Slovakia, almost 9 percent of the population, and the relationship between them and the Slovak majority is not always an easy one. The anthem move seems to have been sparked by the success of a football club in the small town of Dunajská Streda, where most of the population speaks Hungarian (and call the town Dunaszerdahely). The stadium of FC DAC 1904 Dunajská Streda can seat almost thirteen thousand people. The fans are virtually all ethnic Hungarians, and they wave Hungarian flags and sing the Hungarian national anthem at home matches, where it is regularly booed by the much smaller contingent of Slovakian fans.

One of the sponsors of the anthem clause in the new law was Slovak National Party MP and former Slovakian international football star Dušan Tittel. He defended the no-foreign-anthems rule (and made it very clear exactly who it was aimed at) by telling parliamentarians to go and watch a football match in Dunajská Streda when nine thousand fans sing the Hungarian anthem. "I don't think you'd like it," he said.[12]

Once people found out what the new law contained, there was immediate pushback. It turned out that even some ethnic Hungarian MPs had voted for the law without realizing what it meant. They claimed not to have noticed the change concerning the anthems. Slovakia's president Andrej Kiska rescued them from their embarrassing mistake by vetoing the law, making it safe for people to gather in Slovakian public spaces for rousing renditions of "O Canada," "Advance Australia Fair," "La Marseillaise," and even Hungary's "Himnusz," without fear of arrest.

Japan's national song, "Kimigayo," is one of the world's shortest anthems — at just four lines — and also the oldest, being based on a poem from about a thousand years ago. The title is usually translated as "His Imperial Majesty's Reign," and the short poem seems like a fairly benign desire for the emperor to have a long and happy reign. A Japanese equivalent of "God Save the King."

There is no official English language translation — understandable since the Japanese can't even agree on what the lyrics mean in their own language — but it was translated poetically by English author Basil Hall Chamberlain, who was a professor of Japanese at Tokyo Imperial University in the late nineteenth century.

> Thousands of years of happy reign be thine;
> Rule on, my lord, until what are pebbles now
> By ages united to mighty rocks shall grow
> Whose venerable sides the moss doth line.

But the poem is not without controversy. After being set to music in the late nineteenth century, it became Japan's de facto national anthem — and that included the period of the Second World War. The song's close identification with Emperor Hirohito and the appalling war crimes committed in his name has led to many calls for its replacement. Unlike its defeated Axis allies Germany and Italy, Japan did not change its anthem after the war. Not everyone was happy with that decision.

Opposition to the anthem was led by Japan's teachers, who were sickened by the role they played in teaching children to show complete obedience to an emperor who was revered as a god. The playing of the anthem was a key part of that indoctrination. The goal — largely successful — was to create fanatical soldiers who believed the greatest honour was to die for their emperor.

For years after the war, rules on singing "Kimigayo" were largely ignored in schools, without consequence. But a push to enforce compulsory singing of the anthem began in the 1980s. Teachers were ordered to sing the anthem and disciplined if they refused. The extent of the passions at play was tragically revealed in 1999 when the principal of a high school near Hiroshima was caught between the two sides. Toshihiro Ishikawa tried to persuade his teachers to accept the law and agree to play the anthem. They refused, maintaining the anthem with its wartime links was inappropriate for a school. Unable to broker a solution, Ishikawa took his own life.

Teachers continue to voice their opposition to the anthem and have taken their fight to the courts, but without much success. Japan's Supreme Court has sided with the government, finding that even if a teacher felt their freedom of conscience was being infringed, it was their duty as public servants to obey their superiors' orders.

The teachers received some support from a surprising quarter. Emperor Akihito caused a constitutional kerfuffle in 2004 at — of all things — a royal garden party. One of the guests, a Tokyo school-board member, told the emperor he was responsible for ensuring all students and teachers stood for the anthem. He clearly expected to be congratulated, but the reply he got was completely unexpected. Emperor Akihito said, "It is desirable that it not be compulsory."[13]

That may seem like an innocuous thing, but it was a huge deal in a country where the emperor is constitutionally prohibited from expressing any political opinions. When you think about it, though, it seems reasonable that the man who's the subject of the anthem should be allowed to share his views on what is basically his own theme song. And wouldn't it be wonderful if monarchs got to pick their own anthems? Instead of sticking with, say, "God Save the King," why not have each new monarch commission their own anthem and introduce it with a (literal) fanfare at their coronation?

For the moment, though, Japan is stuck with the anthem it has. And despite the collective shock in Japan over their emperor expressing an actual opinion, he repeated it at a news conference the following year. Yes, Emperor Akihito — and his successor, Emperor Naruhito* — held occasional news conferences. Imagine if the British monarch did the same thing. Akihito did balance the scales somewhat by also saying that it was important for schools to respect both the flag and the anthem.

"As they are considered to be symbols of nations, it is essential to respect the feelings people have for them," he said.

And that's where it rests for the moment. Japanese teachers may not like being forced to play the anthem, but they know that refusing to do so can cost them their jobs.

---

* Emperor Naruhito ascended to the Chrysanthemum Throne in 2019 when his father abdicated due to age and ill-health, taking the glorious title of "Emperor Emeritus."

11
EVERYONE WANTS AN ANTHEM

We all used to get on just fine without everyone needing a theme song. It's easy to understand the need for flags. They are visible signs that let everyone know whose territory you are in. Think of them as a slightly more civilized way of peeing against trees and rocks to mark your land.

But anthems? We don't go around singing to each other to let us know whose team we're on. We don't listen out for the sound of music to confirm that we've crossed an otherwise invisible border. They are just recent creations, originally adopted to assure insecure absolute monarchs that the people loved them.

Once we started the whole idea of adopting songs to represent ideas and tribes, it became contagious. If a big song showed that you belonged to a place, then every place had to have one. Don't like the Spanish anthem because you're Catalan? Don't worry, there's a Catalan national song you can sing instead.* If you have

* The Catalan anthem is in the public domain, so there was no problem with the American metal band A Sound of Thunder recording their own take on the anthem in both English and Catalan in 2017. The mother of lead vocalist Nina Osegueda is Catalonian. You should check it out. It's really good.

a national anthem, then you must be a nation. And if you're a nation, you must have a national anthem. You can see why anthems become inevitable.

Of course, not all local and regional anthems are political statements like Catalonia's "Els Segadors" (The Reapers)* or Scotland's "Flower of Scotland." At least not on the surface. Cape Breton, part of the province of Nova Scotia, has its own anthem. "The Island" is a ballad written in the 1970s that honours the coal miners and steelworkers that were the bedrock of the island's industrial past. It recalls how those workers had to fight for their rights against foreign-owned companies. The song reminds the listeners that the island and its people remain strong and unbowed despite losing so much — a rock in the stream. As an anthem, it ticks most of the boxes: emotion, pride, unity created from conflict, and a society born of immigrants working together. But it does ignore one important group: the Indigenous Mi'kmaq who have lived there for ten thousand years — something that is pretty much standard practice for anthems written by settler people.

What the Cape Breton anthem does — like other similar tribal bonding songs — is give people membership in a club. A feeling they belong to something larger than themselves, particularly when they are separated from their ancestral home. There is a reason so many Irish and Scottish folk songs are filled with bittersweet thoughts of remembered places: it's because those places were torn away by forced emigration. The Cape Breton anthem falls into this category.

But where these songs can become problematic is when they exclude, and the more narrowly focused a song is on a group, the more obvious it is when people are excluded. In a small place like Cape Breton, with a population of 130,000, you can know the

* The anthem is about a seventeenth-century war that began with a peasant uprising.

names of the individuals who are left out. On that small a scale, it's a reminder that picking a song to represent the best that you are is a tricky business.

♫

Most regional anthems tend to be popular songs that are adopted precisely because they are so well-known. Virtually every defined regional area has a song that the locals will refer to as their anthem. Sometimes, it comes about because someone just says, "Hey, you should write us an anthem," and then the person actually does, instead of just laughing and buying another beer.

The island of Saint Helena is known to most of the world for precisely one thing. It was where Napoleon Bonaparte was imprisoned by the British after his defeat at the Battle of Waterloo in 1815. Napoleon had already escaped from one island prison, but this time the British made sure he'd never return to France. And having an empire that covered the globe, they had lots of isolated spots to keep him. The place they picked was Saint Helena, a tiny tropical island in the Atlantic between Africa and South America. It was remote then, and it's remote now.

Not many people live there; the population is about 4,300 people. But they have an anthem. It's one of the world's more off-beat anthems, but the islanders — they call themselves "Saints" — have grown to love it. "My Saint Helena Island" is a country song written and recorded by a man who never visited the place but was talked into writing the song by a friend.

Dave Mitchell was an American who had a gig as a part-time DJ with Volcano Radio on Ascension Island in the 1970s. Like Saint Helena, Ascension has some mid-Atlantic strategic importance. The radio station was mostly funded by the U.S. armed forces, which had a major presence on Ascension Island in the form of a military base that features one of the world's longest runways. It was designated as an emergency landing strip for the Space Shuttle. The island was also home to a NASA tracking station in the 1970s, which is what brought Mitchell and others to the island. He worked for Bendix Corporation, which manufactured communication equipment for the space program.

There wasn't a lot to do on Ascension Island when Mitchell lived there, and nothing much has changed since. There's a golf course — built on a lava field and described by many as the worst golf course in the world — and not much else. That's why he ended up volunteering at the radio station. He also played music in a country band at parties across the island, and that's how he made friends with people from Saint Helena. There's no indigenous population on Ascension, and most of the nine hundred or so residents are from Saint Helena and work either directly or indirectly for the military base and supporting services.

Mitchell's style of country music proved popular with the locals on Ascension, and he was encouraged by a friend to write a song about Saint Helena to boost the band's popularity with its audience. While Ascension and Saint Helena are neighbouring islands, they're separated by 1,300 kilometres of ocean. In the 1970s, the only way of making the trip was by boat — a difficult trip. Dave Mitchell had never been to Saint Helena and was understandably reluctant to compose a song about a place he'd never set eyes on.

His friend didn't see that as a problem and gave Mitchell some postcards of the island to inspire him. After staring at the pictures for a couple of days, Mitchell picked up his guitar and wrote the song in a few minutes. It's not exactly a classic — it has lines like "Diamonds they are pretty, so is your fancy cars / But Saint Helena Island is much prettier by far" — but "My Saint Helena Island" was an immediate hit with the Saints on Ascension. In 1975, shortly before he left Ascension for good, Mitchell recorded the song at a studio in Memphis, Tennessee, during a trip home to the United States. He mailed copies of the 45 RPM records to Saint Helena, where it was played by Radio Saint Helena and quickly became accepted as the unofficial anthem of the island.*

Dave Mitchell never set foot on Saint Helena, but he remained proud of his distant connection to the place. He was particularly thrilled that the Royal Mail Ship *St Helena*, which for years was the only regular way of reaching the island, used to play his song whenever it left port.[1]

♫

Forty-eight of the fifty American states have official state songs, from Alabama to Wyoming.† You've probably never heard most of them. But some are very famous — like "Oklahoma!," taken from the Rodgers and Hammerstein musical. Or "You Are My Sunshine" from Louisiana. Georgia has the best of them all: "Georgia on My Mind." If all anthems were like that, then this book would not be necessary.

I have to say that New York really dropped the ball by not grabbing "New York, New York." Maybe they decided against it because it's more about the city than the state.

Then there's Florida's song, "Old Folks at Home" — you may know it better as "Swanee River." There's a certain ick factor to that one, even though the words have been revised to hide its racist past. The song was originally written as a "minstrel" song — a quaint name that conceals the reality that minstrel

* As a British Overseas Territory, Saint Helena's official anthem is "God Save the King."

† New Jersey has never had an official song. Legislators voted several times to adopt "I'm From New Jersey," but the governor obviously didn't like the song and didn't sign the law adopting it. Maryland's state song was removed in 2021 because of its pro-Confederacy lyrics. No replacement was named.

shows featured white singers in blackface performing racist songs and skits about African-Americans* — which is why the original lyrics were written from the perspective of a slave "longing for de old plantation." Today's verses are cleaned up for modern sensibilities. But some people don't think the stain of racism can ever be removed from the song and want it replaced. A new song was picked in 2008 after a state-wide contest. "Florida (Where the Sawgrass Meets the Sky)" was adopted as the state anthem. But "Old Folks at Home" remains the official state song. No one seems to know what the difference is.

So, all those official songs and/or anthems exist. But here's what doesn't happen: when the governor of California goes to visit the governor of Nevada, he isn't met by a band playing "I Love You, California."† In fact, these state songs are rarely played and are mostly heard at formal occasions — like a governor's inauguration or funeral.

However, there are lessons to be learned from these state anthems. First, you can have a song — but you don't have to play it all the time. Second, you can pick the best available song and the best available singer. Think Ray Charles and "Georgia on My Mind." Third, you can follow Florida's example and keep rewriting a nasty song until you get one that sort of works. And finally, you don't need to limit yourself to just one song.

---

* I grew up watching *The Black & White Minstrel Show*, which ran from 1958 to 1978 on BBC despite a continuous campaign to end it. The BBC defended the indefensible with the argument that it was "a traditional show enjoyed by millions for what it offers in good-hearted family entertainment." One critic observed that the same thing was said of throwing Christians to the lions in ancient Rome.

† With so many songs about California out there ("California Dreamin'," "Hotel California," "California Nights") you have to call this out as a missed opportunity but not one too late to rectify. However, the current state song has one major fact in its favour: the composer of the tune was called Frankenstein.

Tennessee has twelve,* including the famous "Tennessee Waltz" and the not-so-famous but truly inspiring "A Tennessee Bicentennial Rap: 1796–1996," which the Tennessee governor's office describes as "the Official Bicentennial Rap song to provide a fun and easy way for citizens and students to learn and retain some of our great state's history."†

The lyrics are mostly lists of great things, places, and people associated with the state, including this classic verse:

> Dollywood and Walking Horse Show!
> Opryland and the Opry Show!
> Whiskey, whiskey — sipping smooth!
> Moon, Moon Pies and Goo Goo Goos!‡

You have to think that maybe Tennessee has got it right: an entire songbook of anthems, with one to suit every occasion. And when musical tastes change, you add another song. Who knows? Maybe a heavy metal or K-pop Tennessee state song. Wouldn't it be great if countries followed the example of Tennessee?

The rest of the world should also pay attention to song selection. Instead of picking a song that no one outside your nation has ever

---

* Tennessee keeps adding new songs to its list of official state songs. In 2023 "Copperhead Road" by Steve Earle became the latest. The irony of having a state song about growing cannabis in a state where the drug is still illegal has not gone unnoticed, particularly as the announcement was made on April 20 — or 4/20, the date used to celebrate pot smoking because of its connection to "420," a popular slang term for pot use.

† It's not a perfect song. One of the historical figures mentioned is Nathan Bedford Forrest, who was a Confederate general, slave owner, and the first grand wizard of the Ku Klux Klan — although he later distanced himself from the white supremacist terror group and spoke out in favour of racial harmony. A bust of Forrest was removed from the Tennessee State Capitol building in 2021.

‡ There's a lot to unpack here. Dollywood is, of course, Dolly Parton's theme park. The Walking Horse Show is an annual celebration of the Tennessee horse. Opryland was a music-based theme park that closed in 1997. The Opry Show is the Grand Ole Opry, home of country music. Tennessee is home to many whiskey distilleries, including Jack Daniel's. Moon Pies are chocolate-covered cookies with a marshmallow filling; they were invented in Chattanooga. The Goo Goo Cluster is a candy bar with marshmallow, nuts, and chocolate.

heard, maybe go for something we can all enjoy. It would make the world a much more relaxed place. I mean, if your anthem was a song like the official Kansas song, everyone — and I mean everyone — would join in. All together now:

> Oh, give me a home where the Buffalo roam
> Where the Deer and the Antelope play;
> Where never is heard a discouraging word,
> And the sky is not clouded all day.

Imagine an international football match where the entire stadium sang along with the anthems. It would be hard to whip up nasty nationalist fervour if the whole world wants to sing your song.

♫

You can understand why people like having a song to identify with their home or why a country wants to trademark its presence with an anthem. But you don't need to be a place to merit an anthem. Some of the most bizarre anthems belong to corporations — many of them bigger than a lot of countries and obviously with egos to match. The idea, at least in some companies, seems to be that if a country can encourage loyalty through song, then a corporation can achieve the same result with its employees.

The world leader in corporate anthems is Japan. For years, many Japanese workers were expected to start the day with a rousing rendition of the company song. It was all about building loyalty. Employees were expected to be dedicated to the company — and in return, the company was expected to offer lifetime employment.

But the idea of working for one company your entire career — or having companies that lasted that long — began to decline in the 1980s. The economic meltdown that hit Japan in the early '90s saw many long-standing companies go out of business. The social contract between workers and employers was broken. The practice of daily singing became less common. Companies still had songs, but now they were more about the brand than the idea of working together. And they were designed to be played rather than sung. The days of thousands of employees singing lyrics like "Fuji! Fuji! Fuji! With one voice, let us sing of a prosperous future!" are largely gone.

But some people obviously miss those days, because occasionally a company song will pop up again in a fit of nostalgia — although it's usually more of a promotional tool than an attempt to boost employee morale. In 2003 a Yokohama firm specializing in building demolition was looking for a way to make itself stand out in a crowded market. So, Nihon Break Kogyo, which translates as "Japan Break Industries," came up with a company song, complete with a video featuring employees doing what they did best — knocking things down.

"We will destroy houses. We will destroy bridges," the singer promises gleefully.[2]

The song proved so popular it was released as a single and made the Japanese pop charts. The company got more demolition work than it could handle. In that way, it ended up being a very successful company song — it definitely improved morale among the employees, even if its pop-rock style doesn't lend itself to a group singalong.

While Japan may have been the most enthusiastic embracer of company songs, it wasn't alone. The company that set the standard for corporate anthems was America's IBM. Its association with music goes back to 1915, when the Computing-Tabulating-Recording Company, as it was then known, established a band at the suggestion of company president Thomas Watson. He went on to build IBM into one of the world's largest and most successful companies. Watson loved music and believed in the power of group singing.

In 1927 the book *Songs of the IBM* was published, the first of many editions that continued into the 1950s. Employees were encouraged to sing the songs at company conventions and gatherings. Such singalongs were often led by company choirs. IBM wasn't alone in promoting group loyalty through music, but it definitely took it to a higher level. The lyrics were sung to popular tunes, like "Auld Lang Syne" and "Yankee Doodle." But the official company anthem — "Ever Onward" — was a unique composition. It's worth quoting one verse in full:

> Ever Onward — Ever Onward!
> We're bound for the top to never fall!
> Right here and now we thankfully
> Pledge sincerest loyalty
> To the corporation that's the best of all!
> Our leaders we revere, and while we're here,
> Let's show the world just what we think of them!
> So let us sing, men! Sing, men!
> Once or twice then sing again
> For the Ever Onward IBM.

While most of the people working at IBM in 1930s were men, women weren't entirely forgotten. The song "To Our I.B.M. Girls" pays tribute to the secretarial staff.

> The office girls surely are always in style,
> They greet you with smiles, their welcome's worthwhile,
> The best in the world are our girls, rank and file.

But most of the songs are dedicated to executives, like Vice-President Otto E. Braitmayer.

> We adore you, Otto Braitmayer
> Our great pioneer,

You're a wise and able leader,
And you always are sincere.

That one is sung to the tune "It's a Long Way to Tipperary," if you want to give it a go in the shower. And you can check out more of the classic IBM songs on the company's website, along with some audio examples.

IBM's dedication to music wasn't limited to encouraging employees to sing; the company even commissioned a symphony from American composer Vittorio Giannini. The short work — it runs a little over eleven minutes — was written to mark the opening of IBM's new world headquarters in 1938. The only available recording appears to be one by the in-house symphony orchestra of Columbia Records. Unfortunately, it's not widely available, but you can listen to it on YouTube. And it fits nicely into our theme of national anthems. As IBM notes in its musical archives, "Above these constant rhythms are heard the different anthems of the nations as they unite their common efforts for the prosperity and the betterment of mankind."

It's easy to mock the IBM songs, but it's worth remembering that these were early team-building exercises. Today's companies may not issue corporate songbooks, but they certainly force employees into other group activities that people often find embarrassing and pointless, like paintball, survival weekends, or the classic "trust fall" — you fall backwards and expect a colleague to catch you.

And the desire for a company anthem hasn't dimmed. It's not entirely clear why. You have to suspect that in many cases it's a vanity project of a CEO — something to play when they run onto the stage at a corporate event. It's hard to imagine the employees of international accounting and consultancy giant KPMG getting together to sing along to the 2001 anthem, "Global Strategy."

> KPMG we're strong as can be,
> A team of power and energy.
> We go for the gold,
> Together we hold
> Onto our vision of global strategy.

And if you're going to commission someone to write a song for you, why would you try to stop people from hearing it? I'm guessing that embarrassment is the main reason why KPMG — and other companies — have done their best to eliminate their corporate songs from the internet. The songs were often so hilariously bad that instead of raising company morale, they became objects of ridicule. And giant corporations generally have a very low tolerance for being mocked.

Unlike IBM, which has embraced its musical past, you generally won't find any information about these songs on company websites. And people who post the songs online have been told by company lawyers to remove them because of copyright issues.

At the behest of company lawyers, YouTube tried to stamp out the KPMG "Global Strategy" song, replacing it with the statement, "This video is no longer available due to a copyright claim by KPMG." However, the original poster resubmitted it with just audio and a cheeky graphic saying, "Sure about that?" So, it's not yet lost to posterity.[3]

Interestingly, KPMG seems less concerned about people seeing the anthem it commissioned in 2015. That's perhaps because "One Firm Anthem" is a more slickly produced symphonic work, more in tune with the company's image of itself. You can still find that video online, but it's not nearly as much fun as the terrible pop of "Global Strategy."

Sadly, the drug company Pfizer has had more success in killing off all online copies of its 2008 anthem, "Excel and Succeed." Or perhaps some artificial intelligence roaming the internet eliminated it in a gesture of goodwill to humanity. By all accounts, the song was in an awful league of its own with lines that include, "Excel and exceed, in our drive to succeed / Pfizer stands united, we were born to lead!"

We can only hope that Pfizer has not managed to destroy all the copies and that it will reemerge one day for us to enjoy.

The list of truly terrible corporate anthems is so long that it's difficult to understand why anyone would want to add to it. There really isn't an upside. Corporate songs are ripe for ridicule. What seemed — presumably — like A Good Idea At The Time can quickly require damage control.

The British security firm G4S released a country-rock style corporate song in 2011, called "G4S: Securing Your World." No expense was spared. American singer-songwriter Jon Christopher Davis was hired to co-write and perform the song. Davis notes on his website that he has "written songs for and collaborated with legends," including Dolly Parton, Billy Ray Cyrus, and Vince Gill. He also promotes his custom music business to create "the sound of your brand."

The song Davis helped write features lyrics like, "Because the enemy prowls, wanting to attack / But we're on the wall, we've got your back." And a chorus of, "G4S! protecting the world / G4S! so dreams can unfurl."

Unfortunately for G4S, the song was recorded just before the 2012 London Olympics. The company won the contract to provide security at the Games but failed to hire enough people to do the job. The British government had to bring in thousands of soldiers and police officers to make up the shortfall. G4S chief executive Nick Buckles admitted it was a "humiliating shambles" that had left the company's reputation in tatters. He said he regretted ever signing the Olympic security contract.

And then people found the song. The reaction was swift, vicious, and, in the light of the CEO's admissions before a British parliamentary inquiry, entirely justified.

Our mission is to maintain the peace,
But make no mistake we'll face the beast.
We'll back him down and make him run,
We'll never leave our post 'til the job is done.

The company tried to distance itself from the song, denying it was a corporate anthem, claiming instead that it was a promotional video used to boost business in the United States. But the damage was done. One exceptionally cruel headline in the *New Statesman* magazine stated, "G4S, Securing the World — Nickelback-Style."[4]

Nick Buckles left the company after the Olympic security debacle with a £1.2 million payoff. The official video of the song was removed from YouTube, but parody versions remain. And Jon Christopher Davis didn't seem to mind the negative publicity associated with his song. In the midst of the security controversy, he posted this in an online forum: "Hey guys — check out the corporate anthem I did for the G4S corporation. Now that the company have got in the news a bit, I thought y'all might like to hear it.... Just so you know, I'm available for your corporate anthem, wedding, or Bar Mitzvah."

And he helpfully supplied a link to the audio of the song. One commentator observed dryly, "Hope he was paid a lot of money for this."

There's nothing new about hubris. When a victorious general returned to ancient Rome, he was often honoured with a triumph — a parade through city streets lined with cheering citizens. But standing behind the general in his chariot was a man with the job of whispering the words "memento mori" in his ear. Remember, you will die. The aim was to remind the conquering hero that fame and glory are fleeting.

A similar task should be assigned to a company employee, so that when an over-exuberant executive utters the words, "You know what we need? A corporate song!" they will immediately whisper in his ear, "Remember G4S!" and save everyone a lot of embarrassment and aggravation.

♫

There's one group that you may be surprised to learn does not have an official song. The United Nations represents 193 countries, all of them with national anthems. But the UN doesn't have one or want one. People obviously assume there's a UN anthem, because they keep asking about it — to the point where the UN has offered up a response to a Frequently Asked Question on its website: "Though many songs have been written about the United Nations or on related themes, there is no official anthem or hymn for the Organization."

You can see why it doesn't have one. The UN's goals are to keep peace, to develop friendly relations among nations, and to encourage respect for each other's rights and freedoms. Let's face it, those goals are basically incompatible with almost all national anthems, which, as we've seen, generally celebrate violence; encourage fighting against real or perceived enemies; expect a deity to back them over all others; and generally ignore women, Indigenous Peoples, and others who don't fit the appropriate national profile.

If the UN were to have an anthem, it would have to be one that all 193 member states could agree to sing. And no matter how bland it was, it would upset someone. If Israel or the United States or North Korea agreed to a set of lyrics, numerous nations would reject them on principle. And even just a line about striving to get along would muster opposition from countries that genuinely don't want to get along with some of their neighbours. Maybe the UN should just adopt the G4S song — after all, the mission statement for both organizations is basically the same: "Our mission is to maintain the peace." But the UN made the sensible decision to walk away from the whole idea.

Well, almost. What the UN does have is a poem, one that was set to music — composed by Spanish cellist Pablo Casals — and first performed with an orchestra and choir for the twenty-sixth anniversary of the UN in 1971. It's never been officially endorsed, used as an anthem, or played in the kind of places or at times an anthem would be heard. So why mention it at all? Because of the words. "Hymn to the United Nations" was written as a poem, and when it's sung, you can't really get the full power of what those words are saying. That's the thing about anthems: people don't pay much attention to the words, because if they did, they probably would have second thoughts about singing them at all. What anthems are about is the shared experience of coming together. The words really don't matter; it's the singing that's important.

But in the case of "Hymn to the United Nations," the words absolutely do matter. They were written by W.H. Auden, one of the greatest poets of the twentieth century. He read his poem at the United Nations — you can listen to it on the UN website. And it's important because it really reads like an anti-anthem. Ironically, it warns people about words, because words offer false promises, and declares that what's important is music, which Auden calls "holy ground, / Where all are Brothers, / None faceless Others."

Beware of words, he says, because "With words we lie, / Can say peace / When we mean war." But song is true, he says. "Let music for peace / Be the paradigm."

> So may the story
> Of our human city
> Presently move
> Like music, when
> Begotten notes
> New notes beget,
> Making the flowing

Of time a growing,
Till what it could be,
At last it is,
Where even sadness
Is a form of gladness,
Where Fate is Freedom,
Grace and Surprise.[5]

So, if you do feel the need for an anthem, listen to Auden. Because he's telling you that you don't. What you do need is to lose yourself in a never-ending cycle of music that promises peace, truth, and change for all. In other words, the very opposite of what anthems are telling us.

12

WHO OWNS YOUR ANTHEM?

National anthems are just songs. Someone wrote them. In many cases, the writers never dreamed the songs would become national symbols. But like any composition, they are subject to the laws of copyright. Of course, that protection varies from country to country and depends on when the work was created. But the basic principle is that the copyright owner is entitled to royalty payments when their work is performed. In many countries, that protection stays in place for seventy years after the composer's death. So, if you write a song when you are twenty and die at age ninety, your song will generate seventy years of royalties during your lifetime and another seventy years of earnings for your heirs.

Once the copyright has expired, it's open season on songs: anyone can sing them, publish the music and lyrics, or create parodies without seeking permission or paying a fee. And even when a song is still under copyright, anyone can record their own version as long as they pay for the privilege.

The musician Prince didn't like anyone covering his songs without his permission but couldn't do anything about it. He addressed that issue in an interview with TV talk-show host George Lopez in

2011: "There's this thing called the compulsory licence law, which allows artists through the record companies to take your music at will without your permission, and that doesn't exist in any other art form be it books, movies...."

He also said that "covering music means your version doesn't exist anymore. A lot of times, people think I'm doing Sinead O'Connor's song or Chaka Khan's song when in fact I wrote those songs."*[1]

And you don't even have to be the author of the song to object to a cover version. American soul legend Etta James took extreme exception to Beyoncé's performance of "At Last" during Barack Obama's inauguration ball in 2009. "That woman he had singing for him, singing my song — she's going to get her ass whupped," James told an audience at a concert in Seattle. "I can't stand Beyoncé. She has no business up there, singing up there on a big ol' president day, gonna be singing my song that I've been singing forever."[2]

Ouch. And rather over the top, considering that James didn't write "At Last." While the song was certainly identified with her, it was written in 1941 and was a chart hit for big-band leader Glenn Miller decades before Etta James made it her own. James later said her comments about Beyoncé were a joke.

The proprietorial feelings expressed by Prince and James show just how much passion is attached to song ownership. So, it's hardly surprising that nations don't like it when their beloved anthems are mishandled. Some countries acquired ownership of their anthems by purchasing the copyright: Canada bought the music and English lyrics to "O Canada" for a nominal $1 in 1970, even though the song did not become the nation's official anthem for another ten

* Sinéad O'Connor had a global hit in 1990 with Prince's "Nothing Compares 2 U." She said Prince didn't like her version of the song. Chaka Khan's 1984 recording of "I Feel for You" was made with Prince's approval.

years. But as we've seen, owning the copyright just means you get paid when it's performed; it doesn't allow you to stop other people from doing whatever they like with the song. It makes sense for the state to own the anthem's rights because otherwise, someone would get paid every time the anthem was played in public. States don't collect royalties on anthems.

When Uganda was preparing for independence from Britain in 1962, it announced a competition for a national anthem. A government committee had the task of selecting the winner. It decided on "Oh Uganda, Land of Beauty," by well-known classical musician George Wilberforce Kakoma. The song received its first public performance at Uganda's Independence Day celebrations on October 9, 1962. Kakoma received a prize of two thousand Ugandan shillings (worth less than $1 today).

Everyone seemed happy. But Kakoma wasn't. He always maintained he had never signed away the copyright to his work. In 2008 he sued the government for forty-six years of royalty payments — one billion Ugandan shillings (around US$250,000 today). The courts ruled against him, saying that when someone creates a work under the direction of the government, then the government owns the copyright.[3]

Kakoma was bitter over the lost royalties. But the family of the man who composed South Korea's anthem had more success. The lyrics to "Aegukga" (Patriotic Song) were written in the nineteenth century, and the author is unknown. Originally, it was sung to the Scottish tune "Auld Lang Syne," probably due to the influence of Scottish missionaries. In 1936 classical composer and conductor Ahn Eak-tai wrote a new tune. The melody and words became the Republic of Korea's anthem in 1948.

It's likely that no one bothered about the issue of copyright at the time: Korea was an occupied nation under brutal Japanese rule from 1910 until Japan's defeat in 1945. The Korean government that initially adopted the anthem was in exile in China. After the war, the Korean peninsula was divided, with the south under American rule and the north occupied by the Soviet Union. Those occupations were meant to be temporary while the victorious powers worked out how to reunify the Korean peninsula under a single government.

That never happened. The Korean War broke out in 1950 when the North invaded the South with the goal of creating a communist state. Three years of brutal fighting followed, with the North supported by China and the Soviet Union and the South backed by a United Nations force led by the United States with support from another twenty countries, including Canada. An estimated 2.5 million Korean civilians were killed, and much of the country was destroyed. The fighting stopped with a ceasefire in 1953, but the war has never been formally ended.

The government that emerged in South Korea was a right-wing dictatorship. Even if it knew there was a copyright issue with the anthem, it probably wouldn't have cared. Political opponents were ruthlessly repressed. It was only in the late twentieth century, after the country transitioned into a democracy, that the copyright issue with the anthem's music finally emerged.

Ahn Eak-tai died in 1965. Under South Korea's Copyright Act, his work was protected until fifty years after his death — until 2015. His Spanish-born wife, Lolita Ahn, inherited his rights. She met Ahn in 1946 while he was working as a conductor with a Spanish orchestra. After her husband's death, Lolita Ahn lived in Spain but retained her Korean citizenship. And in the early 1990s, the Ahn family started receiving royalties for the anthem through the Korea Music Copyright Association, which collects fees for public performances of copyrighted works.

The family didn't get rich from their royalty cheques — estimates published in South Korean newspapers ranged from US$5,000 to $8,000 a year — but Koreans weren't happy about having to pay anything to perform their own anthem. The Ahn family was asked to give up their rights to the song, and in 2005 Lolita Ahn donated the copyright to the South Korean government.

There are a surprising number of anthems still under copyright. That's because so many nations only needed an anthem when they won independence from their colonial occupiers in the second half of the twentieth century. They often adopted the idea of holding a national competition to find an anthem. The smart ones avoided the kind of confusion that led to the court case in Uganda by making it clear the winning entry would become the state's property.

That's what happened in Barbados when it became independent from Britain in 1966. The winning lyrics for its new anthem were composed by one of the Caribbean's greatest songwriters, Irving Burgie — known professionally as Lord Burgess. Burgie was born in New York. His mother was Barbadian, and he grew up surrounded by Caribbean music. As well as writing his own music, he created new versions of traditional songs — including the Jamaican working chant that he turned into the international hit "Day-O," sung by Harry Belafonte.

Burgie died in 2019, which means the copyright to his works remains in place under Barbadian law until 2069. But not the anthem he wrote. The National Emblems and National Anthem of Barbados Act notes that the copyright in the words and music of the anthem is vested in the state.

Even though Barbados got a bona fide hitmaker to write its anthem, that didn't make it a popular ditty that charted worldwide. The number of people recording or playing alternative takes of a national anthem is very small and mostly American. Two versions of "The Star-Spangled Banner" have made the charts: Whitney

Houston's rendition from the 1991 Super Bowl and the 1969 José Feliciano performance described in Chapter 10. The Jimi Hendrix Woodstock performance wasn't released as a single.

It's hard to imagine that the latest K-pop band will gain a breakthrough hit with an anthem recording. But the thought that someone might be able to do such a thing was a big concern in Ireland in 2011. The copyright on the nation's anthem was due to expire in 2012, seventy years after the death of its author. And people worried about the horrors that could be visited on the song unless the state moved to protect it. A columnist in the *Irish Independent* fretted that "heaven knows what sort of abuse will be inflicted on it. Rap versions in the charts, or hip-hop versions in television commercials."[4]

Oh my. Questions were raised in Ireland's parliament, the Dáil. A government minister said they would "look at the possibility of introducing legislation should it be required to ensure that the National Anthem is not being used in an inappropriate context and without due deference such as to render it an object of scorn or derision."[5] Ministers didn't go into detail about what would constitute "scorn or derision." The government did not introduce legislation.

The whole issue was brought back to the boil by some T-shirts and sweatshirts. In 2015 Gaelic football star Paul Galvin released a clothing line through the Irish retail chain Dunnes Stores. The clothes featured lyrics from the anthem. Critics immediately seized on that as the kind of inappropriate use warranting immediate action. A private member's bill was introduced to give the anthem the same legal protection as the Irish flag — but without government support, it didn't go anywhere. The Irish anthem sits in the public domain, unprotected, like many other anthems, relying on the good sense of the country's citizens to treat it with respect. The feared rap version has not yet made it into the charts.

There is understandable confusion over anthems and copyright. Canada grants open access to the anthem, saying it is in the public domain and available for any purpose — including commercial uses — without seeking permission. The Canadian government says, "There is no law or behaviour governing the playing of the national anthem; it is left to the good citizenship of individuals." But what that doesn't do is grant you access to any anthem performance you can find on the internet. Maybe you really love the Anne Murray performance of "O Canada" from the 1992 World Series and want to include it in a podcast. You can't — because someone holds the copyright, likely Major League Baseball.

Think of it this way: Beethoven's *Fifth Symphony* is free and clear of any legal encumbrances. Play it backwards on the piano, arrange it for harmonica, print the music on a T-shirt. Go nuts. But what you can't do is use a recording of the piece by Herbert von Karajan and the Berlin Philharmonic for your latest YouTube project. If you try, the website will likely prevent you from uploading the video, or YouTube will remove it before you can say "*Deutsche Grammophon*." What's copyrighted here is not the music: it's the performance.

And that's led to problems with some national anthems. In 2019 Kenyans were furious when it appeared that a British music production company had acquired the copyright to the country's national anthem. Social media commentators accused the company of "stealing" the anthem. The government became involved. It had the makings of an international incident.

So, what happened? It all began when the owner of an African YouTube channel decided to create one of those online video listicles so popular with viewers. You know the kind of thing: "The Ten Best Cars of All Time," "Top 10 80s Hits." The list that caused a problem was the "Top 10 Best National Anthems in Africa." And number one on the list was Kenya's anthem. So far, so good. But when they uploaded the video, they got a YouTube alert telling them their video infringed on the rights of the song's owner.[6]

Cue a minor internet meltdown in Kenya. The Kenya Copyright Board, a government agency, stepped in to assure the people that a British publishing company had not taken ownership of the anthem. It pointed out that the copyright had expired in 2013 and the anthem was now in the public domain. As a result, it said any copyright claims on the anthem were invalid, and it was working to remedy the situation.

And then it all got sorted out. The publishing company issued a statement, saying, "We do not own, or claim to own, the copyright to the Kenyan National Anthem." But what the company *did* own was a recording of the anthem. It appears the uploaded YouTube anthem performance was mistakenly tagged as the same one owned by the company. It wasn't. YouTube removed the alert, and you can now watch the "Top 10 Best National Anthems in Africa" without worrying that every time the Kenyan anthem is played, a British company earns royalties.

Kenyans have good reason to be suspicious of Western companies appropriating their cultural legacy. The Swahili phrase *hakuna matata* became known worldwide after appearing in the 1994 blockbuster Disney movie *The Lion King*. It's usually translated as meaning "no worries," and like that familiar English phrase, it is in everyday use in Kenya and neighbouring African countries. In other words, Disney didn't invent *hakuna matata*. So, when people realized that Disney had trademarked the phrase, they weren't happy.[7]

Although the trademark was granted in 2003, it wasn't until Disney began promoting its live-action version of *The Lion King* in 2018 that people became aware of what had happened. An online petition was started, calling on Disney to drop its trademark. The founder of the petition wrote, "Disney can't be allowed to trademark something that it didn't invent … the decision to trademark 'Hakuna Matata' is predicated purely on greed and is an insult not only [to] the spirit of the Swahili people but also, Africa as a whole."

Hundreds of thousands of people signed. Disney was accused of cultural appropriation and colonialism. The company explained that the trademark only applied when the phrase was used on clothing along with references to the movie. So, anyone could make a T-shirt with *hakuna matata* on it, but they couldn't include the words "The Lion King" or names or pictures of characters from the film. It also pointed out that many other popular words and phrases have been trademarked, including "Merry Christmas" and "Seasons Greetings." But the company's statement that it "has never and will not prevent individuals from using the phrase" came across as rather paternalistic and didn't do much to placate angry Swahili speakers.

The trademark was still listed as active in 2023. The petition calling for its removal is still accepting signatures. And people across Africa are still saying *hakuna matata* without first checking that no Disney lawyers are within earshot.

♫

It all used to be so much simpler back in the days when you couldn't own creative work. Remember how the tune to "God Save the King" was lifted by numerous nations across Europe? No one was wondering if they had any right to use the music: it was out there, people liked it, so they took it.

When Francis Scott Key wrote "The Star-Spangled Banner" back in 1814, he did it with a specific tune in mind. "To Anacreon in Heaven" was a song composed for a London gentlemen's club in the late eighteenth century. It made its way to the United States and was adopted as the music for many other songs. This practice was so common that a word was coined for it: "contrafactum," meaning "the substitution of one text for another without substantial change to the music." It wasn't even the first time Francis Scott Key had done it; he used the same tune for an earlier song he had written, called "When the Warrior Returns."*

Because this sort of thing happened all the time, no one complained that Key had poached someone else's work. The composer of the tune, John Stafford Smith, was never asked for permission and certainly wasn't paid. He wouldn't have expected it. Smith lived until 1836 and was presumably well aware that others had appropriated his work. He did receive posthumous recognition in the form of a plaque in Gloucester Cathedral, where he was baptized in 1750. It states that "he will long be remembered as composer of the tune of the National Anthem of the United States of America."

The use (or abuse) of Smith's music didn't stop with Key; many other songs were written to the same tune during the nineteenth century. Some parodied Key's lyrics. There's even an abolitionist take:

> Oh, say do you hear, at the dawn's early light,
> The shrieks of those bondmen, whose blood is now
> streaming
> From the merciless lash, while our banner in sight
> With its stars, mocking freedom, is fitfully gleaming?

And the temperance movement also came up with a version, which is actually rather clever:

---

* Other examples of contrafacta include Elvis Presley's "It's Now or Never," which takes its tune from the Italian song "O Sole Mio" and Eric Carmen's hit "All by Myself," which uses a melody from Rachmaninoff's *Piano Concerto No.2 in C Minor.*

> Oh! who has not seen by the dawn's early light,
> Some poor bloated drunkard to his home weakly reeling,
> With blear eyes and red nose most revolting to sight;
> Yet still in his breast not a throb, of shame feeling!

No one got paid for any of this; composers generally produced work on commission. Or they worked as a resident musician in a wealthy or royal household and composed their own material on the side. They often relied on patrons, who helped them financially in return for compositions, which were dedicated to them. Russian composer Pyotr Tchaikovsky was supported for thirteen years by a wealthy music lover who made it a condition of her support that they never meet, although they did carry on an extensive correspondence. Tchaikovsky dedicated his *Symphony No. 4* to her.*

Most composers weren't as fortunate. Beethoven and Mozart gave piano lessons to the children of rich families to supplement their income. Then as now, the real money in the music business was in publishing; music publishers would pay a flat fee for a work and sell as many copies as possible before music pirates and foreign publishers reprinted it without any payment to the composer. Prior to the invention of recorded music, publishers made their money by selling sheet music for people to play at home. Hawkers would stand outside music halls and concert venues offering patrons copies of the songs and music they had just listened to.

A Baltimore music publisher named Thomas Carr was quick to see the commercial possibilities in Scott Francis Key's song. The poem Key called "The Defence of Fort McHenry" was published in

---

* Tchaikovsky's patron was Nadezhda von Meck, a rich Russian widow who lived in seclusion. While she insisted they never meet, the two did bump into each other at least once while Tchaikovsky was visiting one of her estates. They came face to face for a moment but did not speak, and Tchaikovsky later wrote to apologize. He dedicated three works to her, but in an oblique way to preserve the private nature of their relationship. His *Symphony No. 4* was dedicated "to my best friend." The others are dedicated to "B" (for the name of one von Meck's estates) and even more cryptically to an asterisk.

newspapers in September 1814, just days after he wrote it. That was quickly followed by a sheet music version available from Thomas Carr's music store, set to the tune of "To Anacreon in Heaven" but omitting the name of the poet. And like any good publisher, Carr knew how to market his product; Key's uninspiring title was dumped in favour of the one we all know today. The printing was clearly a rush job to capitalize on the instant popularity of the song; the sub-heading is misspelled as "A Pariotic Song."*

Scott Francis Key certainly didn't expect to make money from his work, but then he didn't need to. He was a prominent lawyer and a member of a wealthy, slave-owning family — some people feel that fact leaves an indelible stain of shame on the anthem. But he also had a lot of children — eleven of them — and there wasn't much left for future generations to inherit. In 1926 one of his two surviving grandchildren was found to be "without sufficient food and was in a very distressing condition."

That description was presented to the U.S. House of Representatives Committee on Pensions by the Daughters of the American Revolution (DAR). They petitioned Congress to grant a pension of $1,200 a year to Mary Key McBlair. She was seventy-two-years-old, a widow, and had no children.

Mrs. Frank Foster Greenawalt of the DAR told the committee that McBlair was left "destitute" after the death of her husband, whom she described as "not a very competent lawyer." As a result, McBlair was forced to sell some of her grandfather's relics to a pawnbroker, who returned them, saying, "Madam, I can not take any interest from the granddaughter of Francis Scott Key."

Several committee members were worried about setting a precedent and being "deluged" with pension requests. They said

* One of only eleven known surviving copies of that original printing was sold for US$506,500 at a 2010 auction.

there were many indigent individuals who had rendered great service to the country and were equally deserving of help. But Mrs. Greenawalt was having none of that. "We have only one Francis Scott Key; we have only one million dollar bridge erected to him; we have only one Fort McHenry that Congress is going to restore," she said. "If the Congress of the United States can erect monuments to his memory … they should do something for his granddaughter."

She also warned the congressmen about the optics of turning down the request. "Here is his own flesh and blood starving in the last years of her life for want of a few hundred dollars from Congress. It would really look very bad to turn this down. It would indeed."[8]

Mary Key McBlair didn't live long enough to see her pension. She died in 1927. The "one million dollar bridge" erected in her grandfather's honour still stands across the Potomac River in Washington, DC. A second bridge now bears his name, running across Baltimore Harbor near the historic site of Fort McHenry — the fort that Key witnessed being bombarded by the British in 1814, and where he saw by the dawn's early light that the flag still flew "o'er the land of the free and the home of the brave."

♫

Proving ownership of a song isn't always easy. There have been numerous court cases claiming breach of copyright brought against wealthy pop stars — there's little point in suing a non-wealthy musician — for producing tunes that sound a little too much like another song. George Harrison was found guilty of "subconscious plagiarism" because his 1970 song "My Sweet Lord" was found to be too similar to a 1963 hit by The Chiffons, "He's So Fine."

In perhaps the most bizarre case of a musician being accused of stealing someone else's work, John Fogerty, of the group

Creedence Clearwater Revival, was accused of plagiarizing a song written by ... John Fogerty. In 1970 CCR released "Run Through the Jungle," which was a Top 10 hit for CCR. Fifteen years later, Fogerty recorded "The Old Man Down the Road" as a solo single. It was also a hit. But Fogerty didn't own the copyright to the first song, and the man who did thought they were too similar. So Fogerty was sued for copying one of his own songs. The jury sided with Fogerty.

When it comes to national anthems, no one really seems to mind that Estonia and Finland share the same tune or that "Nkosi Sikelel' iAfrika" is used in whole or in part for the anthems of Tanzania, Zambia, and South Africa. But while you can't stop people from using an anthem tune, it's a different matter when they rip off the version of the anthem that you recorded.

Peter Breiner is a Slovak composer who has also lived in Canada, the United States, and England. He orchestrated and recorded the national anthems used for the 2004 Summer Olympics in Athens. That meant spending ninety hours in a studio with the Slovak Radio Symphony Orchestra to create 204 anthems. In the event, only fifty-six of the tunes were needed for medal ceremonies, but the entire catalogue of recordings is available on the classical music label Naxos.

If you're wondering who would buy a ten-CD collection of the world's anthems, then the answer is supplied by MusicWeb International, which says in its review of the collection: "A mandatory purchase for the nationality/sovereignty anorak.* Indispensable

* The word "anorak" is British slang for a person who is obsessed with a hobby that seems largely irrelevant to the rest of the population. The most famous example of such a hobby is trainspotting, whose enthusiasts stand beside railways and write down the types of engines and rolling stock that go by. The stereotypical trainspotter wears an anorak — a hooded waterproof jacket with deep pockets useful for holding notebooks, pencils, and flasks of tea.

for bandmasters, state musicians, *Mastermind** contestants, Tovey† experts, and organizers of diplomatic events and international visits. Also, any self-respecting major or regional library will want to have this on the shelves."[9]

And Peter Breiner believes that among the purchasers of this collection was the Beijing Olympic Committee.

When Breiner — and others — heard the anthem versions recorded for the 2008 Summer Olympics, they sounded very familiar. Because his arrangements of those anthems were unique. For example, his version of "The Star-Spangled Banner" was criticized by some Americans for being too soothing and gentle. A writer in the *Wall Street Journal* said it played down "the notion of the U.S. as a chest-thumping, butt-kicking, jingoistic powerhouse."[10] So, when people heard what sounded like the same orchestration four years later, they weren't happy. And nor was Breiner. He told the *Washington Post* that he was 100 percent positive that the Beijing Olympic Committee was using his work — and not paying for it.

"My arrangements of public-domain anthems are actually original compositions from a legal point of view," he told the *Post*. "Which means if someone wants to record them, they have to purchase the material."[11]

The suspicion was that someone, presumably in the employ of the Beijing Olympic Committee, listened to Breiner's recordings and transcribed the music. The Beijing Olympics organizers denied copying Breiner's work and said the orchestrations were created by Chinese musicians and recorded by the Beijing Symphony Orchestra. And there wasn't much anyone could do about it, even if

---

* *Mastermind* is a long-running BBC TV quiz show.

† Donald Tovey was a British composer and musicologist best known for his *Essays in Musical Analysis*. He also composed Zanzibar's national anthem, which existed from 1911 until the island merged with Tanganyika to create Tanzania. His anthem is included in the Naxos box set.

the theft seemed clear. China's approach at the time to intellectual property was very lax, so it's not surprising that complaints from the record label were ignored. In the end, all Naxos could do was note on its website that one hundred of Breiner's arrangements were used illegally at the Beijing Olympics.[12]

13

REBEL SONGS FOR A CAUSE

It was a scene of total joy, a familiar one to followers of sports. A winning team, celebrating a monumental victory in the locker room after the game. The players danced and cheered and sang a popular song from one of the country's best-known groups. And because it was 2022, the celebration was captured on video and posted on social media. The reaction was fast and furious. The team was forced to apologize. The victory was tainted, and the players were left confused and uncertain about what they had done wrong and why they were under investigation by police and the sport's governing body. So, what happened?[1]

The occasion was a crucial qualifying game for the 2023 FIFA Women's World Cup. Ireland was playing Scotland in Glasgow. The winning team was guaranteed a place in the World Cup finals. Ireland won, sending the team to the tournament for the first time. The players were instantly national heroes. It was no wonder the players were celebrating and singing. "We sang a hundred songs last night," veteran player Áine O'Gorman told Irish television the next day. Among those songs was Taylor Swift's hit "Love Story." But that's not the one that caused the controversy. The song that went viral had the rather innocuous title "Celtic Symphony"* by The Wolfe Tones.

The Wolfe Tones are an Irish rebel music group famous for their original songs about the country's fight for independence. Although noted for their songs rooted in the past, the group wrote many that were about contemporary events during what was called "The Troubles" in Northern Ireland, which some saw as a continuation of the long Irish fight against British rule. Songs about the outlawed Irish Republican Army, the IRA, feature prominently in the group's repertoire. Two of its most famous albums are *Up the Rebels* and *Rifles of the I.R.A.*

The song "Celtic Symphony" is about a Glasgow sailor who returns home and sees graffiti on the walls of his city, some of it in support of Glasgow Celtic Football Club and some saying, "Ooh ah up the 'RA, say ooh ah up the 'RA." That last line is repeated half a dozen times.

The phrase "up the 'RA" (pronounced "rah") is instantly familiar to Irish people as meaning "up the IRA." And that's what the women of the Irish football team sang in the video recorded after their famous victory. No one watching it could seriously believe the players were cheering on a paramilitary group labelled a terrorist organization in both Britain and the Republic of Ireland. You would be hard-pressed to find a bar in the Irish Republic featuring traditional music that didn't play a similar song on any given Saturday night.†

On this occasion, the song was deemed unacceptable. Politicians and family members of people killed in IRA bombings and

* The word "Celtic" here is pronounced with a soft c. That's because it was written to mark the one-hundredth anniversary of Glasgow Celtic Football Club, a team traditionally supported by descendants of Irish Catholic immigrants to Scotland.

† "Celtic Symphony" hit number one on the Irish iTunes chart after the chanting controversy. Several other Wolfe Tone rebel songs also climbed into the Top 10 in both Ireland and the United Kingdom.

shootings condemned the players and called for disciplinary action. The players were quickly trotted out to issue apologies and assurances that they were not IRA supporters. But the man who wrote the song pushed back against the critics. Brian Warfield, a founding member of The Wolfe Tones, told the *Irish Times* the players were being "persecuted and bullied for a song they like." He went on to say, "Don't tell [me] that you can't sing 'Celtic Symphony' but you can sing 'God Save the King.' Don't give the argument that 'Land of Hope and Glory' isn't a rebel song. It is. In England, they wear poppies and rise them up to 'sir this' and 'sir that' for killing for English expansionism but to kill to gain Ireland's freedom is a terrible crime."[2]

Any song that promotes violence, even if the songwriter thinks it is justifiable, will provoke a backlash. Except for certain songs that are considered to be above criticism. You can guess where this is going. On the same evening the Irish women's football team sang "up the 'RA," they also sang about fighting the English, taking up arms as soldiers, pledging their lives to Ireland, and braving cannon and rifle fire in the cause of freedom. That is exactly the kind of rebel song The Wolfe Tones have been singing for half a century. But no one complained. Because when it's an official national anthem, the lyrics apparently don't matter.

The Irish national anthem is a rebel song. During the fight for Irish independence in the early twentieth century, it was sung by members of the Irish Volunteers, a paramilitary group that evolved into the IRA. And it was sung by rebels during the 1916 Easter Rising against British rule. The song was well established as a popular piece in the country long before it was adopted as the national anthem in 1926. It completed its century-long journey from rebel song to respected anthem in 2011, when the song that was once banned by the British was played during Queen Elizabeth's historic visit to Ireland.

Many other nations also adopted rebel songs as their anthems. For the purposes of this chapter, I am defining rebel anthems as popular songs that became national anthems, as opposed to rebel anthems that were commissioned by governments. For example, most Central and South American anthems are of the rebel type but were specifically written to be national anthems.

The most famous rebel songs to make the leap to respectability are France's "La Marseillaise" and the United States' "The Star-Spangled Banner." Both were written in times of war while the nations fought for survival. And they were both one-hit wonders that achieved what so many writers and composers have tried and failed to do: come up with just the right message at just the right time. They were songs that were needed at the precise moment they were written. The power of sheer familiarity helped propel "The Star-Spangled Banner" to anthem status, even though that took over a hundred years.

"La Marseillaise" caught on faster. As you'll recall from earlier chapters, it was written in 1792 and was quickly adopted as a marching song by fighters from Marseille, which is how it got its name. Just three years later, it became France's first national anthem. But like all good rebel songs, it wasn't loved by the people in power: Napoleon Bonaparte dumped it, and it was banned when the monarchy was restored after Napoleon was overthrown.*

Occasionally, a song becomes so popular that people on both sides of a fight claim it as their own. That's the case with China's anthem, "March of the Volunteers." As described earlier, it started life as a movie theme song before it became popular with both sides in China's civil war as they fought the invading Japanese and each other. The Chinese Communist Party was quick to spot its potential — and its danger if it became a symbol of

---

* The song was readopted as the national anthem by the Third Republic in 1879.

counter-revolutionaries. Adopting "March of the Volunteers" as the national anthem changed it from being a song of revolution to a tool of the state. The rebel song is now part of the establishment. And the establishment doesn't like rebel songs it can't control.

When it comes to rallying the people behind a banner, the Chinese government makes it very clear what kind of rallying is permitted and what banners can be displayed. Most countries are displeased when the wrong national anthem is played at sporting events. But calls for a formal inquiry and a police investigation seem a little over the top, except when the offended country is China. That's what happened in 2022 and 2023 after several sporting events involving Hong Kong teams. Hong Kong is still allowed to compete as a separate entity at international tournaments, despite being part of China. Since being absorbed into China, many people in the former British colony have resisted Chinese efforts to stamp out democracy and free speech. One of the most popular songs at protest rallies was "Glory to Hong Kong."

When you do a Google search for "Hong Kong anthem," "Glory to Hong Kong" is the first thing that appears. It was the song sung at multiple sporting events, played instead of "March of the Volunteers." The Chinese government reacted with fury every time this happened. It refused to believe the wrong anthem was played because of a simple mistake, usually because some lowly paid employee or intern was tasked with downloading the required anthems from the internet. Police inquiries were launched. Sporting organizations were told they could lose funding or be disbanded if the mistake was repeated. Beijing demanded that Google change its search results to remove "Glory to Hong Kong." The company refused.[3]

There are some interesting similarities between the two songs. The Chinese anthem starts with the line "Arise, we who refuse to be slaves." It goes on to say that "Everybody must roar defiance." "Glory to Hong Kong" — which was written in 2019 — takes that opening line, and reworks it as, "Arise! Ye who would not be slaves again." Instead of roaring defiance, it says "our voice grows evermore."

The Hong Kong anthem is a rebel song that China's rulers cannot tolerate. That's the thing with states born out of recent revolutions: they are paranoid about the possibility of someone else organizing a counter-revolution, and they appreciate, and fear, the power of a good rebel song.

Perhaps the greatest badge of honour for a rebel song is to be banned by the authority targeted by the lyrics. In 1907 the United States banned the song that Filipino revolutionaries used during their fight for independence from American rule. The Americans took control of the Philippines after winning its 1898 war against Spain. A three-year fight for independence followed before the insurrectionists were defeated in 1901. During that war, writer and soldier José Palma wrote the poem "Filipinas." It was sung to a tune already accepted as the national anthem of the revolutionary movement. It's a typical rebel song, with lyrics that describe the nation as a holy land. "Never shall its shining fields / Be dimmed by tyrant's might," it goes, before adding that "We behold the radiance, feel the throb / Of glorious liberty."

The Americans, like all conquerors, moved to suppress anything that could be used to inspire nationalism among the defeated people and included the song in a law that prohibited anything that could be used "by the public enemies of the United States in the Philippine Islands for the purposes of public disorder or of rebellion or insurrection against the authority of the United States."[4]

The ban didn't work, and it was repealed a decade later. The song re-emerged as a rebel rallying cry after the Japanese invaded and occupied the Philippines during the Second World War. When the country finally gained independence in 1946, the rebel song that inspired Filipino revolutionaries in their battles against

American and Japanese occupiers became its national anthem. The origins of "Lupang Hinirang" (Chosen Land) are recognized and celebrated by the government, which officially describes the anthem as "a product of revolution, a response to the need of the revolutionary times that gave birth to it."[5]

But once revolutionaries take power, they are generally no longer interested in promoting rebellion. The song that once inspired people to fight is now a legally regulated tool of conformity. The 1998 Republic Act states, "When the National Anthem is played at a public gathering, whether by a band or by singing or both, or reproduced by any means, the attending public shall sing the anthem. The singing must be done with fervour."

The very nature of rebel songs demands passion. Anyone who has been in an Irish bar when a Saturday night band plays "A Nation Once Again" knows that singing with fervour does not come from a legal requirement; it comes from the heart. When you are ordered to sing a rebel song, the whole point of the song is negated. It has become just another of the world's bad anthems.

One of the great rebel-song anthems is "La Bayamesa," which has been Cuba's national anthem since 1902. It was literally written in the heat of battle, and its author died with its words on his lips, giving it a pedigree that's hard to beat. The anthem takes its title from the city where it was written. Bayamo is one of the oldest European settlements in the Caribbean, founded by Spanish explorers in 1513. In 1868 it was the scene of a major battle between Cuban insurgents and the Spanish colonial rulers. The rebels captured the city. One of the fighters that day was a poet, Perucho Figueredo, who was asked to write a song to celebrate the victory. He scribbled down the lyrics while still sitting on his horse, using a tune he had written a year earlier. The song was quickly adopted by the independence movement and became Cuba's anthem when the Republic of Cuba was created in 1902.

Figueredo was captured by the Spanish during the independence war. On August 17, 1870, he was executed by a firing squad. Just before the order to shoot was given, Figueredo shouted out a line from his anthem: "To die for one's country is to live." His body was buried in Havana. A monument in his honour was later erected in Bayamo.

"La Bayamesa" remained Cuba's anthem even after the Communist revolution, but the version sung today is much shorter. Figueredo wrote three verses, but only the first was adopted for the anthem: the other two were dropped because of their anti-Spanish rhetoric. It was felt that calling Spaniards vicious, cowards, and tyrants could be embarrassing when the new country was seeking Spanish investors. What remains, though, is truly a classic rebel song that demands of its singers that they not just lay down their lives for their country, but also give thanks for the glorious opportunity to do so.

Most rebel songs are about the longing of a people to be free of their current (or past) rulers. But sometimes, a rebel song has a much heavier burden to bear: it is asked to actually help create a nation. Indonesia isn't a natural state that is easily defined by geographic or ethnic boundaries. The country consists of more than seventeen thousand islands spread across a huge area between the Indian and Pacific oceans. The population of 275 million is divided into thousands of ethnic and linguistic groups. This is not a nation that came together easily.

Indonesia is a creation of colonialism, but not by one of the big colonizing nations that you might expect. The country was formed out of what was known for more than two hundred years as the Dutch East Indies. There was no logical reason for one country to be created out of such a diverse region, particularly since it is one that was never really fully under the control of its Dutch masters. Most of the history of Dutch rule involved various wars and rebellions. Other widespread colonial possessions, like British India, were split into several countries at independence. But a nationalist movement emerged in the early twentieth century that advocated for a single Indonesian state. And the song they picked for their anthem was a key part of that campaign.

While many people fought against Dutch rule, they didn't do it to set up a new Indonesian state: they just wanted to be rid of the occupying foreigners from where they lived. So there was no traditional pan-Indonesia rebel song that everyone could get behind. And writing a new revolutionary song faced the problem of coming up with a common narrative that few people in the colony shared. An Indonesian journalist decided to give it a go anyway. In 1924 Wage Rudolf Supratman wrote the lyrics and music for "Great Indonesia."

> Indonesia, my nationality
> My nation and homeland
> Let us exclaim
> Indonesia unites!

The one nation idea was a perfect fit for the nascent nationalist movement, which adopted the song and promoted it along with the vision of a united Indonesia. The composition quickly met the highest standard there is for a rebel song: it was banned by the colonial authorities. When Indonesia won independence as a single country after the Second World War, "Great Indonesia" was the obvious choice for national anthem. Sadly, its composer didn't live to see that day: he died in 1938. He left behind perhaps the strangest of rebel song anthems: a work that doesn't meet the usual definition of a rebel song. It doesn't feature calls for an uprising or the glory of dying for a cause. Instead, it extols the virtues of building unity, freedom, and safety for all its people. Of course, that didn't stop the country from falling prey to corruption, civil war, and authoritarian rule, but you have to admire the aspiration of the writer.

If singing a rebel anthem makes a statement, then refusing to sing it can also send a powerful message. Iran's national anthem wouldn't ordinarily make the list of rebel anthems; it wasn't a rebel song that was subsequently adopted by the state, and the lyrics are focused on religion rather than rebellion.*

At the 2022 FIFA World Cup, the eyes of the world were on Iran's footballers. In warm-up games ahead of the tournament, the players had shown apparent support for anti-government protests by refusing to sing the national anthem. And they stayed silent when the anthem was played ahead of their opening game against England. Iran's state television station didn't show the pictures of the non-singing players. But unlike the huge demonstrations in Iran's cities, this was a protest the state could control. There were media reports the players' families were threatened with prison if the team didn't behave. One Iranian politician called for the entire team to be replaced by people loyal to Iran. The head of Tehran's city council warned that "we will never allow anyone to insult our anthem." Whatever was done behind the scenes, it worked. The players all sang at their subsequent games.[6]

* Iran did have a rebel anthem for a brief period following the 1979 revolution. Before Iran was turned into a fully Islamic state under the rule of clerics, it used a popular patriotic song from the 1940s as its anthem. "Ey Iran" (O Iran) is really more of a love poem to the country, but I've put it in the rebel song category for two reasons: it's often sung at political protests, and it was banned by the regime.

Other athletes have also refused to sing the song, and some Iranian fans at the World Cup booed the anthem. So, while the song isn't a rebel song, it certainly provokes rebellious tendencies when it's played.

♫

We started this chapter with the outburst of anger that followed what seemed like an innocent celebration of a sporting triumph. The chorus of "Ooh ah, up the 'RA, say ooh ah up the 'RA" doesn't mean much to people outside Ireland, but the rhythm and rhyme in the words have caught on and been adopted by others. During one of Canada's World Cup appearances in 2022, television cameras went to a bar to show fans watching the game. The boisterous happy crowd had songs to sing. Among them was the catchy chorus, "Ooh ah, Canada, say ooh ah Canada" chanted in exactly the same way as the Irish women performed it a few months earlier. It seems that you can't keep a good rebel song down.

14

A KINDER, GENTLER WAY

Most anthems have few redeeming features beyond familiarity. There's a reason the most bombastic of them are all played the same way: by military bands, as marches. Even when they were never meant to be played that way.

When composer Peter Breiner was asked to arrange and record all the world's anthems for the classical music label Naxos, he didn't realize it would be a controversial project. Naxos wanted to create a definitive set of anthems that could be used at international events like the Olympics. That required getting every country's Olympic committee to approve the recorded anthem. In the book *The Story of Naxos*, by Nicholas Soames, Breiner explained why Poland rejected his recording of their anthem. "They wanted me to record the anthem again. 'Make it more like a march,' they insisted. 'It is not enough like a march!' My response was: 'It is never gonna be a march unless you grow a third leg, because the anthem is in *three*. It is a Mazurka!'"*[1]

---

* A mazurka is a traditional Polish folk dance. It's not really designed to be marched to. And given that the title of the anthem is "Dąbrowski's Mazurka," after a Polish national hero, that shouldn't have come as a surprise to the Polish Olympic Committee.

But you can see why the Poles wanted a march, because that's what we expect from mighty nations: a war song, designed to whip people into a nationalist frenzy and, in some cases, to literally persuade citizens to march to battle. War is frequently glorified, and laying down your life for your country isn't a sacrifice — it's an honour. There's nothing good or positive about these violent songs. The Poles should be happy they have a dance tune for their anthem.

Even more common than violence is God. Sometimes, they appear together, but as we've seen, a deity pops up in the vast majority of national anthems — mostly directly (as in anthems that call on God to save the monarch) or obliquely, with indirect references to religious symbols or imagery.

When you remove all the anthems that feature religion or violence or both, you're left with fewer than forty songs. Take out the ones that are sexist (by honouring only sons and fathers) or describe their country as a Fatherland or Motherland, and you are down to a handful of anthems that are non-violent, non-sectarian, and non-sexist. Out of the 193 full UN members, just thirteen have anthems that meet that criteria. And three of them have no lyrics.

Think about that. Only ten countries in the world have national anthems that meet the kind of basic criteria that we'd expect from an elementary school play. And even some of those are problematic. We'll get to that in a moment. But imagine you were asked to set the terms of reference for a new national anthem. What criteria would you want to include?

Fortunately, this has happened. So, there are guidelines out there. In 2015 Switzerland, which probably leads the world in consulting with its citizens on all sorts of decisions, decided to review its anthem. The problem was that no one seemed to like the old one. And while that's generally not something that would come up in day-to-day conversation, it does periodically make news in a sadly predictable way. Because of sports. If people become passionately engaged with anthems, it's almost always because of sport — and usually football (of all varieties). As we've seen, there are many super-patriots who judge a football player's commitment to their country not by the number of goals they score but by the enthusiasm with which they sing the national anthem. And the Swiss players generally don't sing.

There are reasons for that. It's a very religious anthem in a country where about a third of the people don't identify with any religion. It also suffers from being one of the few anthems with multiple official versions, one for each of the four national languages: German, French, Italian, and Romansh. Unlike the Canadian anthem, which has completely different French and English versions, the four Swiss versions of the anthem are fairly direct translations. So, at least the Swiss are all singing basically the same song. But try singing your Romansh anthem while the player to the left of you is belting out the German lyrics and your teammate on the other side is doing the same in French. Or Italian. It's understandable why the players tend to either stay silent or just mouth the words.

Now there's an obvious issue here that you may have already spotted: the Swiss aren't about to give up any of their languages, so no matter what song they are expected to sing, it's going to sound like a multilingual mess. Changing the anthem isn't going to inspire Swiss football players to start singing unless they can all agree to sing the same words.

But there's another reason for not singing the "Swiss Psalm." Lots of Swiss people apparently think it's boring. It's been described by some critics as "more like a biblical weather forecast than a national anthem."[2] And when you look at the words, you can see why. The opening lines set the standard, "When the morning skies grow red, / And o'er their radiance shed, / Thou, O Lord, appeareth in their light."

And it goes on like that for four verses, taking us from sunrise to sunset and the starry sky of night, tossing in grey mist, dark clouds, and thunderstorms. And a lot of God, of course. People clearly don't care much about the anthem — although some obviously care that football players don't sing it — but it turns out they don't care that much about changing it either.

Given the lack of enthusiasm for the anthem, it was easy to find people who wanted a new one. Leading the charge was the organization the Swiss Society for the Common Good (SSCG), which is a non-profit group that has played a key role in fighting poverty and promoting equality, fairness, and education for more than two hundred years. In 2013 it launched a national competition for a new song to replace the anthem. The rules stated that the winning entry had to reflect Swiss values of democracy, fairness, diversity, freedom, and peace as well as "measuring the well-being of society by its weakest members."

Also important was that the song should be easy to sing. It was suggested that it also be based on the existing melody, but that wasn't essential. Entries could be in any of the official languages but had to be easily translatable. A prize of ten thousand Swiss francs was offered to the winner.

A total of 206 entries were considered by a thirty-person jury. The number was eventually whittled down to three finalists. The songs were translated into the four official languages and recorded by a choir. The winner was decided in an online vote, with the result announced in a televised concert in 2015.

The new anthem also got an official English translation:

> White cross on a shining red,
> Woven by a common thread:
> Freedom, independence, equality.
> Open to the world in solidarity,
> Swiss are one in peace and diversity.
> Free are we who freely speak,

> Strong as we protect the weak.
> White cross on a shining red,
> Sign of Switzerland, the path we tread.

The Swiss Society for the Common Good submitted the lyrics to the government, which said thank you, put them in a drawer, and promptly did nothing — beyond making a commitment to take a look and then, at some point in the future, maybe asking voters to decide in a referendum. The Swiss are keen practitioners of direct democracy, but they also don't like to rush things. It took until 1971 before a referendum granted women the right to vote.

The SSCG, which also plays a big role in promoting national unity and organizing national day celebrations, is encouraging people to adopt the anthem themselves, by singing it at public events and eventually squeezing out the old anthem by sheer force of numbers. It's an ongoing campaign.

The Swiss anthem winner certainly meets the standards set out by the contest organizers. It definitely isn't violent, sexist, or sectarian. And it identifies with Switzerland and Swiss values through the imagery of the flag, although the cross reference is unfortunate but unavoidable unless the Swiss also decide to change their flag.*

But the proposed Swiss anthem nicely captures the dilemma at the heart of national songs. In order to whip up the kind of fervour they are designed to create, they have to be passionate. They have to reference terrible fights for national survival, love for a homeland that transcends life itself, and a tribal sense of belonging. You need the bombs bursting in air. The march toward victory. The passion of liberty or death. Somehow, being one in peace and diversity just doesn't quite cut it. The message is wonderful. The delivery lacks

---

* The cross is, of course, the ultimate Christian symbol. When the Red Cross was founded in Geneva, it took the Swiss flag as the inspiration for its logo and reversed the colours: a red cross on a white background. That decision meant the humanitarian group was not welcome in Muslim countries, which led to the creation of the Red Crescent symbol.

the passion, emotion, and connection that anthems are supposed to deliver. It's more of a mission statement.

"Hold on," I hear you say. "I thought this was all about why anthems are terrible and should be dumped — or at the very least, made nicer. So shouldn't you be praising this new Swiss anthem?"

Ah. Got me. But I just can't do it. Because I recognize that people want to sing songs that connect with them emotionally. Yes, we need to get rid of nasty, militaristic, bloodthirsty anthems. But we need to replace them with songs that inspire and move us, songs that come from the heart and aren't inextricably tied up with nationalist tropes and love of God and the military. The Swiss song just seems too ... nice. If you define your nation as your flag, then maybe you have a problem figuring out exactly what you stand for.

They should really have added another option to their voting process: none of the above. Just go with the music.

If, like the Swiss, we set out to select an anthem that meets the modern criteria of being inclusive and kind — but also inspires — where should we go looking? Are there songs out there that can move people to tears without also promoting a brand of nationalism that glorifies violence and tribalism?

Well, yes. Not in my list of two-hundred-plus national anthems — but if we look at songs that people sing in crowds, we can find some that can melt even the hardest heart.

One of the world's most famous football clubs is Liverpool, which plays its home games at Anfield. Although it's been remodelled a few times — particularly in the early 1990s when it was converted to an all-seated stadium — Anfield has been home to the club since it was founded in 1892.

I've only been there once, back in the days when the areas behind the goals were still terraces, stepped concrete spaces where fans stood pressed tightly against each other, swaying back and forward with the crowd. That practice came to an end in England after the

1989 Hillsborough disaster, when a police decision to open gates to allow spectators to push their way into an already overcrowded stadium led to the deaths of ninety-seven people, most of them crushed to death while standing upright. Liverpool was playing that day; I and many others watched the disaster unfold on live television.* A report on the disaster recommended the removal of standing-only areas in stadiums to ensure that crowd sizes would be limited to the number of seats available.

Back in the late '70s, though, crowds were still packed uncomfortably together. Fortunately, I am tall enough to see over most crowds. A boy or a short man — and fans in those days were mostly men — had to pick their spots to see the game.

I can't remember who was playing Liverpool that day. Probably Arsenal. I know I was at the Anfield Road end of the stadium, which is where visiting fans were gathered. At the other end of the stadium was the famous Kop,† where the most dedicated Liverpool fans traditionally stood.

Regular season football games in most countries are not usually graced by the presence of national anthems — that's generally reserved for major finals and international games. But that doesn't mean there isn't music. And Liverpool is the place to go to hear the greatest football anthem of them all.

In 1963 Liverpool band Gerry and the Pacemakers recorded the Rodgers and Hammerstein song "You'll Never Walk Alone" from the musical *Carousel.* Lead singer Gerry Marsden gave a copy to

---

* This was my second experience of football tragedy: I was in Glasgow in January 1971 when sixty-six people were crushed to death in a crowd at the traditional "Old Firm" New Year's fixture between Rangers and Celtic. I didn't know about it until I saw the newspaper headlines the following day.

† It is named after Spion Kop, a hill in South Africa, which was the site of a battle in 1900 during the Boer War. The naming wasn't to commemorate the battle, but rather because the shape of the hill resembled the steep sloped terraces of early twentieth-century football grounds. There are several Spion Kop stands, but Liverpool's is the most famous.

the Liverpool manager, who loved it, and the song was immediately adopted as the Liverpool anthem. The fans on the Kop started singing it and have never stopped. I have never forgotten how powerful that song sounded as it swept around Anfield that day.

The club adopted "You'll never walk alone" as its motto and worked it into the club crest. The words can also be found on the gates to one of the stands at Anfield. Other clubs have songs. Other clubs even sing "You'll Never Walk Alone," but the song never has the emotional impact that it has in Liverpool. When sung at Anfield, it is a magnificent anthem, with no baggage and massive goodwill.

"Walk on, walk on with hope in your heart and you'll never walk alone."

Much better than marching on with hate in your heart and the bodies of your enemies underfoot.

I'm not really suggesting "You'll Never Walk Alone" as a national anthem for Switzerland or any other country, but I guarantee it would generate far more passionate singing at any event than even the most resounding version of "God Save the King."

Another stadium, a few years later. Actually, several stadiums in different countries at different times but with one common element: Ireland was playing. Yes, there were national anthems before the kick-off, but when it comes to supporting their team during the game, the Irish fans don't favour their anthem: they have a stronger weapon. The green-clad parts of the stadium burst into "The Fields of Athenry."

This is a traditional Irish ballad, or at least it is in the style of one, because the song itself was only written in 1979. But it's easy to sing, and the theme of a young man deported to Australia for stealing corn* for his starving family during the Irish famine reson-

---

* The corn the protagonist was accused of stealing isn't what North Americans call corn. In Britain and Ireland, corn refers to all cereal grains, like wheat and barley. North American corn is called maize.

ates with Irish people. Not exactly a pick-me-up, but it's an anthem that rolls and rumbles around a stadium with purpose and passion. If this song was played as a national anthem, people would show up for an event just to hear it and then applaud at the end.

♫

You may remember that my database on national anthems yielded just ten songs that don't have lyrics that espouse violence, sexism, or religion. One of those songs is Japan's anthem, which we know to have a very troubled past, even if the words themselves seem innocuous.

Another is from North Korea, which is somewhat surprising; given the recent antics of its ruler, you'd almost expect the song to be filled with revolutionary fervour or expressions of loyalty and love to the Dear Respected Comrade Leader. And you'd be sort of right. The official anthem, "Aegukka" (Patriotic Song), is rarely sung inside North Korea. It's reserved for international sporting events and the rare visits of foreign dignitaries. It comes across as a nice song about the beauty of Korea and its thousands of years of culture.

Sadly, the songs most North Koreans think of as their national anthems are entirely predictable; "Song of General Kim Il-sung" and "Song of General Kim Jong-il" eulogize the grandfather and father of the current leader, with the former being one of the most played songs in the country. I won't trouble you with the lyrics. Let's just say they aren't critically important, but it's worth remembering that other anthems also sound like they are the theme songs of a personality cult. "God Save the King" perhaps?

The very short list of least-offensive anthems includes one of the strangest. Moldova's national anthem is a hymn of praise, not to the nation but to its language. This is odd because there is no

Moldovan language; the official language of Moldova is Romanian. Moldova is another of the countries that emerged from the collapse of the Soviet Union. It had a long history as a principality under the rule of the Ottoman Empire before it was ceded to Russia in the early nineteenth century. It became part of Romania after the First World War but fell back under Russian control in 1940. After declaring independence in 1991, Moldova adopted the same national anthem as neighbouring Romania, which was obviously going to create a lot of confusion — particularly as the anthem's title is "Awaken thee, Romanian!" Four years later, it approved a new anthem of its own: "Limba noastră" (Our Language).

The anthem is taken from a twelve-verse poem that is entirely about "our language" — a language that is never actually named, but given that it was written in Romanian and is sung in a Romanian-speaking country, it's reasonable to assume the language must be Romanian.

The anthem describes the language as "a treasure that surges from deep shadows of the past," a "burning flame," the "greenest leaf" of the country's forests, and "a necklace of rare gems." It's actually quite delightful, although the Soviet-era music does seem a little too triumphal to suit the rather wistful and ethereal lyrics.

It's the performance of the music that often lets anthems down. They are so identified with military bands and marching troops that even the nicest words and best tunes can be lost in the huge arrangements of mass choirs and national supremacy. For example, the Republic of Kazakhstan has an anthem you can envisage being sung as a gentle song by a soloist.

> Sky of golden sun,
> Steppe of golden seed,
> Legend of courage —
> Take a look at my country!

But the music demands a mighty delivery, so it tends to sound more like the kind of tune that's played while tanks and missile launchers roll past the reviewing stand.

You get the impression with anthems that everyone involved in the process, from writing them to approving them to singing them, is just a little bit too uptight. That's understandable. You're dealing with a song that is representing a nation. It has to sound proud and dignified and aspirational. But as we saw with Switzerland's proposed new lyrics, sometimes the right ingredients just don't produce a tasty meal.

Singapore's anthem seems to hit all the right notes but somehow falls a little flat. It's hard to take issue with the sentiment, "Come, fellow Singaporeans / Let us progress towards happiness together," but it doesn't really *soar* in the way you'd hope. Even though the anthem actually uses the word "soar" — "Let our voices soar as one / Onward Singapore." You want to like it, you feel that you should, but it just seems a little too buttoned-down and corporate to inspire much emotion.

Sad to say, we're not going to find a kinder, gentler anthem among the few that are left to us. Australia is on the shortlist, but as we've seen in Chapter 6, "Advance Australia Fair" isn't short of critics. Mongolia's anthem has a poignant tone that makes it easy to listen to, and you can't really complain about the words — rather than promising dire retribution against enemies, past and future, it promises to strengthen relations with all honest nations of the world, which is a refreshing thought that most anthems don't bother to share. But it's hard to imagine it bringing tears to your eyes.

It's possible to go backwards with anthems. Niger was originally on my shortlist of least-offensive songs, but it replaced its anthem in 2023 with one that includes references to a fatherland as well as proud warriors who are prepared to die in defence of the nation. The original anthem was criticized for lines that seemed to show gratitude to France for granting the country its freedom. It says something about the country's rulers that they chose to spend time on creating a new national song — instead of focusing on more urgent issues. Niger is one of the poorest countries in the world and faces problems of violence, drought, and food shortages.

It's rather surprising that countries like Niger don't actually have really nasty anthems. Any country that emerged from years of brutal and unwanted colonialism would be perfectly entitled to seek a little musical payback. But most chose a different route, which is a lesson many other nations — including the empire builders of yesterday and today — could learn from. Look at the example of the Democratic Republic of the Congo,* formerly known as Zaire and before that as the Belgian Congo. It's one of the largest countries in the world, and for more than twenty years, from 1885 to 1908, this vast territory was the personal property of the Belgian king, Leopold II. It's hard to get your mind around the idea of a single individual basically owning most of central Africa. But it happened.

Leopold was not a benevolent ruler. Private companies were allowed to operate with impunity to extract rubber, the colony's main export. Leopold established a private army to force people to gather the rubber, often by holding their families hostage. Millions of people — estimates run as high as ten million — died while Leopold accumulated vast wealth from his private colony. The atrocities committed in his name were so awful — even by the standards of European brutality in Africa — there was an international outcry.† The most notorious scandal was the rule that every bullet fired by Leopold's army had to be accounted for; missionaries and

---

* Somewhat confusingly, there are two countries often referred to simply as "the Congo." The Republic of the Congo, also known as Congo-Brazzaville, is a much smaller neighbour of the Democratic Republic of the Congo.

† Joseph Conrad's novel *Heart of Darkness* drew on his experiences while working for a Belgian company in the Congo during its time as a personal possession of Leopold.

other visitors to the country reported that soldiers kept their records by cutting off the hands of people they had shot. The soldiers sometimes collected extra hands from living victims.

The reports of abuse were so extreme they even outraged the British government, which wasn't exactly known for its kind treatment of colonized people. A British diplomat was sent to investigate. Roger Casement's report to Parliament in 1904 confirmed the many reports of inhumane behaviour, enforced labour, and indiscriminate killings.

"The punitive measures undertaken to this end had endured for a considerable period," Casement wrote. "During the course of these operations there had been much loss of life, accompanied, I fear, by a somewhat general mutilation of the dead, as proof that the soldiers had done their duty." He recorded two cases of mutilation that he came across. "One, a young man, both of whose hands had been beaten off with the butt ends of rifles against a tree; the other a young lad of 11 or 12 years of age, whose right hand was cut off at the wrist."[3]

Casement was so troubled by what he saw that he helped set up the Congo Reform Association, which campaigned for an end to the Belgian king's personal rule of the Congo. The association's work and the public outcry following Casement's report led to international pressure on Belgium to end Leopold's private control of the Congo, which occurred in 1908. The Congo was ruled by Belgium until its independence in 1960.*

None of that horrible history is reflected in the country's anthem, "Debout Congolais" (Arise, Congolese). There is a reference

* Roger Casement was much praised for his Congo report and was later knighted after investigating reports of human rights abuses in Peru's rubber industry. But his experience as a British diplomat turned him against imperialism. Casement, who was Irish, became involved with the fight for Irish independence and was arrested after trying to get German military support for the 1916 Irish Easter Rising. This occurred while Britain and Germany were enemies in the First World War. Casement was found guilty of high treason and executed.

to being united in the struggle for independence, and the people are encouraged to hold up their heads after being bowed for so long, but the rest is all about moving forward in peace and building a country more beautiful than before. Given the horrors inflicted on the nation by outsiders, it's remarkably restrained and optimistic.

In fact, many of the world's newer countries have chosen to take the moral high road when it comes to their anthems — unlike the nations who fought their way to independence in the nineteenth century. Perhaps the appalling violence of the two world wars made newer nations less inclined to glorify the idea of dying for one's country.

That's certainly the case throughout the Caribbean, where every nation has its roots in slavery. We tend to link slavery most strongly with the United States and its civil war, but far more enslaved Africans were shipped to the Caribbean to work — and die — on sugar plantations run by the British, French, Dutch, Danish, and Spanish. Today's Jamaicans, Barbadians, Dominicans, and residents of other islands we tend to think of only as holiday destinations are largely descended from African slaves. There has never been a true accounting of this crime against humanity, but most of the nations of the region have not adopted warlike anthems calling for revenge or retribution.

There are exceptions — island neighbours the Dominican Republic and Haiti both had wars of independence that are reflected in their violent anthems — but the countries that had a more peaceful path to independence opted for anthems that are focused on love, justice, and peace. The words of Dominica's anthem do not deal with the island's history of slavery, rebellion, and oppression.

> Isle of beauty, isle of splendour,
> Isle to all so sweet and fair,
> All must surely gaze in wonder
> At thy gifts so rich and rare.

Saint Lucians sing of the "fairest isle of all the earth." The anthem of Saint Vincent and the Grenadines peaks of "a haven, calm, serene" where "the sunshine ever beams."

These countries have not forgotten their past — they just choose to turn their heads toward the future, unlike some of their former colonial rulers, who still relish their role as former overseers of the world.

♫

There is a strange nostalgia in Britain for its empire, which many people view as a source of pride. A 2020 survey found more than 30 percent of Britons were proud of their empire and almost a third thought the countries they colonized were better off as a result.[4] The brutal realities of the empire — from the slave trade to preventable famines that killed millions — are rarely discussed in Britain. For generations, India was considered the "jewel in the crown" of the British Empire, which it was, both literally and figuratively. The British drained the subcontinent of its immense wealth, including the Koh-i-Noor diamond, one of the largest in the world at more than 105 carats. It now forms part of the British Crown Jewels. India and Pakistan have asked for its return.* The British have refused, presumably on the grounds that if they started handing back valuable items taken from one country then lots of other countries (and the British Empire at its height controlled a quarter of the globe) would show up with long lists of their own missing items.

Indians were not generally happy about being occupied by the British, and they periodically rose up against their rulers. The

* Pakistan's claim to the diamond is based on the fact that the part of Punjab where the diamond was surrendered to British forces is now in Pakistan. Afghanistan also claims the diamond on the grounds it was previously owned by the Afghan royal family and was stolen by the father of Maharajah Dalip Singh, who gave it to the British.

British history books call these uprisings "rebellions" or "mutinies," but the Indians view them somewhat differently, describing them as "wars of independence." When Britain finally relinquished control of India in 1947, it was just three years after a famine in Bengal that killed up to three million people. That famine was just one of many that occurred in British-ruled India. About a million people died in the violence that followed independence, when the country was partitioned into India and Pakistan, and millions more were displaced. Both countries had excellent reasons within very recent memory to adopt anthems with pointed messages aimed at their former ruler. And yet they did not.

Both Pakistan and India adopted spiritual songs, Pakistan's is more openly religious, as you would expect in the Islamic Republic of Pakistan. But there's no threat of violence or bitterness at past wrongs in either song. And really, it would be hard to blame them if they tossed in a line about giving back what you stole or demanding an apology for centuries of occupation.

India also showed good taste in selecting its anthem writer: the Bengali poet Rabindranath Tagore, who was awarded the Nobel Prize for Literature in 1913, becoming the first non-European winner. He wrote the poem that eventually became the Indian national anthem in 1911. He also composed the music and translated the poem into English. But wait, there's more: you can actually see and hear him singing the anthem that he wrote. There's a video clip on YouTube. And he also wrote the poem selected by Bangladesh as its anthem. "Amar Sonar Bangla" (My Golden Bengal) contains the truly amazing lines, "In spring, O mother mine, the fragrance from your mango groves makes me wild with joy! / Ah, what a thrill!" It makes you want to visit Bangladesh in spring.

While we're on the subject of spring, the Czech national anthem uses similar imagery, and when sung as a solo, is wistful and simply gorgeous.

> Where my home is, where my home is,
> Water roars across the meadows,
> Pinewoods rustle among rocks,
> The orchard is glorious with spring blossom,
> Paradise on earth it is to see.

We're on the right track with that kind of anthem. There is nothing there but love and gentleness. And that's a good thing in an anthem, right? I guess it depends on the anthem — and on the listener. In 2004 Maureen Dowd, a columnist for the *New York Times*, didn't think much of the version of the U.S. anthem played at that year's Olympic Games. She wrote, "Our warlike national anthem has been transformed, from blaring horns to peaceful, soothing strings."[5]

That comment captures both the problem and the solution when it comes to national anthems; perhaps what we need to do is focus less on substance and more on style. If we can't change the song, then change how it's presented. In 2021 two Australian sisters completed a somewhat strange mission that took them nine years to prepare for. Teresa and Augnes have a wonderfully evocative surname: "Joy." The young women, of Indian origin, decided to learn all 193 anthems of UN members in their official languages — about one hundred of them. On World Peace Day 2021 (a United Nations–sanctioned holiday celebrated each year on September 21), the sisters stood up in St. John's Cathedral in Brisbane and started singing the national anthem of Afghanistan. They continued, without interruption or accompaniment and singing entirely from memory, until they arrived at Zimbabwe's anthem some six hours later.

They weren't setting out to establish a record — although they did. They wanted to promote peace and eliminate fear and hatred. They've created the Augnes and Teresa Peace Foundation to raise money to help women and children around the world. They want to take their anthem show on the road to perform it in different countries. That's because Augnes and Teresa have a refreshingly different attitude toward anthems, as Teresa explained in an interview with the Australian news organization SBS Malayalam.* "When we sing national anthems, it's uniting everyone. It's basically unity. That's what we feel. When we sing all other countries' national anthems, we all feel united because they sing together with us."

Her sister agrees. "We are singing because national anthems are the binding source for citizens of a nation irrespective of social, economic, or political differences," Augnes Joy said. "That's why we chose national anthems. Whenever we sing it's like showing that everyone is one and no matter what nationality you are, we're all one and national anthems join us together."[6]

While it's not my take on national anthems, I can't help but admire the Joy sisters for their infectious enthusiasm about the prospects of securing world peace, one anthem marathon at a time. And they're right about one thing — something you can check for yourselves on their website, augnesandteresa.com. When they sing the anthems — and they sing them beautifully — you hear them as simple songs that can be judged purely on artistic merit. The lyrics haven't changed, but much of the rhetorical power is drawn out of them, as poison is sucked from a wound, by the innocent delight the sisters clearly get from performing the songs. They genuinely believe people can be brought together through singing national anthems, not driven apart. And when the singing is just the words — with no band, no orchestra, no agenda set by a musical director demanding a militaristic rhythm — then the nature of even the most violent songs is changed.

The Joy sisters think national anthems can be a force for good. They want the United Nations to establish a World National

---

* SBS Malayalam is targeted at Malayalam-speaking Australians. The language is spoken by about thirty-eight million people in southwestern India, where the Joy family comes from.

Anthem Day. On their website, they state: "When we as individuals sing these national anthems on World National Anthem Day, a unique atmosphere of oneness will be created and that, in turn, will create a common platform conducive to World Peace and a heightened sense of Humanity."

I'm not convinced the world's problems can be solved through a giant hand-holding concert where we all sing each other's national anthems. But it may be one way of making our anthems more acceptable; if we can't change the words, then change how they are sung so they become kinder and more gentle by the nature of their delivery.

15

THE SOUNDTRACK OF NATIONALISM

Do nations really need theme songs? The question is a bit of a set-up because we're leaping straight to the answer. Which is obviously, no. Nation-states and empires rose and fell for thousands of years without any need for a soundtrack. There was no imperial Roman song that the citizens dutifully performed. The Spanish took over large chunks of the world without needing to advertise their arrival with a band. When Shakespeare wanted King Henry V to inspire his troops, he didn't burst into song; he rallied them with words, "We few, we happy few, we band of brothers; for he today that sheds his blood with me shall be my brother."

Anthems are relatively recent creations, dating back to that Saturday evening in London's Drury Lane Theatre in 1745. They are an add-on to the national symbols that most states have used for centuries — flags and coats of arms. Most countries protect those symbols in their laws — but no one seems very sure what protection, if any, should be applied to anthems. Dozens of countries have precise rules about how the national flag should be treated — and penalties for desecrating it. That list includes many countries that are liberal democracies — like Austria, Italy, New Zealand, and Switzerland.

Other countries — like the United States, Britain, and Canada — don't protect the flag. The U.S. Supreme Court held in 1989 that flag-burning was a form of constitutionally protected free speech. But there are ongoing attempts to override that ruling by adding a Flag Desecration Amendment to the Constitution. Canada has no law about how its flag should be treated. Nor does the United Kingdom.

Even those countries that do protect their flag don't often take action against protesters — except in countries like China and Russia, where the very act of protest itself is likely to lead to arrest, whether or not a flag is in flames. But occasionally, governments elsewhere do take action.

Perhaps the strangest case of all was the one taken against Mexican poet Sergio Witz Rodriguez. In 2001 a literary magazine published his poem "Invitación (La patria entre mierda)." Witz wrote it to show his anger at the government's failure to tackle Mexico's economic and social problems. The poem describes using the Mexican flag as toilet paper and calls it a "rag" that dogs lie on and that represents nothing.[1]

Your average literary journal doesn't reach a large audience, but the poem eventually came to the attention of a former military officer, who filed a police complaint against Witz. The poet was arrested and charged under Article 191 of Mexico's Federal Penal Code, which states: "One who insults the coat of arms of the Republic or the national flag, in word or action, shall be imprisoned from six months to four years and/or fined 50 to 3,000 pesos."

It took almost seven years to get the case resolved. In 2008 Witz was found guilty. The prosecution wanted a jail term, but the judge imposed a symbolic fine of fifty pesos (about US$2.50). The judge said that the fine, the minimum allowed for in the law, would "discourage antisocial behaviour by those who threaten the cultural heritage of our country and the national symbols that represent it."

Most countries — at least, most countries where any kind of dissenting opinion is allowed — don't go to such extremes to protect national symbols. And anthems are hard to protect. It's easy to declare a song an official anthem and publish the approved lyrics — but what do you do if someone sings it in a different key? And how do you tell the difference between someone who's just mangling the anthem because they're a bad singer and someone who is deliberately distorting it? What's the difference between Roseanne Barr's notorious anthem performance at a San Diego Padres game in 1990 and Jimi Hendrix's Woodstock anthem in 1969? Both were perfectly legal in the United States — but would definitely break China's anthem law, which forbids altering the lyrics or performing the anthem in a distorted way.

National anthems are modern constructs that we've adopted as a way to create a common sense of national identity. The fact that they tend to be more exclusive than inclusive doesn't really matter. It's a way of showing that we're all on the same side — or of spotting those who are not. But it's not a timeless tradition. Of the 193 UN members, just three have anthems dating back to the eighteenth century (and one of those — France's — hasn't been an anthem continuously). Twenty were adopted in the nineteenth century, and the remaining 170 are products of the last 120 years. Most of them only became official in my lifetime, although some of the tunes or the words date back longer than that. The point is anthems weren't seen as an essential part of national life until relatively recently. In some cases, they were only created because it would be embarrassing not to have one — not because of a pressing national need.

Costa Rica, along with the other Spanish territories of Central America, gained independence from Spain in 1821 but didn't become a fully independent state until 1848. It immediately adopted a coat of arms and a flag (both still in use today) but apparently didn't see any immediate need for an anthem. Then, in 1852, four years after the establishment of the First Costa Rican Republic, the United States and Britain sent diplomatic delegations to the new country to open embassies. Suddenly, the absence of an anthem became an issue. The president ordered the director of the Costa Rican Military Band to compose an anthem in time for the reception of the new ambassadors. It was a rush job, done in just a few days — and there was no time for lyrics. The Costa Rican anthem remained an instrumental until the late nineteenth century, when several sets of lyrics were proposed, but none caught on with the public. A national competition was held in 1903, and the winning lyrics were later adopted as the anthem. The tune composed in such a hurry for the nation's first big diplomatic event has stood the test of time.

Other nations have also stumbled into national anthems almost by accident. In 1888 the new sultan of Perak visited London. Perak, on the Malay peninsula, was then part of the British Empire. It is now a state of Malaysia. Queen Victoria had just celebrated her Golden Jubilee, and Sultan Idris wanted to pay his respects. It had already become the practice for visiting heads of state and monarchs to be greeted by their national anthem. A protocol officer asked the sultan's staff for the music so that a band could play Perak's anthem as he arrived to meet the queen.

It was a moment of acute embarrassment because Perak did not have an anthem and up until that exact moment hadn't needed one. But the sultan's quick-thinking aide-de-camp didn't want to admit that and told the queen's representative they had forgotten to bring the sheet music — but he could whistle the tune if someone could be found to write down the notes. This was done, and the creative aide whistled the song "Terang Bulan" (Bright Moon), which was popular in Perak at the time. The sultan arrived to see the queen accompanied by his brand-new national anthem.* The queen was obviously impressed by her visitor. In 1892 the sultan was appointed an Honorary Knight Commander of the Order of St. Michael and St. George, which entitled him to use the letters KCMG after his name and to call himself "Sir."

Lyrics were later composed that praised the sultan and wished him a long life. The song also turned out to be remarkably long-lived. When the Federation of Malaysia was created in 1957, the new country needed an anthem as well. It launched an international competition, but despite receiving more than five hundred entries, none was deemed appropriate. Several major composers were invited to give it their best shot — including Benjamin Britten and William Walton, who had composed the march for Queen Elizabeth's coronation. But the anthem selection committee didn't like their efforts either and instead decided to go with a tune that had been right in front of them all along: the state anthem of Perak. New lyrics were written, and the anthem whistled up all those years ago in London is now the official anthem of Malaysia.[2]

The lack of importance attached to picking a national anthem is interesting and instructive. When Pakistan came into existence following the partition of British India in 1947, it had a flag ready to fly on Independence Day. But there was no pressure to have a national anthem ready for the same occasion. There were a few lacklustre efforts to compose an anthem over the next couple of years, but it wasn't until 1950 that it became a priority. The government wanted an anthem to play when the shah of Iran paid a state visit. It ordered the National Anthem Committee, which had spent a year failing to find a suitable song, to come up with a winner — and quickly.

* Another version of this story claims this actually happened a few years later, when the sultan arrived for the coronation of King Edward VII in 1902, but the official website of the current sultan of Perak goes with the Queen Victoria story.

Fortunately, one of the committee members was also an accomplished composer. Ahmed Ghulam Ali Chagla produced a tune that proved acceptable. There was no time to write lyrics, but that wasn't really considered a problem as long as the band had something to play when the shah arrived. It took another four years to approve the words, and the new anthem was first sung in public in August 1954.

And that's how many anthems came to be: chaotically created, not because they're really needed, but because convention demands that every country must have one. National anthems are the neckties of a nation's symbols — no one really knows what they are for or why they became important, but if you don't have one, then you won't be allowed into polite society. And like a lot of ties, they tend to be last-minute purchases, adopted without much consultation about whether they are appropriate to the occasion.

If you doubt that countries don't really care much about their anthems, think about what would happen if an international organization told nations to change their flags because they were too big or had too many colours or stripes. Probably not going to happen. But when FIFA and the Olympics tell nations to rewrite their anthems to suit an arbitrary time slot, not only do nations comply without objection, they actually adopt those truncated songs as the new norm.

Occasionally, citizens (who are rarely if ever consulted about this kind of thing) do push back. FIFA's anthem rule limits the songs to ninety seconds or less. That's not a problem for countries with short anthems, but there are some nations — particularly in South America — which have much longer stories to tell. Brazil's anthem lasts almost four minutes, and the singing doesn't even begin until after thirty seconds of a musical overture. The cut-down version for football games runs for about a minute.

In the build-up to the 2014 World Cup in Brazil, the country was seething with protests over economic hardship. People were furious about the huge cost of staging the tournament. But Brazilians love their football team, and the fans wanted to make sure the players knew that the protests against World Cup spending weren't aimed at them. They poured their passion into the pre-game singing of the anthem. And once they started singing, they wanted to finish the whole song. FIFA's version wasn't long enough for the fans, so they kept singing after the music stopped.[3]

This began at warm-up games for the 2014 World Cup and continued during the tournament itself, starting with the opening match against Croatia. The music stopped after a minute, but the players and fans just kept going, the faces of the singers shining with joy. The players spoke afterwards about how the singing gave the team extra motivation, and they did go on to win the game. However, there are limits to the power of music. Brazil crashed out of the World Cup in the semi-finals, losing 7–1 to eventual champions, Germany. But they did score a victory over FIFA, which hasn't moved to try and stop the extra-long anthems, probably because it recognizes that it couldn't do it anyway.

Other countries' fans are now following Brazil's lead and insisting on a complete performance of their anthems. It's happened at games involving Chile and Colombia, both of which have anthems much longer than FIFA's ninety-second limit. While this kind of musical uprising works at team games where there are lots of people to do the singing, it's unlikely to catch on at the Olympics, where medal ceremonies are quieter affairs. But as we've seen, the Olympic movement hasn't always been comfortable with the idea of anthems. And countries have shown themselves to be quite happy with dumping their anthems if that's what they have to do to be allowed into the Olympic club.

Russia's underwhelming punishment for mass-doping its athletes included a ban on its name, anthem, and flag at the 2020 Summer Games and 2022 Winter Games. The team was known officially as the Russian Olympic Committee (ROC), but, of course, everyone just called them "Russians." And while we're on the topic of Russia, the 1980 Moscow Olympics were boycotted by much of the world because of the Soviet Union's invasion of Afghanistan. The United States led the boycott, but several of its traditional allies participated, including Britain, Australia, and France. They showed their disapproval of Russia's actions by abandoning their flags and anthems, opting instead for the Olympic tune and the five-ring flag when on the podium. One event in cycling produced medallists from three of those countries, which meant all three banners raised at the medal ceremony were the Olympic flag.

One country has been forced to adopt a special anthem for sporting events. Taiwan may seem like a regular nation, but China views it as a rebel province that will one day be reabsorbed into the country, by force if necessary. When the defeated Chinese nationalist forces fled to the island of Taiwan in 1949 after losing the civil war, they maintained the fiction that they were the legitimate government of all of China. So, Taiwan kept the national anthem "Three Principles of the People." The victorious Communists didn't care about losing the song; they had "March of the Volunteers" to use instead. But the Chinese are determined to prevent Taiwan from being recognized as an independent nation. Beijing uses its huge diplomatic and financial clout to ensure only a handful of small countries have official diplomatic relations with Taiwan. And China won't tolerate the playing of the official Taiwan anthem or the use of its flag at international occasions. So, the only way Taiwan can compete in events like the Olympics and the World Cup is by calling itself Chinese Taipei, flying a special flag, and playing a different anthem, which is very sensibly called the "National Flag Anthem."

All this goes to show that you don't actually need an official national anthem to do anything. You can play any song you like, use the Olympic anthem, or whip up a tune at the last minute. As long as it's played by a military band, you can be pretty certain most people will stand to attention and look appropriately respectful. After all, most of us have never even heard the national anthems of all 206 Olympic nations — and likely never will, because a lot of those countries have never won a gold medal or indeed a medal of any colour. And if they did, they could play a medium-paced orchestral version of the current local number-one pop song and we'd be none the wiser.

The truth is, that's how some of our national anthems were picked in the first place; they were popular songs that captured the right mood at the right time and just never went away. That is how a patriotic ditty set to a tune composed for an English gentleman's club became America's anthem and how a song written for a propaganda movie about fighting the Japanese ended up as China's.

It's important to remember there are two parts to a national anthem — or indeed to any song. The music. And the lyrics. The problem with anthems is rarely the tune. Sure, it's possible to object to some anthems on artistic grounds, but that would be like arguing whether the Beatles are better than Beethoven; it's a subjective opinion that doesn't have a correct answer. And it's the music that contains the power to move us; just reciting the words to an anthem would have little impact and would often leave people bewildered, because they wouldn't understand what they were hearing. Anthems are filled with strange poetic phrases like "the blood of our sires which hallows the sod," "from the shafts of strife and war," and "twilight's last gleaming." Those are all English-language anthems; other languages are no better.

When we hear an anthem that thrills us — like Russia's or France's — we usually have no idea what the words mean. A

Russian choir singing the Soviet Union anthem sounds just as inspiring as the same choir singing the current lyrics. If you're not a Russian speaker, they could be singing the instructions to operate a dishwasher and sound just as good.

The problem with the world's anthems, which should be very clear by now, is not the notes but the words. When Germany wanted to sever any possible links between the post-war state and Nazi rule, it changed the words of its anthem — but not the music. Russia dropped — then brought back — its Soviet-era anthem, again with new words. Numerous countries around the world have reworked their anthems to suit the changing times, sometimes by tweaking, as in the case of Canada and Australia, and sometimes by starting over, as South Africa did. Others have edited for length and content, as Argentina did when it removed the most violently anti-Spanish verses.

Perhaps countries should start thinking of their anthems as a sort of national mission statement. In that case, it should be periodically reviewed, like any set of values and intentions. Does this anthem convey the best image of ourselves to the world? Is it clear and easily understood? Does it represent the entire nation? Does it exclude some people? Are we proud of the message it sends?

Now, it's very possible the citizens of some countries think the role of their anthem should be to show how willing they are to die for their nation — and how horribly you will be killed if you choose to mess with them. They *want* a big, belligerent, don't-mess-with-us anthem. But maybe they should think about that a little and ask themselves how they would feel if the same message was set down in clearer language and presented to them as a requirement of citizenship. Americans would recognize this as a beefed-up Pledge of Allegiance — one that sets out in much more detail what you would actually be prepared to do for your country, no questions asked.

Here are some of the things that national anthems of different nations expect their citizens to do:

- Water the earth of your nation with the blood of your enemies (France and Mexico)
- March over the bodies of your foes as you rush toward the battlefield (Vietnam)
- Build a wall with your own flesh and blood to keep out your enemies (China)
- Promise to fight to the death when called upon (Mexico, Albania, Tunisia, and many more)
- Swear to die before you would live as slaves (Bolivia, Ireland, and others)
- March toward cannons (Portugal and others)
- And believe in God, because with God's blessing we will win (lots).

If we take those messages and use them as a basis of a contract with your country, you'd be agreeing to the following:

> If called upon, I promise to grab whatever sharp object is to hand or a gun if it's available. Despite no training in being a soldier, I promise to march as quickly as possible toward the enemy. Along the way, I promise to slaughter as many people as I can and to make sure their blood pours into the soil. I will march shoulder-to-shoulder with my comrades toward the enemy's guns, and when they fall in combat, I will build a defensive wall from their bodies. I promise never to stop fighting until victory is won or I die gloriously on the battlefield. I know a martyr's death guarantees

> me a place in heaven because God is on our side. Failure to live up to the terms of this contract will mark me as a traitor who should be killed.*

Okay, I admit to artistic exaggeration. No national anthem contains all those horrible things — but almost all feature one or more of them. So perhaps it would be more constructive to come up with a statement of what you think your anthem *should* say and then apply that test to the actual words. Something like:

> Our national anthem represents all our people and does not exclude based on gender, race, language, or religious belief (if any). It praises our country's natural beauty and our desire to live peacefully. While we love our nation, we know other countries are equally beautiful and deserving of our respect. We do not believe in war to settle differences or consider death in battle to be a glorious ending. And we look to build a better future for all children, one marked by democracy, unity, and understanding.

If that is your baseline, then it knocks out any anthems that feature violence, sexism, and a deity. Which is pretty much all of them. And isn't that a good thing? It brings us back to my initial point: national anthems are terrible songs, so why bother with them? But I know that getting rid of anthems is a forlorn hope. Perhaps what we should focus on is limiting the damage they do.

We've seen how anthems are a relatively recent development for countries and that they are frequently replaced, shortened, or

* This contract only applies to men. If you're a woman, it's your job to proudly give birth to the future soldiers who will do all this dying.

rewritten. They are not sacred documents that must be preserved untouched to maintain a nation's honour. Most of the world's anthems were only adopted within my lifetime.* Many of the older ones are products of their time, revolutionary songs that have questionable relevance in today's world. What we need is a plan to update them.

The first thing to do is defang them. Make them nice. This will have the added bonus of reducing their effectiveness as ultranationalist symbols. It is precisely their nastiness that makes anthems attractive to right-wing opportunists who want to force people to sing them. Governments help with that by militarizing anthems. They are often played at public events by military bands accompanied by warplanes screaming over stadiums and trailing smoke in the relevant national colours. If you weaponize the anthem by using it like that, it becomes easy to spot your enemies: they are the ones not singing; the ones without hands on their hearts; the ones who keep their hats on; the ones who reject national symbols for religious or moral purposes; the ones who kneel to demand racial equality. The anthem becomes a tool of the state, not a song for the people.

But there is hope — because the tone of an anthem often decides how it is perceived. For example, it's hard to imagine Finland as an aggressive military nation based on its anthem, which is slow and melodic and entirely about the beauty of the country.† On the other hand, it's hard to imagine anything peaceful when you hear "La Marseillaise." It gets you fired up and ready to fight — which

* I was born in 1959. Of the 193 UN nations, 108 have anthems that were officially adopted after my birth.

† One shouldn't underestimate the Finns as a military force; they ground down the mighty Russian army in the 1939–1940 Winter War, only yielding when their forces were exhausted and out of supplies. They may have technically lost the war and a lot of territory, but they secured their independence and humiliated the Soviet Union.

is precisely the point. But even if you have a mighty, we're-number-one anthem, a slight adjustment can make a big difference.

Let's go back to José Feliciano's performance of "The Star-Spangled Banner" in 1968, which caused so much damage to his career. His gentle, folk-jazzy, acoustic guitar rendition wouldn't raise many eyebrows today, but the reason it upset so many people at the time was because it was so different. This is a song that makes you slow down, think, and remember — the polar opposite of the all-in 1991 Super Bowl version by Whitney Houston, which had everything tossed into it: an incredible voice, all the military support you could imagine, flags, cheering, and warplanes flying overhead. This is the kick-ass jingoistic chest-thumping American anthem that gets people all riled up and ready for battle.

When you listen to the two versions, you can *feel* the difference. Feliciano leaves you calm and relaxed and ready for the ballgame to come. Houston's performance leaves you pumped up on adrenalin, high-fiving with your buddies, and impatient for gladiatorial action on the football field.

Anthems can do what you want them to do: inspire you for battle or instill quiet pride in your nation. But what we don't need is to play them all the time. In most countries, the anthem is only played occasionally — at big sporting events or major national occasions. Some countries start the school day with a recorded performance of the anthem. Some insist it be played every day on radio and television. For example, in Thailand the anthem is broadcast at 8:00 a.m. and 6:00 p.m. and is also broadcast on loudspeakers in parks, railway and bus stations, and other public spaces. People are expected to stop what they are doing and stand to attention.

However, that kind of daily interaction with an anthem isn't the norm in much of the world. In countries where the pressure to declare loyalty to the state is less intense, people can go for months without ever hearing their national anthem. The United States (and to a lesser extent, Canada) is a bit of an outlier in that respect. It can be perplexing for European visitors to attend a sporting event in either country and hear the relevant national anthem being played before a fairly mundane regular-season club game. This does not happen at equivalent events in Europe.

The practice of playing patriotic songs in American stadiums appears to date back to the Civil War. The earliest recorded example was in 1862 when "The Star-Spangled Banner" (still decades away from becoming the national anthem) was played before a baseball game.[4] That started a habit of occasionally playing the song at games, but it didn't become embedded in the culture until another war.

On September 6, 1918, the Boston Red Sox and Chicago Cubs played the first game of the World Series. The country had joined the First World War the previous year, and over a million American soldiers were fighting in Europe. Acts of patriotism were everywhere as the country, which had been reluctant to join the war in the first place, sought to unite behind its military. The *New York Times* reported on what happened that day:

> As the crowd of 19,274 spectators — the smallest that has witnessed the diamond classic in many years — stood up to take their afternoon yawn, that has been the privilege and custom of baseball fans for many generations, the band broke forth to the strains of "The Star-Spangled Banner." The yawn was checked and heads were bared as the ball players turned quickly about and faced the music. Jackie Fred Thomas of the U.S. Navy* was at attention, as

* Thomas was the Red Sox third baseman. He was on leave from the navy to play in the World Series.

> he stood erect with his eyes set on the flag fluttering at the top of the lofty pole in right field. First the song was taken up by a few, then others joined, and when the final notes came, a great volume of melody rolled across the field. It was at the very end that the onlookers exploded into thunderous applause and rent the air with a cheer that marked the highest point of the day's enthusiasm.[5]

The crowd's reaction was so enthusiastic that the band played the song again the next night … and the next, and then the Red Sox hired a band to do the same for the games in Boston. A tradition was born. It was quickly adopted by other professional sports. The arrival of public-address systems allowed the use of recordings, which helped spread the practice to places that couldn't afford a band.

The Second World War cemented the tradition. It seemed that no occasion was too small to be honoured by a rendition of the national anthem, and so was born the strange unique-to-America custom of Terrible Anthem Singers as everyone who believed they could carry a tune was trotted out to give it a go.

But what's needed is not *more* anthem singing: it's *less*. Backing off from the anthem is a better way of making it special and important rather than a daily test of patriotism. This can be done.

Goshen College is a private liberal arts institution in the city of Goshen, Indiana. It was founded in 1894 by Mennonites, a Christian group with a strong commitment to pacifism. A national anthem that glorifies fighting makes a lot of Mennonites uncomfortable. The small college doesn't have a strong athletic presence, but it does field some teams. And it didn't play the anthem before games.

There aren't enough U.S. Mennonites to allow the college to only recruit from within their religion. About 70 percent of the students are from other denominations, and some of those students noticed the absence of the pre-game anthem. In 2010 they were granted permission to play "The Star-Spangled Banner" before a baseball game. It didn't go down well on campus. There was strong pushback from staff, students, and alumni. So, the college came up with a compromise: Goshen College teams would be allowed to play a song before their games, but it would have to be "America the Beautiful." The College Board said the song "fits with our national sports tradition and honours this country while better resonating with our Christ-centred core values."[6]

Some teams play it, while others just get right to the sport. No one seems to mind or to question the patriotism of the college students.

♫

We're almost at the end of our journey. And I hope we've learned that anthems don't have to be terrible songs, and they don't have to be permanent or exclusive. They don't even have to have lyrics — if Spain can manage to struggle along as a nation without a song to sing, then so can the rest of us. Nor do they have to be played as military marches. If a nation really believes in peace and unity — and without fail, all nations claim those as underlying principles of their existence — then jettison the military association with your song. Better yet, pick different songs or different performances to suit the occasion. New Zealand and Denmark have two official anthems. Why should the rest of us restrict ourselves to one? And if there has to be a national song, make sure the words reflect your country in a positive light. It seems almost insulting to point out that things would be better without the fighting, the overwhelming maleness, and the appeals to God. That should be obvious.

As the leaders of any successful organization or business can tell you, a vital part of staying relevant is undergoing constant review. When it comes to anthems, this isn't about rewriting history. It's about recognizing that what seemed like a good idea two hundred years ago may not be quite as pertinent today. It's understandable that a nation emerging from a bloody war of independence would use that conflict to define national unity: we all went through this together and emerged with a common purpose. That's what led to the anthems of South America, Ireland, the United States, Algeria, and more. But it's so easy to get trapped by these songs; they become familiar and comforting. Just suggesting that perhaps they need to be reassessed is viewed as anti-patriotic. That is why we should build in the idea of regular reviews. Give a National Anthem Committee the responsibility to review the anthem every ten years or so to make sure the ideas and language are still doing their job. And to do that, you need to know what the job is: get that mission statement written.

Don't roll your eyes; every nation has detailed specifications governing its national flag. For example, the Government of Canada defines the country's flag as "a red flag, twice as long as it is wide (proportion 2:1, or sixty-four units in length and thirty-two units in width or depth). In its centre is a white square the width of the Flag, with a single stylized eleven-point red maple leaf in the centre. The flag is horizontally symmetric."[7] In the National Flag of Canada Act, the Maple Leaf is described as "*the* symbol of the nation's unity" (emphasis added) and that it "represents the principles of freedom, democracy, courage, and justice upon which our great nation is based." It also says the flag represents all citizens of Canada and acknowledges those who have sacrificed their lives for the nation.[8]

So, the flag gets a mission statement. But the anthem? Nothing. The National Anthem Act attaches absolutely no significance to the national song. This tiny law says just two things: it specifies the words and music to "O Canada" and confirms they are in the public domain. That's it. Nothing about how the anthem must be performed or when or what it represents. Simply adding a declaration that states the importance of the anthem to the nation and a clause that requires a review every few years doesn't seem unreasonable.

FINAL VERSE

A song is a mantra, something you repeat over and over. We need peace, we need giving, we need love, we need unity. I want the whole world to sing this song.

— Michael Jackson

When I was at boarding school in Scotland, students were required to attend religious services in the school chapel. The school was not run by a church or religious group, but it clearly saw as a key part of its educational role teaching children to love God and country. And that apparently required the occasional singing of the national anthem. In those days — the early 1970s — there was no real debate about what constituted the national anthem of Scotland. At least, no debate in the conservative circles that governed what are strangely known as "public schools" in the United Kingdom, which actually means very, very private. The national anthem we were required to sing was "God Save the Queen."

I did not like the song and refused to sing it. As a twelve-year-old, I had only the most tenuous grasp on the concept of republicanism, but I definitely knew I didn't agree with the idea of a hereditary monarch. Nor did I understand why I was being asked to celebrate as head of state someone who was obviously English, even if the song appeared in the Church of Scotland hymnal. However, this was not an issue that was up for discussion. Schools in those days were allowed to use violence to control disobedient students. There were many occasions when I ran afoul of authority and was beaten with a cane. Refusing to sing the national anthem was one of the offences that merited corporal punishment. I learned from that lesson not to submit to authority but to subvert it. I could not be beaten into singing the anthem, but I did recognize the need to avoid further pain. So, I opened and shut my mouth without making any sound during future mandatory anthem performances.

What struck me — along with the cane — was the peculiar logic that forcing me to sing the anthem would turn me into a loyal subject of Her Majesty. It seemed clear to me even then that forcing someone to pledge allegiance to a symbol was more likely to make them resent it than admire it. In many ways, that is the whole point of anthems. It doesn't matter if you like the song or agree with its message, because its role is to unite people and force dissenters out into the open. When the words "please stand for the national anthem" are spoken, it's a brave or foolish individual who chooses to remain seated.

Most countries have protocols for what to do during their national anthems. For example, the United States enshrines anthem etiquette in its Code of Laws, even though there is no means of enforcing it or specified punishment for those who don't follow along. It states that from the first to last note of the anthem, "all persons present except those in uniform should face the flag and stand at attention with the right hand over the heart. Those present in uniform should render the military salute. When not in uniform, men should remove their headdress with their right hand and hold it at the left shoulder, the hand being over the heart." It also says that if no flag is displayed, "all present should face toward the music and act in the same manner they would if the flag were displayed." Individuals in uniform are expected to salute for the entire playing of the anthem.[1]

That may not be an enforceable law, but many people believe it should be. We saw that during the "take a knee" protests against racial injustice begun by NFL player Colin Kaepernick in 2016. The practice spread to include other players, then other teams, and even other sports inside and outside the United States. The adverse reaction was swift and predictable, led by President Donald Trump, who said anyone kneeling during the anthem was a "son of a bitch" who should be fired.[2] But not all powerful people condemned the kneeling athletes. The owner of NBA team the Dallas Mavericks decided in 2020 to stop playing the anthem before his team's home games. Mark Cuban wasn't alone in opposing the playing of pre-game anthems. The then coach of the NBA's New Orleans Pelicans also joined in. Stan Van Gundy said in a tweet that "all the talk about national anthem protests begs the question — Why do we even play the anthem before games? Why do we have to honor our country before we play a game? We don't play the anthem before movies, plays, etc. It makes no sense. Let's end the practice and just play."[3]

But there were far more powerful forces involved. The NBA, facing public and political backlash, intervened and ordered all teams to play the anthem. Mark Cuban complied but released a statement saying, "We respect and always have respected the passion people have for the anthem and our country. But we also loudly hear the voices of those who feel that the anthem does not represent them. We feel that their voices need to be respected and heard because they have not been."[4]

Lawmakers in Texas decided to make sure he wouldn't change his mind, passing what came to be known as the Star-Spangled Banner Protection Act. It requires pro sports teams that accept public money from the state to play the national anthem before games.

♬

People who protest during national anthems are rarely protesting against the idea of anthems in general. They are usually opposed to that anthem in particular (because it is exclusionary) or because of what it represents (a country or government they don't like) or because a nation fails to live up to the ideals expressed in the anthem (not everyone feels like they are living in the land of the free). Anthems have become so embedded in our culture that getting rid of them is as unlikely as eliminating national identities.

The British historian Eric Hobsbawm introduced the term "invented tradition" to describe what he called "a set of practices, normally governed by overtly or tacitly accepted rules and of a ritual or symbolic nature, which seek to inculcate certain values and norms of behaviour by repetition, which automatically implies continuity with the past."[5] He pointed to the pageantry surrounding the British monarchy as an example of what appear to be ancient rituals but were, in fact, largely made up during the nineteenth and early twentieth centuries. An example is the pageantry surrounding state events like the opening of Parliament or the coronation of a new monarch. Those costumes, carriages, and solemn symbols were deliberately created in the nineteenth century to boost public support and reverence for the monarchy.

Queen Victoria was not a much-loved ruler. In 1864 a protestor pinned a notice to the fence surrounding Buckingham Palace. It stated that "these commanding premises to be let or sold in consequence of the late occupant's declining business."[6] Sentiments like that were widespread, leading to fears of a rise in republicanism. That threatened not just the monarch but the entire ruling class. Leading politicians decided to rebrand the monarchy to make it more popular with the people. One of the tools they used was to encourage singing the national anthem, which was usually confined to royal events. It wasn't even played at Queen Victoria's coronation in 1838.

National anthems and other state symbols — like flags, statues, and ornate public buildings often built in a classical style reminiscent of ancient Rome — seek to bind people together with a single approved mythology. This is no accident. These symbols and national myths have been carefully crafted. Think of the idea of American Exceptionalism, which argues that the United States is inherently different from (and better than) all other nations. China is now creating similar national myths to bolster its arrival as a global superpower, promoting a history of five thousand years of peaceful civilization. Virtually every country — large and small — has its own version of this, often tied to a heavily edited version of history and usually rooted in military victories (or where no such victories can be found, built around glorious defeats — like the Battle of Kosovo, a fourteenth-century fight that is at the heart of Serbian national identity).

Entire populations are convinced their way of life and beliefs are better than anyone else's. They don't do this independently. Left to our own devices, our priorities are our families, communities, and a safe and comfortable life. Convincing people that their tribe is the best tribe takes work. Passions must be whipped up, national myths must be created, and perceived injustices must be invented, distorted, or exaggerated. Entire government departments are devoted to this kind of project, even in countries we view as liberal democracies. Think of how education has become a battlefield in the United States, with history in particular treated as a weapon.

In China, the only "correct" version of anything is the one promulgated by the state and protected and adjusted to suit the needs of the Communist Party. That is how Tian Han, the author of China's national anthem, went from being a hero to an enemy of the state who died in prison, only to be restored to national hero status after his death.

Rewriting history to suit the state's interests has always been a tool of government. Having myths to build your nation around is pretty much Job One in the nation-building handbook. This is how we create stereotypes of ourselves and of others. Canadians are tolerant and polite. Americans are loud and arrogant. The French are rude. Germans are militaristic and demand obedience to the rules. Italians are disorganized and passionate. Part of creating our own national myth is to make us different from others so that we see our society as exceptional and others as flawed.

When the reality of a nation's history fails to live up to expectations, then we just change the past. When Queen Victoria and her husband, Prince Albert, visited Balmoral Castle in the mid-nineteenth century, they fell in love with the estate and bought it. But the fifteenth-century castle already on site didn't meet Prince Albert's idea of what a Scottish castle should be. It was cold, small, and uncomfortable. He ordered it to be demolished, and a new castle was built, complete with the turrets, walls, and crenelations that an ancient Scottish castle should have. At least in the mind of nineteenth-century architects. As a castle, it's as real as Cinderella's Castle in Disney World, but it has been seamlessly woven into the manufactured tradition of the British royal family and its ancient roots.

The fact that Queen Elizabeth died at Balmoral was worked into this narrative to show how Scottish people were united in their grief and therefore united in their support for the royal family and, by extension, the United Kingdom. Anyone watching television coverage of the days following the queen's death would have believed that Scotland was a royalist nation, even though an opinion poll taken months earlier showed that just 45 percent of Scots favoured keeping the monarchy, as opposed to 58 percent for the United Kingdom as a whole. Many Scots may have sung "God Save the Queen" to honour the end of Elizabeth's reign, but that does not mean the British anthem will now replace "Flower of Scotland" as the de facto national song.

♫

If a national anthem is closely tied to the state itself, then criticizing the anthem becomes a challenge to authority. That is true even in countries where dissent is allowed. But we need to separate blind acceptance of invented tradition from the truth of what our symbols are saying. The vast majority of anthems are not nice songs. If we expect our laws and public standards to be flexible instruments that change with the times, then it is reasonable to expect our national symbols to evolve as well. It is perfectly legitimate to question why the motto of Canada is *A Mari Usque Ad Mare* — a Latin phrase taken from the Bible meaning "From Sea to Sea." Few people in Canadian public life quote the Latin words, but many actually think the motto is in English and reads "From Sea to Sea to Sea" (which recognizes the often-overlooked fact that Canada actually has three coastlines, touching the Pacific, Atlantic, and Arctic Oceans). Changing the motto to reflect what people think it already is has been proposed.[7] One day it may happen.

It was that need to adapt for different times that led to Australia's decision to acknowledge its Indigenous population by tweaking the words of its anthem. Not everyone thinks the change went far enough, but at least it shows a willingness to make adjustments that reflect a new world. And here's the thing about inclusive changes to national anthems: once made, they become the new invented tradition, and all that previous opposition melts away. No one is seriously campaigning to restore the old sexist language to Austria or Canada's anthems.

An important part of creating a new tradition is familiarity. Anthems are recognized not because they are good but because they are comfortably familiar. If you play a song often enough, it can be easy to confuse quantity with quality. One of the greatest pioneers of rock and roll was Chuck Berry. His influence has been cited by all the great bands and performers of rock music. When he was inducted into the Rock and Roll Hall of Fame, the citation said, "While no individual can be said to have invented rock and roll, Chuck Berry comes the closest of any single figure to being the one who put all the essential pieces together." But despite all that, Chuck Berry only topped the Billboard Hot 100 singles chart once. That happened in 1972 with the risqué novelty song, "My Ding-a-Ling." A dispassionate observer unfamiliar with Chuck Berry but looking at his best-selling records could reasonably conclude that "My Ding-a-Ling" was one of his best songs and not, as *Rolling Stone* described it, one of "22 terrible songs by great artists."[8]

We cling to our national anthems not because they are great songs but because we have been taught to believe they represent the culture, history, and essence of our nations.

♫

In explaining the term "invented traditions," Eric Hobsbawm wrote about "creating emotionally and symbolically charged signs of club membership." Signs such as standing for a national anthem or proclaiming loyalty to a flag. These new traditions can be quickly created because the very act of designating a national symbol means that it automatically commands "instantaneous respect and loyalty." In other words, if we're told a particular song is our national anthem, and we're expected to stand up and sing it, then we're going to accept it quickly and without question. A new and instant tradition will have been born. "*C'est la vie*," as Chuck Berry said in one of his more critically acclaimed songs, "it goes to show you never can tell."

That easy acceptance of brand-new "traditions" is both depressing and reassuring. Yes, it makes it hard to change our anthems, but it also means that if enough pressure is applied, a new or improved anthem can be adopted with as much enthusiasm as the old one.

As we saw in Chapter 1, music is an essential part of human existence. We just can't manage without it. No public or private event — whether a political rally, a wedding, a funeral, or a commercial product launch — can be held without a soundtrack. We associate key events in our lives with the music that surrounded them and remain firmly and intransigently convinced that *our* music — the music of our youth — was the best, whether that was the 1960s, '70s, '80s, '90s, or early 2000s.

However, the love of music does not mean we have to accept the inevitability of today's national anthems. We've seen how they can be changed — and why they need to be changed. There is also a lingering nasty colonial legacy at their heart. Anthems are the product of European nations, which then spread the practice around the world, with the result that virtually every anthem follows the same Christian hymn-like structure and Western-style musical instruments and arrangements. For example, the diverse traditional music of a country like Kenya is not in any way connected to its national anthem, which — quite frankly — could be transferred with only minor editing to almost any other country in the world. Where are the djembe drums in the national anthem of Mali? Or the didgeridoos in Australia's song? Why does Canada's national anthem not reflect the culture of its Indigenous people — the throat singing of the Inuit or the traditional dance and drum music of the

Cree? And consider this: when anthems are commissioned for international sporting events like the World Cup or the Olympics, they are recorded by traditional symphony orchestras using traditional Western instruments.

A rare exception to that Western dominance of anthem-type occasions is the haka performed by the New Zealand rugby team, the All Blacks, which, as we saw in Chapter 3, has the power to intimidate the toughest opponents. As a statement of national identity, it is a far more inspiring and unique expression of New Zealand culture than the bland "God Defend New Zealand." It's certainly more widely known. So why not take one of the many haka and use that as your anthem? Or compose a new one?

The flaws at the centre of almost every anthem are fixable. At the simplest level, the words can be disposed of altogether, thereby removing much of what is problematic about national songs. But if words are wanted, then make them universal; let them speak to everyone, not just those in your own country. Traditions don't have to be ancient. As we've seen, they can be manufactured to suit the occasion. So invent new ones. And make them welcoming. Make them nice.

We end on a moment of opportunity. When Queen Elizabeth died, the British national anthem immediately changed from "God Save the Queen" to "God Save the King." This didn't happen through some legislative change or official order. In fact, there are absolutely no rules about the British anthem. It's not enshrined in law. The official royal family website notes, "there is no authorised version of the National Anthem as the words are a matter of tradition. Additional verses have been added down the years, but these are rarely used."

There you have it. A matter of tradition. It began spontaneously in 1745 at London's Drury Lane Theatre and then never went away. It's the anthem because it has the authority of familiarity. It began as one man's act of patriotism, and it can be ended in exactly the same way — by one man, if he is prepared to seize the moment.

We don't have a good sense of what the various kings and queens down the years thought about the anthem. You have to imagine it must have felt a little awkward for them on first hearing people sing it. After all, put yourself in the position of standing to attention while hundreds or thousands of people sing a song about you. It's believed that George V (the current king's great-grandfather) was not a fan. It's been claimed he wanted "Jerusalem" as the national anthem, and there's certainly plenty of evidence he loved that song. When he learned it wasn't to be played at a concert to mark his Silver Jubilee in 1935, he insisted it be included, telling officials that "if there's no room for it, I shall go down myself to the platform and whistle it."[9] Sadly, the audience was denied the spectacle of seeing the monarch whistling on stage.

The current king is also a big fan of the music of "Jerusalem" composer Sir Hubert Parry. King Charles III presented a BBC film about the composer in 2011. And he has also gone on record about "non-politically correct" language in the current anthem. It's not entirely clear which phrases concern him, but it seems likely he was referring to the lines calling on God to scatter the king's enemies and to "Confound their politics, / Frustrate their knavish tricks."[10]

Audiences still flock to the Theatre Royal on Drury Lane, as they have since the first theatre was built on the site in 1663. It's always enjoyed royal patronage. The current building has hosted every monarch since it opened in 1812. Queen Victoria was a big fan. One of George VI's last public appearances was to see the musical *South Pacific* with his daughter, Princess Elizabeth, the day before she left on a Commonwealth tour that was cut short when her father died. The current king visited as the Prince of Wales.

And this is the opportunity that King Charles III can seize. It is the perfect time and place to start a new tradition. Take a Saturday night off and escort the queen consort to Drury Lane for the latest musical presented by theatre owner, Sir Andrew Lloyd Webber. At the end of the night, as the applause dies down and the cast is assembled on stage, give a discreet nod from the Royal Box to the orchestra leader, who is expecting the signal. The house lights go up. That will be the cue for Adele, Ed Sheeran, and Dua Lipa to walk on stage. The audience, which is busy gathering bags and coats in preparation to stream out into the late London evening, pauses in some confusion. They recognize the singers, of course, but what are they doing there? What is going on?

The performers wait until everyone has settled down again. Then Adele speaks. "We are here tonight by Royal Request," she says, gesturing toward the king, who waves back in acknowledgement. He is one of only a handful of people who know what is about to happen.

"We've been asked to sing a very special song," Adele continues. "One that I guarantee will be a bigger hit than anything any of us have ever recorded." She laughs, and Ed Sheeran and Dua Lipa join in. The audience, excited now, breaks out in sporadic applause. Adele waits for silence before continuing. "The song we've been asked to sing is a patriotic one. Ladies and gentlemen, I must ask you to stand for our new national anthem."

ACKNOWLEDGEMENTS

Writing seems like such a solitary pastime. Just the writer and a blank page. Then words. Sentences. Chapters. A book. I did it by myself. So, who is there to acknowledge? There was no one else in my office when I wrote this. And yet, as I write these words, I think I see something out of the corner of my eye. There is a shadow — no, shadows — floating around me. Slowly they solidify and separate. I am not alone. I am surrounded by a crowd. They are watching, pushing me forward, shaking their heads in disapproval, applauding success, and refusing to allow me to contemplate failure.

There is Miss Blakeney, who encouraged me to write page after page of stories and even read them to the class in the high school on Harcourt Street in Dublin. There is Auntie Bun — really my great aunt — who was the first author I really knew; her novels about girls' schools in the 1930s, which were on my grandmother's bookshelves in Glasgow, I devoured as a child. There is my Uncle Ron, who give me my first proper typewriter — a massive metal machine that needed to be pounded into submission.

Many of the faces I don't recognize or can't put a name to — people who offered maybe a sentence of encouragement at just the right time, enough to keep me filling sheets of paper even if they went no further than a drawer in my desk. I always dreamed that one day, there would be a book with my name on it. I just didn't know how to make it happen.

The shadows have dispersed. Now I am surrounded by people who are very much alive, though no more physically present than the ghosts of the past. I thought that writing the book would be the hard part, but getting a book into the hands of a reader takes a lot of work. Fortunately, much of that work is done by other people. I would not have written this book if it was not for the Masters of Fine Arts in Creative Nonfiction program at the University of King's College in Halifax. In particular, my mentor Ken McGoogan gave me invaluable tips on structure and chapter arrangement and was unfailingly supportive when my confidence waned. My fellow students Jenny Chen, Amy Fish, John Larsen, and Fay Martin (alphabetical order, my friends, because your contributions were equal!) refused to tolerate any suggestion of giving up, no matter how high the rejection pile became. Believe me, there were days when I was ready to hit "delete" on the whole project.

And then, one day, there was Kathryn Lane from Dundurn Press, writing in an email that she was enjoying the book I had submitted and asking if I would be interested in talking to her. I had always believed that if my book landed on just the right person's desk, then it would immediately click with them. Kathryn was that person. You can't get a book published without a champion, and that's what she became.

The team at Dundurn have been unfailingly supportive. No matter how many I name, some will be inadvertently left off the list. I apologize. I will mention my editor, Dominic Farrell, who, despite an insistence on inserting Oxford commas throughout the text, in every other way managed to make it better. He caught every stupid mistake I made. Art director Laura Boyle and production designer Karen Alexiou managed to turn a concept into a cover.

Finally, there is one more ghost, who taught me the harsh realities of life as a writer. Peter Driscoll was the author of several bestselling thrillers, at least one made into a major movie with Michael Caine and Sidney Poitier. I met him in the early 1980s at the Irish public broadcaster, RTÉ. Peter was working the overnight shift on the radio news desk. I had read a couple of his books — they were the kind of popular novels that were sold at airport bookstores for reading on the beach. I couldn't understand why someone who was such a successful writer would want to work the newsroom graveyard shift. That is when he explained to me the realities of being a full-time writer: very few people make money doing it. Despite his bestselling status, he needed another job to pay the bills. That's the truth about writers: we do it because we love it and because we can't help ourselves.

Thank you to everyone who has put up with me while I figured that out.

NOTES

Overture

1 London newspapers conveyed the alarm felt by the city's populace following the surprising initial success of Bonnie Prince Charlie's uprising. The *Daily Advertiser* of September 26, 1745 — two days before the Drury Lane Theatre performance described in the opening paragraphs — made a call to arms. "We may suffer ourselves to be deluded, cheated and abus'd, and we may open our eyes when too late, if we act at this time as if we thought ourselves secure. Shall a few faithless Scotch, aided by the ever-faithless French, dare to impose a King on us? No, let us no longer hesitate; let us banish all animosities, and with hearts entirely English, let us express ourselves openly to each other; let us as one man unite; let us arm ourselves boldly in the defence of our King and country; let us stand firm; let us drive out the common enemy."

2 The music historian Charles Burney delivered his verdict on Susannah Cibber's voice in his 1785 book *An Account of the Musical Performances in Westminster-Abbey, and the Pantheon, May 26th, 27th, 29th; and June the 3d, and 5th, 1784. In Commemoration of Handel.* Perhaps not the catchiest of titles. It's worth noting that Burney did slightly damn with faint praise in the words leading up to the quote, which I chose to omit, when he said, "whose voice,

though a mere thread, and knowledge of music, inconsiderable; yet, by a natural pathos ..." etc.

3 The Reverend Patrick Delany is described in the *Compendium of Irish Biography* (Alfred Webb, 1878) as "an eloquent preacher, a man of wit and learning." There is a bust of him on display in the library at Trinity College, Dublin. His outburst at the premiere of the *Messiah* in Dublin is recorded in the entry for Susannah Cibber in volume 10 of the *Dictionary of National Biography* (Leslie Stephen, ed., 1887).

4 The quotes from the *Daily Advertiser* and *General Advertiser* are taken from the archived newspapers provided in digital form by the British Library. They are accessible with a subscription or through university or some public libraries. The *Daily Advertiser* article also notes that the audience at the Theatre Royal "were agreeably surpriz'd" by the performance of "the anthem of God save our noble king."

5 Frances "Fanny" Burney's descriptive diaries reveal a caustic and surprisingly modern take on eighteenth-century life. For example, in her entry from Weymouth on July 8, 1789, she also describes how during her stay she dined with her female friend, while the gentlemen of the company kept to themselves. "I like this much: I see them just enough to keep up sociability, without any necessary constraint." Burney married a French army officer who had fled to England from the French Revolution. She became known as Madame d'Arblay. Her husband was broke, but the couple was rescued from poverty by the success of Fanny's novel *Camilla*. Her diaries are still in print and available digitally for free through the online Project Gutenberg.

6 The lines by Alfred Lord Tennyson come from his poem "The Charge of the Heavy Brigade at Balaclava" (not to be confused with his more famous "Charge of the Light Brigade" from the same battle). The closing lines from the Epilogue are:

And here the Singer for his Art
Not all in vain may plead
'The song that nerves a nation's heart
Is in itself a deed.'

7 For the purposes of my database, I identified the 193 UN anthems as religious, violent, sexist, or using gender-specific terms like "fatherland" or "motherland." Where possible, I worked with official translations, but it's not a foolproof process. For example, the official translation of Slovenia's anthem (taken from the government website gov.si/en/topics/national-symbols) gives the first line as "God's blessing on all nations," but the Slovenian text makes no mention of God; a literal translation would be "long live all nations." Japan's anthem has no overt religious references, but there are echoes of the Shinto religion in some of its imagery. I put both these anthems in the "not religious" column. The ten countries with relatively problem-free lyrics are: Andorra, Australia, the Czech Republic, Japan, Kazakhstan, Moldova, Mongolia, North Korea, Singapore, and Slovenia.

1: Living for Music

1 Andrew Fletcher of Saltoun (an estate near Edinburgh; Saltoun Hall remains in the Fletcher family to this day) published his comments in a book with the catchy title *An Account of a Conversation Concerning a Right Regulation of Governments for the Common Good of Mankind: In a Letter to the Marquiss of Montrose, the Earls of Rothes, Roxburg and Haddington, from London the First of December, 1703.*

2 Benedict Anderson introduced me to the concept of "simultaneity," which I still struggle to pronounce. The quote comes from his book *Imagined Communities: Reflections on the Origin and Spread of Nationalism* (New York: Verso, 2006).

3 Daniel Weinstein et al., "Singing and Social Bonding: Changes in Connectivity and Pain Threshold as a Function of Group Size," *Evolution and Human Behavior* 37, no. 2 (March 2016). It is available online.

4 The quote from *The Art of War* comes from the 1910 edition translated by Lionel Giles. This is available as a Project Gutenberg eBook. I love Project Gutenberg.

5 Jean-Jacques Rousseau is better known as a philosopher than as a music critic (he came up with the idea of a "social contract"). But he

was also a composer of some note and published his *Dictionnaire de la musique* in 1767. The quote about the impact of music on Swiss mercenaries is taken from the 1779 English translation by William Waring, available online as a Google book.

6 The word "nostalgia" was created by medical student Johannes Hofer in a dissertation presented to the University of Basel in 1688. An English translation of his *Dissertatio Medica de Nostalgia, oder Heimwehe* was published in the *Bulletin of the Institute of the History of Medicine* in August 1934.

7 Dr. J. Theodore Calhoun was an army surgeon during the American Civil War. His comments about getting homesick soldiers to "man up" were published in the *Medical and Surgical Reporter* (February 27, 1864) and were taken from the paper "So Lonesome I Could Die: Nostalgia and Debates over Emotional Control in the Civil War North" by Frances Clarke, published in the Winter 2007 volume of the *Journal of Social History*.

8 Like many scholars in the sixteenth century, Richard Stanihurst (or Stanyhurst) wrote in Latin. His history *De Rebus in Hibernia Gestis* was fully translated for the first time in 2012 by the Centre for Neo-Latin Studies at University College Cork under the English title *Great Deeds in Ireland*.

9 The announcement of the award of the Victoria Cross to James Richardson was published in the official British Government journal *The London Gazette* on October 18, 1918, Supplement 30967. The publication is available online at thegazette.co.uk.

10 The quote from British commando Tom Duncan, recalling hearing Piper Bill Millin's bagpipes during the D-Day invasion, comes from Millin's obituary in the London *Daily Telegraph* on August 18, 2010.

11 The quote from Vladimir Lenin about the role of the state in controlling art comes from the German Communist activist Clara Zetkin, who conducted a series of interviews with the Russian leader in 1920 on the role of women in the revolution. Her comments were published in the book *Lenin on Literature and Art* (Moscow: Progress Publishers, 1967).

12 The translation of Heinz Valk's newspaper editorial calling for a Singing Revolution is taken from the introduction to Guntis Šmidchens's book

The Power of Song: Nonviolent National Culture in the Baltic Singing Revolution (Seattle: University of Washington Press, 2014).

13 "Crossmodal Transfer of Emotion by Music" was published in *Neuroscience Letters* 455, issue 2 (May 15, 2009).

2: To Arms!

1 Argentina's anthem was changed in March 30, 1900, when President Julio Argentino Roca issued a presidential decree: *El himno nacional contiene frases que fueron escritas con propósitos transitorios, las que hace tiempo han perdido su carácter de actualidad; tales frases mortifican el patriotismo del pueblo español y no son compatibles con las relaciones internacionales de amistad, unión y concordia que hoy ligan á la Nación Argentina con España.*

2 The Chinese movie *Children of Troubled Times* 風雲兒女 was released in 1935 along with a soundtrack album featuring the theme song, "March of the Volunteers." The full movie is available on YouTube, but sadly there are no English subtitles.

3 President Xi Jinping's remarks as reported in the *Washington Post*, July 1, 2021.

4 As well as extolling the virtues of the Chinese national anthem, the State Council Information Office of the People's Republic of China also offers this official translation of the lyrics:

Arise, we who refuse to be slaves;
With our very flesh and blood
Let us build our new Great Wall!
The peoples of China are at their most critical time,
Everybody must roar defiance.
Arise! Arise! Arise!
Millions of hearts with one mind,
Brave the enemy's gunfire,
March on!
Brave the enemy's gunfire,
March on! March on! March on, on!

5 The musician Arn Chorn-Pond told his story to the Holocaust Memorial Day Trust. He continues to talk about his life during

Khmer Rouge rule, his escape, and his subsequent return to Cambodia. His story has inspired an opera, *Where Elephants Weep*; the children's book *A Song for Cambodia* (Michelle Lord, New York: Lee & Low, 2008); and the novel *Never Fall Down* (Patricia McCormick, Toronto: Corgi Children's, 2013).

6 As told to *Phnom Penh Post* reporter Khouth Sophak Chakrya on August 8, 2022.

7 The promo clip for the Six Nations rugby tournament may not have pleased the BBC, but it's fortunately still available for everyone to watch on YouTube.

8 George Orwell's article "The Sporting Spirit" appeared in the *Tribune* newspaper on December 14, 1945. The entire article can be read at the Orwell Foundation: orwellfoundation.com.

9 The official Scottish government response to the anthem petition came on February 15, 2015. It added some other suggestions for a possible future anthem: "Our national song should be an anthem for all the people of Scotland with our diverse heritage and traditions. Scotland has many fine tunes, both traditional and contemporary, including 'Flower of Scotland,' which could be stirring national anthems, but it is important that any choice has wide public support. It is also important to note that other songs share 'Flower of Scotland's' special resonance, not least through their use at major events. For example, 'A Man's a Man for A' That,' sung by Sheena Wellington at the 1999 opening of the Scottish Parliament, or 'Scotland the Brave' used at the Commonwealth Games between 1958 and 2006 — and 'Freedom Come-All-Ye' was performed by South African soprano Pumeza Matshikiza at the opening ceremony of the 2014 Games."

3: Humming Along

1 The entire front page of the Cardiff *Evening Express* on Saturday, December 16, 1905, was devoted to the result of the game under the headline "Victory!" However, what stands out is the large cartoon with the caption "Scalp Hunting" showing what is presumably meant to be a club-wielding Māori heading toward Wales with scattered

skulls in his wake and the scalps of all the other teams the All Blacks had defeated tied around his waist. It is complemented by a second panel showing a Welsh dragon asleep with a bloated belly under the headline "A Big Meal." Few people would be offended by the dragon.

2 Pierre de Coubertin's words form the basis of the Olympic creed. See olympics.com/ioc/faq/olympic-symbol-and-identity/what-is-the-olympic-creed.

3 The head of the Scottish Football Association held a news conference to try and defuse the situation. As reported in the *Guardian* on September 8, 2010, he said, "I was embarrassed and extremely disappointed by the disgraceful behaviour of some of our supporters during the Liechtenstein national anthem. The Scotland fans have worked hard to earn their reputation throughout the world as fun-loving and respectful followers of football. Last night, those who chose to boo our opponents' anthem only served to tarnish that reputation. I apologise unreservedly to our visitors for the crass reaction to their anthem." That hasn't stopped the Scottish fans from booing "God Save the King." At a game against England in September 2023, the booing was so loud the BBC Radio commentator said, "If you couldn't hear 'God Save the King' at home, I'm not surprised."

4 In his autobiography, *Full Time: The Secret Life of Tony Cascarino* (New York: Scribner, 2013), the football player revealed that after he was recruited for the Irish team, he applied for an Irish passport. He'd played three games for his new country when he got a letter back from the Irish Embassy in London. "Finally, the envelope arrived, and they were all there, all my mother's documents — and a letter saying it had been declined. It seemed odd but I didn't follow it up. I didn't need to. I had won three international caps. And for the next eleven years, I continued playing for Ireland with my British passport."

5 In the RTÉ television documentary *Division: The Irish Soccer Split*, aired May 22, 2019.

6 Adem Ljajić was speaking to journalists on May 28, 2012. "Adem Ljajic Released from Serbian National Football Team over Refusal to Sing National Anthem," Huffington Post UK.

7 Sebastian Gorka, speaking on his show *America First with Sebastian Gorka* on Salem Radio Network on July 10, 2019. He served as a deputy assistant to President Trump in 2017.

8 "Name That Tune: Northern Ireland Peer 'Amazed' at Spanish National Anthem Silence at Euros ... Before Realising There Are No Lyrics," *Belfast Telegraph*, July 7, 2021.

4: Badly Played and Monotonous

1 Avery Brundage was speaking in Tokyo on October 24, 1964, the final day of the Summer Games. As quoted by the Associated Press. "Victory Ceremony, Anthems at Games Are Criticized," *New York Times*, October 25, 1964.

2 Blog entry quoted in Jennifer Lanthier's article "Rosie MacLennan: Gold Medal Trampolinist at the 2012 Olympics," *University of Toronto News*, August 7, 2012.

3 Julia Hoyt was an American actor, socialite, and newspaper columnist. She generally wrote about etiquette and fashion, but in 1924 she took what the *Bridgeport Post* described in promoting her columns as "a little jaunt to Europe," which coincided with the Paris Summer Olympics. "Americans in Olympics Prove Good Sports of Whom Country May Be Proud," Minneapolis *Star Tribune*, August 19, 1924.

4 From the official report of the 1932 Lake Placid Olympic Games, archived in the library of the Olympic Studies Centre.

5 Quoted by Allen Guttman in his 1984 book, *The Games Must Go On: Avery Brundage and the Olympic Movement* (New York: Columbia University Press).

6 Perhaps the oddest part of this very formal exchange between cousins is that it took place in 1946, almost a year after Germany's defeat. Having received the request for royal approval from Prince George's father, the British Foreign Office deliberated on what it somewhat laconically called a "rather nice problem" before delving into the ancestry of the people involved and technicalities of the relevant Act of 1772. What makes the king's reply (suggested by the lord chancellor) so odd is the reference to the state of war still existing between the countries. Despite Germany's unconditional surrender in 1945, the

formal cessation of hostilities between the two countries didn't take place until 1951. The correspondence relating to Prince George of Hanover's marriage is documented in the British National Archives and is available online using the file reference LCO 2/3371A.

7 The debate over ending the use of flags and anthems at Olympic medal ceremonies is recorded in the minutes of the sixty-seventh session of the International Olympic Committee in Mexico City October 7–11, 1968, as supplied by the Olympic Studies Centre.

8 Lord Killanin's comments appeared in the book *The Olympic Games: 80 Years of People, Events and Records*, edited by Killanin and John Rodda (London: Barrie and Jenkins, 1976). He served as IOC president from 1972 to 1980 and only agreed to take the job if the IOC paid his expenses (previous presidents had largely funded the role out of their own pockets). He then proceeded to run the Olympic movement out of his house in Dublin with a phone, a fax machine, and a single secretary. Those were different times indeed.

9 From *Olympism: Selected Writings*, Pierre de Coubertin, edited by the International Olympic Committee (2000).

10 From *This Great Symbol: Pierre de Coubertin and the Origins of the Modern Olympic Games*, John J. MacAloon (Milton Park, Abingdon-on-Thames, U.K.: Routledge, 2008).

11 From *Nazi Games: The Olympics of 1936*, David Clay Large (New York: W.W. Norton, 2007).

12 The letter to the Melbourne Olympic Committee was publicised at the time, but the author's name wasn't revealed. The original letter is now held by the National Library of Australia. It wasn't until 1986 that John Wing was publicly identified as the writer. Wing didn't attend the closing ceremony but watched a replay later on television. He said that "the athletes seemed to be doing what I wanted them to do. But I wasn't sure it was because of my letter or whether the organisers had planned it." He didn't come forward in response to newspaper appeals for the author's identity, because he hadn't told his father about the letter and was worried that he would be upset. "Melbourne 1956 Olympic Games — the Historical Closing Ceremony," from the Australian Olympic Committee website.

5: God Loves Lots of Countries

1 It was clear from the newspaper coverage of the St. Paul's service that Jeremy Corbyn was in for a rough ride from the right-wing press. The London *Daily Mail*, which has never met a Labour Party leader that it liked, was particularly gleeful, noting that "Mr Corbyn, who was dressed in non-matching jacket and trousers and had failed to properly button his shirt, was branded a 'disgrace' and a 'traitor' by critics" (September 15, 2015).

2 The number of people in the pews on Sunday continues to fall. The most recent average attendance figure from the Church of England was 605,000 in 2021, but it seems unfair to use that number as representative of a trend, given the impact of the Covid-19 pandemic. It is fair to say that the average age of attendees isn't getting any younger.

3 See "US Church Membership Falls Below a Majority for First Time," gallup.com, March 29, 2021.

4 "God Defend New Zealand Got What It Deserved," Radio New Zealand Online, June 25, 2018.

5 New Zealand prime minister Jacinda Ardern was asked by a citizen if she would consider changing the words of "God Defend New Zealand." She responded in a letter quoted in the January 31, 2020, edition of the *New Zealand Herald*, saying that any move to change the song would "not be taken lightly in view of the anthem's national, historical, and constitutional significance. An official change would require significant public consultation and there would need to be a considerable groundswell of support before this would be considered." Ardern is no longer prime minister.

6 "Must Raise National Flag and Sing Anthem to Reopen Church," *Bitter Winter*, July 4, 2020.

6: Changing Times

1 Deborah Cheetham explained her position on the Australian anthem in an opinion piece in the Australian publication *The Conversation*. "Young and Free? Why I Declined to Sing the National Anthem at the 2015 Grand Final" was published on October 19, 2015.

2 The lyrics for the proposed revised Australian anthem were written by Judith Durham, Kutcha Edwards, Lou Bennett, Camilla Chance, and Bill Hauritz. The words and a video of the song can be found on the website for the Dulwich Centre. Judith Durham's open letter about the anthem can be found on scribd.com/document/288682201/Open-letter-regarding-Advance-Australia-Fair-from-Judith-Durham.

3 "Germans Outraged as U.S. Plays Nazi Version of Anthem," Reuters, February 12, 2017.

4 "Dutch Broadcaster Apologises After Subtitling German National Anthem with Nazi Lyrics," *Independent*, June 30, 2021.

5 "Russian Footballers Demand Anthem Lyrics," CNN, August 2, 2000.

6 "El Himno," Antonio Caballero writing in *Semana*, June 1, 1997.

7 The Colombian court decision can be found at corteconstitucional.gov.co/relatoria/1997/C-469-97.htm, "Sentencia C-469/97," Corte Constitucional de Colombia.

8 "Cannes Star Denounces 'Racist' Marseillaise at Festival Opening," *Times* (London), May 14, 2014.

9 "French Justice Minister Under Fire for Refusing to Sing Marseillaise 'Karaoke,'" *Guardian*, May 12, 2014.

10 "Sen. Harkin's Swan Song: Changing the National Anthem," *Washington Post*, December 19, 2014.

11 "Our Anthem: Should It Be Replaced?" Newsweek Feature Service, as printed in the *Dayton Daily News*, March 10, 1969.

12 "'Lift Every Voice and Sing' Would Be Both Symbolic and Substantive as Our National Hymn," James Clyburn writing in *USA Today*, February 8, 2021.

7: Making Room for Women

1 "BBC Announces First Female Chairman," *Daily Mail*, August 30, 2014.

2 "Businesswoman Rona Fairhead the Preferred Choice for Next BBC Trust Chairman," *Daily Telegraph*, August 31, 2014.

3 "Call Me Chairman Says New Female Head of the BBC Trust in Blow to Political Correctness at the Corporation," *Daily Mail*, October 9, 2014.

4 "Why Women Who Fish Are Still Fishermen," *Walrus*, April 27, 2017.

5 "National Anthem Won't Change: PMO," CBC News, March 5, 2010.

6 *Proceedings of the Standing Senate Committee on Social Affairs, Science and Technology*, 42nd parliament, issue 13, online (December 14, 2016) (Kelvin Ogilvie, chair, et al.).

7 Canada, *Debates of the Senate*, March 28, 2017 (Joan Fraser, Liberal Party of Canada), sencanada.ca/en/content/sen/chamber/421/debates/105db_2017-03-28-e.

8 From the column "Opinion: Let's Continue to Sing 'Thy Sons Command,'" Ted Ryczko, inquinte.ca, February 27, 2017.

9 In an August 2019 interview with journalist Anna-Maria Wallner on the website for Arbeit an Europa (Work on Europe), an organization that promotes European unity.

10 "Merkel Dismisses German Official's 'Gender-Neutral' National Anthem Proposal," *Newsweek*, March 5, 2018.

11 "Lebanese Newspaper An-Nahar Publishes a Special Edition in Honour of Women," executive-bulletin.com, November 4, 2019.

12 "Costa Rica Anthem Stays as Is," *Inside Costa Rica*, February 8, 2011.

13 "About One-in-Four U.S. Hispanics Have Heard of Latinx, but Just 3 Percent Use It," Pew Research Center, August 11, 2020.

8: The Verses We Don't Sing

1 "National Anthem Lyrics Prompt California NAACP to Call for Replacing Song," CBS News, November 8, 2017.

2 From the *Hampshire Chronicle*, May 19, 1800, from the British Library newspaper collection.

3 For more on James Hadfield and how his case changed how the British legal system viewed insanity, check out the blog series "James Hadfield, The French Revolution and the Redefinition of Insanity," by Sophia Gal, on the Bethlem Museum of the Mind website.

4 Michael Kelly's account, including the hastily written lyrics for the national anthem, can be found in his memoirs, *Reminiscences of Michael Kelly*, vol. 2, 1826.

5 The "Children's Verse" of "La Marseillaise" is as follows:

We shall enter the (military) career
When our elders are no longer there,
There we shall find their dust
And the traces of their virtues. (repeat)
Much less keen to survive them
Than to share their coffins,
We will have the sublime pride
Of avenging or following them!

6 "The Economist's Playlist of National Anthems," *Economist*, December 19, 2017.

9: Abandoned Anthems

1 "'The Old Lady Was Glaring About': When Dublin's Queen Victoria Statue Was Removed," *Irish Times*, July 23, 1948.

2 "Schiller's Shadow in Salisbury," *Times* (London), August 28, 1974.

3 From Reuters, as published in the *New York Times*, September 28, 1975.

4 When you look at the opening lyrics of "Preamble," you can see why people weren't exactly thrilled by it.

We people of Micronesia
Exercise sovereignty.
Establish our Constitution
Of Federated States.

5 As quoted in *American Popular Music and Its Business: The First Four Hundred Years. Volume II: From 1790 to 1909*, by Russell Sanjek (New York: Oxford University Press, 1988).

6 "What Lincoln Said in His Final Speech," history.com, October 18, 2015.

7 "University of Mississippi Bans Confederate 'Anthem' Dixie," *Guardian*, August 24, 2016.

8 There are a number of versions of the Biafran anthem available, but the one that reaches inside and moves something extraordinary within me is by Nigerian opera singer Igbojekwe Chioma. It's worth listening to and easily found online.

10: Don't Mess with My Music!

1 *Dad's Army*, series 5, episode 3, "A Soldier's Farewell," aired October 20, 1972, on BBC.

2 "'I'm Not with Any Political Party', Says Petitioner Shyam Narayan Chouksey," *Indian Express*, December 1, 2016.

3 "Supreme Court of India, a Record of Proceedings, Writ Petition No. 855/2016," available on the Indian Ministry of Information and Broadcasting website.

4 "Moviegoers Called 'Pakistani Terrorists' for Not Standing Up During National Anthem in Theatre," *India Times*, October 29, 2019.

5 "Belgian Politician's National Anthem Gaffe," *Telegraph* (London), July 23, 2007. The original clip is available on YouTube.

6 Jimi Hendrix's appearance on the *Dick Cavett Show*, on September 9, 1969, can be found on YouTube and other websites, including jimihendrix.com.

7 From the *Detroit Free Press*, October 8, 1968. José Feliciano's anthem performance is easily found online.

8 It's always delightful when you can actually watch and listen to statements like Bernard Brook-Patridge's comments on punk rock. Because he said it on camera, it's on the internet for posterity.

9 The failure of the Sex Pistols to top the charts is recalled in "Still a Fascist Regime? Sex Pistols' God Save the Queen Reissued to Mark Platinum Jubilee," *Guardian*, May 3, 2022.

10 Frank Laboeuf's strong words came in an interview with the program *La Vestiare* on SFR Sport on March 12, 2018.

11 Zhang Haiyang's comments to Xinhua were quoted by the Associated Press on August 28, 2017.

12 "Nationalism Seeps into Slovak Football Club," DW (Deutsche Welle), June 3, 2019.

13 "Japanese Emperor's Statements Stir Controversy," NBC News, October 29, 2004.

11: Everyone Wants an Anthem

1 Much of the information about Dave Mitchell and his St. Helena anthem comes from the website sainthelenaisland.info, where you can also listen to the song.

2 "Demolition Company's Jingle Becomes a Smash Hit," *Japan Times*, December 30, 2003.
3 "KPMG Hits Wrong Note as Its Anthem Rocks the World," *Guardian*, December 8, 2001.
4 "G4S Has a Theme Song. It Is Awful, as You Would Expect. G4S, Securing the World — Nickelback-Style," *New Statesman*, July 13, 2012.
5 © United Nations. Published with permission.

12: Who Owns Your Anthem?

1 Prince appeared on *Lopez Tonight*, April 13, 2011 (on YouTube). The issue is further explored in "Prince and the Copyright Compulsory License Scheme," ipwatchdog.com, May 10, 2011.
2 "Beyoncé Slammed by Etta James for Singing 'At Last' at Inaugural Ball," MTV, February 5, 2009.
3 "Prof. George Wilberforce Kakoma: Development of the Uganda National Anthem," blackhistoryheroes.com, April 8, 2012.
4 "Soldiers Are We — God Save Our Anthem!" *Irish Independent*, November 2, 2011.
5 From the official transcript of the Houses of the Oireachtas, Seanad Éireann Debate, vol. 245, no. 8, January 28, 2016.
6 "UK Firm Speaks Out on 'Owning' Kenya National Anthem Copyright," *Nairobi News*, February 6, 2019.
7 "Hakuna Matata™? Can Disney Actually Trademark That?" *New York Times*, December 20, 2019.
8 The hearing into granting a pension to May Key McBlair is recorded in the official minutes of the Committee on Pensions of the House of Representatives for March 30, 1926.
9 From the review of the ten-CD national anthem collection on the MusicWeb International website.
10 "Changing Our Tune," *Washington Post*, August 26, 2004.
11 Philip Kennicott, "Anthem Arrangements Raise a Red Flag over Authorship, *Washington Post*, August 22, 2008, washingtonpost.com/wp-dyn/content/article/2008/08/21/AR2008082103668.html.
12 The listing for the 2013 edition of the Complete National Anthems of the World on the Naxos website notes, "Peter Breiner is one of

the world's most recorded musicians, with over 180 CDs released. His arrangements of national anthems of all participating countries were used during the Olympic Games in Athens in 2004 and illegally in Beijing in 2008."

13: Rebel Songs for a Cause

1 "Ireland Apologise for Singing Pro-IRA Song After Reaching Women's World Cup," *Guardian*, October 12, 2022.
2 "Irish Team Being 'Persecuted and Bullied' for Singing 'Ooh Ah Up the 'Ra', Songwriter Says," *Irish Times*, October 12, 2023.
3 "Lost for Words After Latest Hong Kong Anthem Gaffe," *South China Morning Post*, March 2, 2023.
4 Published in the *Official Gazette of the Republic of the Philippines*, Act No. 1696, s. 1907.
5 From a description of the Philippine national anthem on the website of the Philippine Embassy to Australia.
6 "Iran Threatened Families of National Soccer Team, According to Security Source," CNN, November 29, 2022.

14: A Kinder, Gentler Way

1 Nicolas Soames, *The Story of Naxos: The Extraordinary Story of the Independent Record Label That Changed Classical Recording for Ever* (London: Piatkus, 2012).
2 "Contest Aims to Get Swiss Singing a Different Tune," *New York Times*, December 13, 2023, nytimes.com/2013/12/12/arts/international/contest-aims-to-get-swiss-singing-a-different-tune.html.
3 Roger Casement, British Parliamentary Papers, 1904, vol. LXII. It's available as a searchable eBook on the Project Gutenberg website, which means you don't have to plough through all sixty-five volumes.
4 "UK More Nostalgic for Empire than Other Ex-colonial Powers," *Guardian*, March 11, 2020.
5 "W.'s Big Fat Greek Pride," *New York Times*, August 19, 2004.
6 "Brisbane Sisters Set a World Record Singing Anthems of 193 Countries for World Peace Day," *SBS Malayalam*, September 21, 2021.

15: The Soundtrack of Nationalism

1 "Poet Fined for Insulting Mexican Flag, Calls Ruling Threat to Free Speech," Associated Press, as published in *Banderas News*, May 2008.

2 "Origin of the Perak State Anthem," *SembangKuala*, July 25, 2009. Also see "The Story of Sultan Abdullah's Exile in the Seychelles and Malaysia's National Anthem," *International Magazine Kreol*, February 9, 2015.

3 "As Protests Simmer, Brazil's National Anthem Soars at World Cup," Reuters, June 20, 2014.

4 "How Sports Met 'The Star-Spangled Banner,'" NPR, September 6, 2018.

5 "Red Sox Beat Cubs in Initial Battle," *New York Times*, September 6, 1918.

6 "National Anthem at Goshen College," Goshen College website.

7 Canada.ca, "Description of the National Flag of Canada," Government of Canada, last modified March 31, 2023, canada.ca/en/canadian-heritage/services/flag-canada-description.html.

8 National Flag of Canada Act, S.C. 2012, c. 12, llaws.justice.gc.ca/eng/AnnualStatutes/2012_12/page-1.html.

Final Verse

1 "Conduct During Hoisting, Lowering or Passing of Flag," US Flag Code §177. It's not just Americans who are governed by this flag etiquette. The code also records that "aliens should stand at attention."

2 "Donald Trump Blasts NFL Anthem Protesters: 'Get that Son of a Bitch off the Field,'" *Guardian*, September 23, 2017, theguardian.com/sport/2017/sep/22/donald-trump-nfl-national-anthem-protests.

3 "Dallas Mavericks' Short-Lived National Anthem Policy Shows Issue Persists," *NBC News*, February 11, 2021.

4 "Mavericks' Mark Cuban Relents on Anthem After NBA Reiterates Policy," Sportsnet, sportsnet.ca/nba/article/nba-teams-will-play-national-anthem-games.

5 Eric J. Hobsbawm (editor and author) and Terence Ranger (editor), *The Invention of Tradition* (Cambridge: Cambridge UP, 1983).

6 "How Elizabeth Ensured the Monarchy Survived," *Spectator*, September 11, 2022.

7 "One Man's Obsessive Campaign to Change Canada's Official Motto," *Maclean's*, February 13, 2018.

8 "22 Terrible Songs by Great Artists," *Rolling Stone*, June 15, 2016. "The only Number 1 hit that the greatest rock & roller of all time ever scored was a limp-dick joke. Originally cut as a negligible novelty number by New Orleans music great Dave Bartholomew in 1952, Berry first overhauled the song as "My Tambourine" in 1968, then soon afterward introduced concert audiences to this naughty rewrite. As though the sing-along hit (recorded at the Lanchester Arts Festival in Coventry) wasn't already too long, there's an overly engorged eleven-and-a-half-minute version on *The London Chuck Berry Sessions* — proof, once and for all, that a bigger ding-a-ling is not always a better one."

9 "Happy Birthday Jerusalem! Celebrating the Life of England's Unofficial National Anthem," Royal Albert Hall website.

10 "Full Text of Charles's Tribute," CNN, June 4, 2002. His concluding comments were: "So, your majesty, we are all deeply grateful to you and, in the words of the non-politically correct second verse of the national anthem, you have defended our laws and certainly given us cause to shout with heartened voice, 'God Save the Queen.'"

INDEX

ABOUT THE AUTHOR

David Pate was a veteran journalist with decades of experience in all media: online, print, radio, and television. He reported from more than twenty countries. His list of writing credits is long and includes the CBC, BBC, ITN, RTÉ, ABC (Australia), the *Irish Times*, the *Sunday Tribune* (Ireland), the *National* (Scotland) as well as many other newspapers, both online and in print. He was hired by CBC News to help launch its all-news television channel in 1989 and continued working for the CBC as a senior producer and executive producer until 2020, when he left to attend the Master of Fine Arts in Creative Nonfiction program at the University of King's College in Halifax, Nova Scotia. While researching this book, he also produced a podcast, *National Anthems: The Worst Songs in the World*, which is available to download.

Born in Glasgow, Scotland, David immigrated to Canada in 1989 with his family. In addition to writing, his other passion was diving. He became a PADI Scuba Instructor in 2016 and was a familiar face in Nova Scotia's diving community, spending most of his free time in the Atlantic Ocean.

David passed away suddenly in February 2024 before this book was published.